The Translator and Editor

EMILY WILSON is a professor of classical studies at the University of Pennsylvania. She is the author of *Mocked with Death: Tragic Overliving from Sophocles to Milton; The Death of Socrates: Hero, Villain, Chatterbox, Saint*; and *The Greatest Empire: A Life of Seneca*. Her translations include *The Odyssey* by Homer, *Seneca: Six Tragedies*, and four tragedies by Euripides in *The Greek Plays*. She is the editor of the Bloomsbury *Cultural History of Tragedy*, Volume 1.

For a complete list of Norton Critical Editions, visit
wwnorton.com/nortoncriticals

A NORTON CRITICAL EDITION

Sophocles
OEDIPUS TYRANNOS

A NEW TRANSLATION

SOURCES

CRITICISM

Translated and Edited by

EMILY WILSON
UNIVERSITY OF PENNSYLVANIA

W. W. NORTON & COMPANY
Independent Publishers Since 1923

W. W. Norton & Company has been independent since its founding in 1923, when William Warder Norton and Mary D. Herter Norton first published lectures delivered at the People's Institute, the adult education division of New York City's Cooper Union. The firm soon expanded its program beyond the Institute, publishing books by celebrated academics from America and abroad. By mid-century, the two major pillars of Norton's publishing program—trade books and college texts—were firmly established. In the 1950s, the Norton family transferred control of the company to its employees, and today—with a staff of five hundred and hundreds of trade, college, and professional titles published each year—W. W. Norton & Company stands as the largest and oldest publishing house owned wholly by its employees.

Manufacturing by Maple Press
Book design by Antonina Krass
Production manager: Stephen Sajdak

Library of Congress Cataloging-in-Publication Data

Names: Sophocles, author. | Wilson, Emily R., 1971 - translator, editor.
Title: Oedipus Tyrannos : a new translation, sources, criticism /
  translated and edited by Emily Wilson, University of Pennsylvania.
Other titles: Oedipus Rex. English (Wilson) | Norton critical edition.
Description: First edition. | New York, N.Y. : W. W. Norton & Company,
  2022. | Series: A Norton critical edition | Includes bibliographical
  references.
Identifiers: LCCN 2020030705 | ISBN 9780393655148 (paperback)
Subjects: LCSH: Oedipus (Greek mythological figure)—Drama. | Sophocles.
  Oedipus Rex. | Royal houses—Greece—Thebes—Drama. | Thebes
  (Greece)—Kings and rulers—Drama. | LCGFT: Drama. | Tragedies (Drama)
Classification: LCC PA4414.O7 W55 2022 | DDC 882/.01—dc23
LC record available at https://lccn.loc.gov/2020030705

W. W. Norton & Company, Inc., 500 Fifth Avenue, New York, N.Y. 10110
          www.wwnorton.com
W. W. Norton & Company Ltd., 15 Carlisle Street, London W1D 3BS

1 2 3 4 5 6 7 8 9 0

Contents

Introduction

The Plot

Many first-time readers of Sophocles' play will already know the shocking skeleton of Oedipus's story: he killed his father and married his mother, and had children with her, without knowing what he was doing. The mythical background is familiar to readers today, and would have been well known in its broad outlines to Sophocles' original audience. This is a drama not of surprise, but of suspense: we watch Oedipus discover the crucial buried truth about himself and his parentage, of which he, unlike us, is ignorant. The mystery that is gradually revealed to the spectators in the course of Sophocles' play is not what the leader of Thebes has done, but how he will discover it and how he will respond to this terrible new knowledge.

The legend goes that Laius, son of Labdacus and ruler of Thebes, learned long ago from the Delphic oracle, sacred to Apollo, that his son would kill him. When Laius had a son by his wife, Jocasta, he gave the baby to a shepherd to be exposed on Mount Cithaeron. Exposure, a fairly common practice in the ancient Greek world, involved leaving a baby out in some wild place in the knowledge that it would likely die. The practice allowed parents to dispose of unwanted children without incurring the blood guilt of killing a family member directly. Laius increased the odds against the child's survival by piercing and binding his feet so there was no chance he could crawl away. This detail of the myth seems to imply that the child was already several months old, although exposure was supposed to be performed on neonates. Like many elements of the Oedipus story, it is not very plausible: it is likely a detail added to the story to explain his name, which was imagined to come from the verb *oideo*, "to swell," and *pous*, "foot": Oedipus is the child with swollen feet. Exposure in real life almost always results in a dead baby; by contrast, exposed babies in ancient Greek myth and literature always survive, usually rescued by the kindness of lower-class or enslaved strangers. The mythical shepherd felt sorry for the boy and saved his life. He was adopted by the childless king and queen of Corinth, Polybus and Merope, and grew up believing himself to be their son.

One day, according to Sophocles' version of the myth, a drunken dinner party guest claimed that Oedipus was not the son of Polybus. Oedipus went to Delphi to seek the truth of the story, and the oracle warned him that he would kill his father and marry his mother. Oedipus fled Corinth and ran away, in the direction of Thebes. At a place where three paths crossed, he encountered his real father, Laius, without knowing who he was; they quarreled, and Oedipus killed Laius. When he reached Thebes, he found the city oppressed by a dreadful female monster, a Sphinx—part human, part lion, often also depicted in Greek art with the wings of an eagle and the tail of a snake. The Sphinx refused to let anybody into the city unless they could answer her riddle: "What walks on four legs in the morning, two legs at midday, and three legs in the evening?" She strangled and devoured all travelers who failed to solve the riddle. But Oedipus gave the right answer: "A human." Human beings crawl on all fours in infancy, walk on two feet in adulthood, and use a cane in old age. Oedipus revealed that he fit his name in a second sense: the verb *oida* means "I know" or "I have seen," so Oedipus the "Swell-Foot" became Oedipus the "Know-Foot." The Sphinx was defeated, and Oedipus was welcomed into the city as a savior. He married the newly widowed queen, Jocasta, and took over the throne.

When Sophocles' play begins, Oedipus has been ruling Thebes successfully for many years and has four children by Jocasta, two sons and two daughters. But a new trouble is afflicting the city. Plague has come to Thebes, and the dying inhabitants are searching for the reason why the gods are angry with the city. Oedipus, who dominates the stage from beginning to end, assures the desperate Priest and his young companions that he is entirely in control of the situation. He is the single ruler of the city, the man on whom all inhabitants depend, second only to the gods. He has already taken action and thinks he knows exactly what to do. The play traces the gradual process of investigation by which the buried family secret becomes public knowledge, and it shows how Oedipus's civic, social, and domestic power is undone, as is his confidence in his own superior cognitive abilities, even as he continues to struggle for control.

The play is often described as being about human agency and human knowledge. Oedipus has solved the riddle of the Sphinx, which is the life story of every physically abled human being. The play explores the possibility that Oedipus's ostensibly exceptional story might be a kind of parable for all human experience. After the protagonist has learned the truth, the Chorus treats his horrible journey from ignorance to knowledge as a paradigmatic instance of the precarity that characterizes all human lives: "O generations of mortals, / I count you as equal to nothing, / even when you are alive" (lines 1186–88).

But even in this same ode, the Chorus also insists on Oedipus's exceptional achievement (in solving the riddle of the Sphinx) and his exceptional power, telling him, "you have received the greatest of honors" (line 1203). Oedipus may be in certain ways paradigmatic of all humanity, but he is not at all typical. Sophocles is interested in the intersection between Oedipus's vulnerability, which we all share, and his extraordinary privilege—as well as his extraordinary curse. Oedipus can be seen as an extreme test case of the idea that all "generations of mortals" are blindly subject to the vicissitudes of fortune and the unknown will of the gods. On the other hand—and the play allows for both of these incompatible possibilities—the story of Oedipus can represent the specific pitfalls that adhere to a position of extraordinary privilege. Enslaved people, women (including those who are not enslaved), and less powerful men are represented as quite different from Oedipus, because they never imagined they could do and know everything.

Historical Contexts and Politics

We do not have any external evidence for the exact date of *Oedipus Tyrannos*. It is usually dated to around 429 B.C.E., because the plague with which the play begins is not a traditional part of the Oedipus myth, but seems highly reminiscent of Thucydides' description of the great plague at Athens, which struck in 430 B.C.E.[1] The opening descriptions of the horrific suffering caused by disease would have been personally shocking to audience members in a city that had recently lost about a quarter of the population to the same kind of devastating plague. If this dating is right, the representation of plague in Thebes, right after the plague in Athens, would have underlined one of the central questions the play poses to its Athenian audience: whether Thebes is like or unlike Athens.

In terms of political structure, the real Athens and the mythical Thebes initially seem quite different. Athens was a direct democracy: all adult male citizens had the right to speak in assembly meetings, to vote directly in important decisions (such as whether to go to war), and to be elected to public office (by vote or by lot, depending

---

1. Some scholars have disputed this dating; for instance, Bernard Knox argues in "The Dating of the *Oedipus Tyrannos*" (*American Journal of Philology* 77.2 [1956]: 133–47) that the play may have been composed in 425, after a later outbreak of disease in the city. Others have argued, unconvincingly, that this kind of reference to contemporary events is antithetical to tragedy and that therefore the play must have been performed in a year when plague was not on the minds of citizens. See also Robin Mitchell-Boyask, *Plague and the Athenian Imagination* (Cambridge, Eng.: Cambridge UP, 2008).

on the office). Athenian male citizens had far more microscopic personal control over the actions of their political community than the citizens of modern representative democracies. By contrast, the Thebes of the play is presented as a society in which a single individual (*tyrannos*) is the ruler. But there seems to be some meaningful confusion about whether all the Thebans are equally willing to acknowledge Oedipus's absolute authority.

Oedipus defines himself as a one-man ruler, a *tyrannos*, as do those around him. The word did not have the same connotations in fifth-century Greek as its English derivative "tyrant," which always suggests illegitimate and abusive exertion of power (as do near-synonyms like "dictator" or "autocrat"). The word *tyrannis* ("one-person nonhereditary government") is not necessarily negative, although from the perspective of Athenian democrats, it often could be; Sophocles' audience would have included men who sympathized with nondemocratic systems of government, such as oligarchy and tyranny. The word *tyrannis* implied a system in which one person ruled without sharing power, as opposed to an oligarchy ("rule of the few," in which a limited number of people, usually wealthier and more privileged people, share power), or democracy ("rule of the people," in which many people, including some who are less wealthy, share power; "many" did not, of course, mean everybody; the majority of inhabitants in Athens—including all enslaved people, women, and immigrants—were exluded from democratic participation). The word "equal"—*isos*—recurs multiple times in Sophocles' tragedy, reflecting a concern over whether anyone else is equal to Oedipus. Oedipus insists on his own singularity. But Tiresias, the blind old prophet who knows the signs of the gods, declares, "Even if you are sovereign [*tyrannos*], still the right / to answer must be equal [*isos*]" (lines 407–08)—a principle that echoes the Athenian right, afforded to all citizens in the democracy, of *isogoria*, or "equal right to speech in public." Creon, Oedipus's brother-in-law, seems suspicious of Oedipus's desire to assert lone, superior authority over his equals; he implies that Thebes is less democratic than oligarchic, in that power might be shared between the three members of the royal household (Oedipus, Jocasta, and Creon). The play creates an important ambiguity about what exactly the political system of Thebes is or ought to be.

Moreover, a fourth system of government was also common in the ancient world: hereditary monarchy, or *basileia*. In political terms, the central irony of the play is that Oedipus imagines that he is a *tyrannos*—a ruler with no dynastic claim to the throne of Thebes—and discovers only far too late that he is actually a *basileus*, a king whose father was the previous ruler. The play's common Latin title, *Oedipus Rex*, and its anglicization, *Oedipus the King*, are therefore spoilers.

Sophocles' Oedipus has often been compared to one of Athens's own most famous and dominant leaders: Pericles, who served as a leader and general (*strategos*) in the city-state from the 460s to his death by plague in 429 B.C.E. Pericles was a dominant figure in the city for several decades; he expanded democratic institutions and pushed for strategies of military expansion. In 451, Pericles advocated for new citizenship laws, which mandated that Athenian citizens must have two citizen parents. This meant that Pericles' own children by his partner Aspasia, who was an immigrant with permanent resident status (the Athenians called them "metics"), became ineligible for citizenship. Oedipus imagines that his children are, like those of Aspasia and Pericles, only half native-born; but he turns out to be wrong. The play explores a case where being too native, with parents who are too intimately connected to their place and to each other, is much worse than being half-foreign. The play is not making a direct comment or suggestion about public policy on immigration or miscegenation between native Athenian and immigrant populations, but it provides a mythical and dramatic language for thinking about these topics. Sophocles' Oedipus, like Pericles, is a decisive, charismatic man, whose public, political decisions conflict with the reality of his household. The play's preoccupation with the blurred distinctions between native-born and immigrant Thebans, and with the various ways that a child might be legitimate or illegitimate, resonates with the sociopolitical concerns of Athens in this time.

Sophocles seems to invite comparisons between the real Athens and the mythical Thebes. Oedipus himself has qualities that many Athenian men in the audience might have recognized in themselves. He is quick-witted, decisive, optimistic, irascible, self-confident, proud, patriotic, brave or rash, both pious and skeptical in his attitudes toward religion, and a committed believer in the power of human reason. The play is engaged, at least in sideways, looking-glass fashion, with current Athenian preoccupations of the mid-fifth century. If the usual dating is correct, the play was produced at the very beginning of Athens's decades-long war with Sparta and its allies—the Peloponnesian War (431–404 B.C.E.)—fought for imperial dominance of the Greek-speaking world. As Thucydides evokes in his fictionalized version of a speech given by Pericles in the first year of the war (included in the Comparative Sources section of this volume, pp. 66–68), it was a time of enormous pride among citizens in Athens's ability to fight off invaders, to expand its imperial dominance, and to maintain social and political systems that were imagined to be superior to all others in the Greek world. Sophocles could not have known how costly the war would be, in terms of the city's prosperity and the massive loss of human life;

but his play hints at dark possibilities. A contemporary Athenian could have seen Sophocles' Thebes as a vision of how a proud, prosperous community could fall apart, partly as a result of its own overconfidence and lack of true introspection. Thebes could be seen as a world either away or all too near at hand.

Key Themes and Imagery

In his *Poetics*, the philosopher Aristotle—writing in distant Macedon a century after *Oedipus Tyrannos* was first produced, and probably basing his opinions primarily on written scripts rather than dramatic performances—describes the play as the finest of all tragedies.[2] It includes two plot patterns that he thought were essential to good drama: a reversal of fortune (*peripeteia*) and a recognition (*anagnorisis*). Aristotle famously cites Oedipus as an example of someone whose fall into misfortune is the result not of bad deeds or evil character, but of some "mistake." The Greek word used is *hamartia*, which connotes an inadvertent failure to hit a target, like a dart that misses the bull's-eye. Twentieth-century critics often applied the different and modern concept of a "tragic flaw" to Oedipus, suggesting that we are supposed to see the disastrous events of the drama as fundamentally the protagonist's own fault; but this interpretation is not justified either by Aristotle or by the play. An important consideration against it is that in his later play *Oedipus at Colonus*, Sophocles makes Oedipus give a compelling self-defense: "How is my nature evil—/ if all I did was to return a blow?"[3] There is a clear distinction in ancient Greek thought between moral culpability—which is attached to deliberate, conscious actions—and religious pollution, which may afflict even those who are morally innocent. Readers must decide for themselves how far they think Sophocles goes in presenting Oedipus as a flawed, sympathetic, or even admirable figure.

Another popular modern approach to the play has been to see it as a classic "tragedy of fate," in which a man is brought low by destiny or the gods. Here, we need to be particularly careful to distinguish the myth—which can plausibly be seen as a story about the inevitable unfolding of divine will—from Sophocles' treatment of the myth in his play, which creates a more complex relationship between destiny and human action. Before Sophocles, Aeschylus had produced a trilogy that dealt with the family of Laius and Oedipus.

2. The passage is included in the Comparative Sources section of this volume, pp. 73–75 below.
3. See the extract from *Oedipus at Colonus* on pp. 69–71 below.

This does not survive, but it likely showed the gradual fulfillment of an inherited curse. In Sophocles' play, our attention is focused less on the original events and their causes (the killing of Laius and the marriage to Jocasta) than on the process by which Oedipus uncovers what he has done.

Oedipus is defined from the beginning of the play as a clever man (*sophos*), the only person capable of solving the riddle of the Sphinx. Cleverness or wisdom—*sophia*—was a fraught topic in the culture of Athens in the 430s. "Sophists" (*sophistai*, "wisdom-teachers") had been coming to Athens for the past few decades. These men were usually, like Oedipus, immigrants from different Greek-speaking cities: for instance, Protagoras came from Thrace, Gorgias from Sicily, and Prodicus from Ceos. The sophists charged wealthy fathers fees to teach their adolescent sons new skills in rhetoric and analytical thinking, including (depending on the teacher) training in the nascent fields of metaphysics, epistemology, linguistics, ethics, mathematics, astronomy, and physics. The presence of new, sophistic forms of learning in Athens was a source of pride and suspicion. Some citizens worried that these clever outsiders might be destroying traditional Athenian family values and traditional religious beliefs—anxieties that would come to a head a generation later, in 399 B.C.E., with the trial and execution of Socrates, who was often seen as a sophist. Oedipus has a certain amount in common with the sophists in general and Socrates in particular: he is an exceptionally intelligent man who claims, ironically, to know nothing ("Know-Nothing Oedipus"). The play examines the costs and limitations of Oedipus's particular brand of cleverness, compared to the very different kinds of *sophia* and knowledge that the prophet Tiresias and the oracle at Delphi possess.

The riddle of the Sphinx defines humanity by the number of feet we use at different points in our lives. Sophocles seems to suggest that the name "Oedipus" is particularly closely associated with feet: as we have seen, it can be read either as "Know-Foot" (from the verb *oida*, "I know," and *pous*, "foot"—an appropriate name for the man who guessed the Sphinx's riddle); or as "Swell-Foot" (from the verb *oideo*, to swell—a reminder of the baby Oedipus's wounded feet). On the first interpretation of his name, Oedipus seems like an Everyman figure, a representative of all humanity: he is the one who truly understands the human condition. On the second, we are reminded of the ways in which Oedipus is not like us: his feet mark the fact that he was cast out by his parents, rejected from his city, and has, unwittingly, done things that seem to make it impossible for him to be part of any human community.

Like all Athenian tragedies, *Oedipus Tyrannos* was composed to be performed in the Theater of Dionysos, at the Great Dionysia, the

civic festival for Dionysos, god of theater and wine. But the god
who lurks behind the whole action of this play is not Dionysos but
his brother Apollo, the god associated most closely with plague,
prophecy, and the light of the sun, with enigmas and revelations.
Gods sometimes appeared on stage in Athenian tragedy, but in this
play, Apollo works always behind the scenes, and the human actors
struggle to identify and interpret his mysterious will. Sophocles
multiplies the number of oracles and messengers in the story, and
Apollo presides over the complex unfolding of the truth.

Oracles are only one of many types of riddling, ambiguous,
or ambivalent language used in the play, which is particularly concerned with all kinds of interpretation. Dramatic irony—a term that
refers to moments when the audience hears a meaning of which the
speaker is unaware—is another particularly important reminder that
words may have more than one sense. For instance, Oedipus comments that Laius was "so unlucky / in fathering" (lines 259–60) and
asserts, "I fight for him, as if he were my father" (line 262)—speaking
more truly than he knows.

The interplay between literal and metaphorical meanings forms
an essential technique in the play. Sophocles creates a relationship
between literal and metaphorical blindness, between the light of
the sun and the light of insight, between Oedipus as "father" of his
people and as real father to his own siblings, and between sickness
as a physical affliction and as a metaphor for pollution.

Through linked patterns of imagery, Sophocles explores the central questions of who Oedipus is, what a family is, and what it means
to be in a place or a community. Plague, disease, and blood exist;
they are also recurrent metaphors for the state of corruption and
pollution. The instability of circumstances is explored through
repeated references to weather, storms, and the city as a ship,
tossed at sea. Thebes is located inland, in central Greece; the image
of the city at sea, tossed by the waves, conflates this mythical land-
locked community with the real island city of Athens.

There are repeated puns and plays on the word "foot," especially
in the opening scenes of the play, and on physical posture: sitting,
standing, falling. It is as if Sophocles repeatedly challenges his audience to solve and resolve the riddle of the Sphinx, by reduplicat-
ing and reiterating the enigmatic fact that people find themselves
in different positions at different moments: our feet hold us upright
only temporarily. Hands are also important in this play, as the body
part associated most closely with action and agency, especially with
killing. The play makes us ask ostensibly childish but profound
questions: whether we can depend on our feet and whether we are
what we do with our hands.

The most important body part of all in this play is the eye, which is repeatedly associated with knowledge. The verb *oida*, "I know," is also the perfect tense of the verb "to see" (*idein*): Sophocles' play is a meditation on the close association in Greek culture, language, and imagination between sight and knowledge. The eyes are imagined to be the most reliable sources of clear knowledge; many Athenians would have assumed that autopsy, or eyewitnessing, ought to be the best, most reliable basis for information. But the murder of Laius, for which there was a surviving eyewitness, remains hidden for a whole generation, as does the story of how Jocasta's baby was exposed. The truth about origins, about guilt, about pollution, and about divine will turns out to be difficult or impossible to determine through physical eyesight alone. Oedipus begins the drama with two functioning eyes, but as the blind prophet Tiresias tells him, he is metaphorically "blind" to the truth. It is only by questioning and listening, using his ears rather than his eyes, that Oedipus finds his circuitous path to the truth. In the final sequence, after he "sees" the truth about his own past and his parents, he puts out his own eyes—and wishes he could also stop up his ears, to shut up all the orifices that provide cognitive access to the world.

This play, like all Athenian tragedies, was performed entirely by male citizen actors wearing masks; in the final scene, Oedipus must have worn a mask marked or blindfolded to depict his gouged eyes. The self-blinding provides a belated physical representation of the fact that Oedipus was, up to this point, metaphorically blind. At the same time, it also seems to be a counter to his earlier blindness—as if it is only by becoming blind like Tiresias that he can see the truth. Oedipus himself seems to suggest that he has blinded himself to assert his own agency: "self-handed, I did it," he declares (lines 1331–32). In contrast to the unconscious, unknowing actions of killing Laius and sleeping with Jocasta, Oedipus puts out his eyes in full knowledge of what he is doing. But paradoxically, the self-blinding is also represented as a deliberate choice to give up knowledge and further vision, a refusal to look at his parents in the underworld. The final scene of the play poses the question of whether Oedipus is more or less in control of his own body—his feet, his hands, his eyes, his ears—now that he knows his own history, the history of his body.

Another central, ostensibly childish but profound question that runs through the play is, What is a parent? Oedipus imagines himself to be the biological son of Merope and Polybus, of Corinth; but they turn out to be his adoptive, not biological, parents. The story of Oedipus's exposure on the mountaintop as a tiny child prompts an ongoing meditation in the play about the relationship between two different models of parenting. Is a parent the one who produces or generates the child (like a seed—an image that recurs in the drama)? Or is the real parent the one who raises or cares for the off-spring? The Greek word *trephein*—"to raise," "to nurse," "to take care of"—is associated with parents, but also with the childcare done in elite families by enslaved women, the nurses (*tropheis*) who breast-fed and took care of little children.

One of the horrors of Oedipus's story, apart from parricide and incest, is the realization that biological parents do not always pro-vide care for their offspring. Moreover, the play imagines the com-munity of a city or country as another kind of family, with citizens as children raised or cared for by a fatherlike ruler. Oedipus seems, at the start of the play, to be the adoptive father of the Theban people. His real heritage, as trueborn son of Thebes, makes it impossible for him to foster the city without destroying it.

The bodies of babies, as the ancient Greeks well knew, are formed out of the bodies of their parents. There were competing medical theories in the fifth century B.C.E. about the precise mechanisms by which this process of generation happened, and specifically about whether both parents provide material to form the fetus, or just the father. The play's imagery creates very distinct ways of imagining fatherhood versus motherhood. Fathering is, in the images of the play, like planting a seed or sowing or plowing a field, or entering the "harbor" of a woman's body; the mother is like the field from which children are harvested, or the harbor into which boats enter. Jocasta's body is presented not in terms of what it can do or experi-ence or be aware of (in contrast to the body of Oedipus); rather, her body is a place, one that becomes horrific when it is entered, used, or possessed by father and son. Within the narrative of the drama, Oedipus and Jocasta experience the same revelation and undergo the same journey, from ignorance to knowledge; both respond with violence against themselves, when they understand the truth about their own polluted bodies. But we are given hardly any access to the interiority of Jocasta's thoughts and feelings about her terrible family history; her body remains inside the house, not out on stage, and the Messenger emphasizes that Oedipus draws all attention from her to himself: "he made it / impossible to watch her suffer-ing" (lines 1252–53). In the final sequence of the play, the associa-tion between female bodies and places is turned around: the daughters of Jocasta and Oedipus, the products of a body in which too many men have placed themselves, are seen by their father as pitiably placeless or unplaceable.

If the mother is like a place, places are also like mothers in this play; place-names and city-names in Greek are female, and the land is imagined as the mother of those who are born in it. Oedipus's uncertainty about his place of origin is represented as an uncertainty about his true mother: he is the son of Corinth, of Thebes, and of the crossroads where the three paths meet. He is also the child of Fate (another feminine abstraction), and most emphatically, he is born from Mount Cithaeron, the mountain that nurtured and saved him from death. In each case, the subaltern human beings who actually nurtured the child—the biological mother in whose womb he grew, the foster mother, the enslaved men who adopted and saved the baby—are erased from the narrative, and instead he is represented as born like the first humans of myth, from Mother Earth. An important myth in Athenian lore and ideology was that of autochthony: the Athenians boasted that their ancestors had always lived in Attica, in contrast to other, more diasporic Greek populations. Sophocles' Oedipus is a test case of the most extreme possible form of autochthony, born directly from the ground in multiple places. The play poses questions about where exactly a person comes from: the bodies of parents, or the earth, or the community?

A third childish, profound question running through the play is, How many? How many people are in your family? How many people are you? As we have seen, the play repeatedly uses terms for "equal," *isos*, and interrogates whether Oedipus is or is not "equal" to other members of the ruling elite in Thebes. Sophocles also creates an important confusion about how many people killed Laius; the testimony of witnesses is inconsistent on this crucial factual point. This is partly a useful plot device, to make it a little bit more plausible that the murder of Laius languished unsolved for so many years. But Sophocles turns it into a deeper thematic thread. Oedipus declares, emphatically, "One man can be equal to a group" (line 845). And the play traces ways in which Oedipus, through inhabiting many apparently incompatible roles in the city and in his family, is indeed equal to a group, a plurality: he is father and son, son and killer, ruler and outcast, savior and curse.

Athenian tragedy was performed in the open air, in a theater that included a large round dancing area, the *orchestra*, for the choral choreography, and a wooden stage called a *skēnē* that included doors to go in or out of the house or palace. Actors could enter or exit from three possible directions: stage left, stage right, and through the central stage doors. Entrances from off the sides of the stage— like that of Creon in the first scene—take much longer, such that the audience can see the character approaching for some time before she or he reaches the stage. *Oedipus Tyrannos* makes use of the dramaturgical possibilities of this space in its staging of the ways that other places affect and shape the central visible space, which is the public arena of Thebes. We have entrances from Delphi, from Corinth, and most momentously, from Mount Cithaeron, all of which affect and change the play's action—as well as exits and entrances from the house, the location of the marriage bed that has held Jocasta along with both her husbands. The stage itself becomes a new kind of crossroads, where multiple places and communities are joined together.

A play whose secret you already know might seem unlikely to be interesting. But it is impossible to be bored by *Oedipus Tyrannos*. The plot races to its terrible conclusion with the twisting, breakneck pace of a thrilling murder novel, while the contradictory figure of Oedipus—the blind rationalist, the polluted king, the dutiful killer of his father, the son and husband of Jocasta, the hunter and the hunted, the stranger in his own home—is a commanding presence, who dominates the stage even when he can no longer see.

The Playwright

Sophocles was a generation younger than Aeschylus and had an unusually long, successful, productive, and apparently happy life. He was born at the start of the fifth century, around 496 B.C.E., in the village of Colonus, which was a short distance north of Athens. His family was probably fairly wealthy—his father may have owned a workshop producing armor, a particularly salable product at this time of warfare—and Sophocles seems to have been well educated. An essential element in Greek boys' education at this time was studying the Homeric poems, and Sophocles obviously learnt this lesson well; in later times, he was called the "most Homeric" of the three surviving Athenian tragedians. He was said to be a good-looking, charming boy and a talented dancer. In 480 B.C.E., when he was about fifteen or sixteen, he was chosen to lead a group of naked boys who danced in the victory celebrations for Athens's defeat of the Persian navy at Salamis. The beginning of his public career thus coincided with his city's period of greatest glory and international prestige.

Athens became the major power in the Mediterranean world in the middle decades of the fifth century, a period known as the "golden" or "classical" age of Athens. The most important political figure in the newly dominant city-state was Pericles, a statesman who was also a personal friend of Sophocles', and who particularly encouraged the arts. Pericles seems to have instituted various legal measures to enable the theater to flourish in his time: for instance, rich citizens were obliged to provide funding for theater productions, and the less wealthy may have had their theater tickets subsidized.

The prosperity of Sophocles' city took a sharp turn for the worse around 431 B.C.E., when the poet was in his mid-sixties. The Peloponnesian War, between Athens and Sparta, began in that year and lasted until after Sophocles' death. Soon after the outbreak of war, Pericles died in a terrible plague that afflicted the whole city. In the last decades of the century, the city became increasingly impoverished and demoralized by war.

Sophocles worked in the Athenian theater all his life. He made some important technical changes in the theater, including the introduction of scene painting, and the increase of the chorus members from twelve to fifteen. His most important innovation was bringing in a third actor (a "tritagonist"); previous tragedians had used only two actors. This practice allowed for three-way dialogues, and a drama that concentrates on the complex interactions and relationships of individuals with one another. The chorus in Sophocles became far less central to the plot than it had been in Aeschylus; this is part of the reason why Sophocles' plays may seem more "modern" to twenty-first-century readers and audiences.

Sophocles has also seemed "modern" in his acute depiction of human psychology and human relationships. The gods are largely absent in most of Sophocles' extant plays, and human beings struggle to interpret their obscure intentions. Sophocles' people are intense, passionate, and often larger than life, but always fully human. They often adopt positions that seem extreme, but for which they have the best of motives. These tragedies ask us to consider when and how it is right to compromise, and to measure the slim divide between compromise and selling out. Clashes between stubborn heroism and the voice of moderation are found in all Sophocles' surviving plays.

Contemporaries gave Sophocles' talent its due. He won first prize at the Great Dionysia for the first time in 468 B.C.E., defeating his older rival, Aeschylus; he was still under thirty at the time. Sophocles would defeat Aeschylus several more times in the course of his career. His output was large: he composed over 120 plays. The seven that survive include the three Theban plays, dealing with Oedipus and his family: *Oedipus Tyrannos*, *Antigone*, and *Oedipus at Colonus*. These were written at intervals of many years, and were never intended to be performed together. The other four surviving tragedies are *Ajax*, about a strong-man hero who is driven mad by Athena—and the consequences of that madness; *Trachiniae*, about Heracles' agonizing death by mistake at the hands of his jealous wife, Deineira; *Electra*, which focuses on the unending grief and rage of Agamemnon's daughter after her father's murder; and *Philoctetes*, about the Greek embassy to persuade an embittered, wounded hero to return to battle in Troy. The dating of most of these plays is uncertain, although *Philoctetes* is certainly a late play, composed in 409 B.C.E. The judges at the Great Dionysia loved Sophocles' work: he won first prize over twenty times and never came lower than second.

Sophocles seems to have been equally popular as a person, known for his mellow, easygoing temperament, his religious piety, and his appreciation for the beauty of adolescent boys. We are told that he had "so much charm of character that he was loved everywhere, by everyone." He was friendly with the prominent intellectuals of his day, including the world's first historian, Herodotus. He participated actively in the political activity of the city; he served under Pericles as a treasurer in 443/442 B.C.E., and was elected as a general with him in 441/440 B.C.E. After the Sicilian disaster in 413 B.C.E., in which Athens lost enormous numbers of men and ships during a failed naval expedition in the Peloponnesian War, Sophocles—then in his eighties—was one of ten men elected to an emergency group formed for policy formation. Sophocles' participation in public life suggests that he was seen as a trustworthy and wise member of the community. He may have been responsible for welcoming Asclepius, the god of medicine, into the city's pantheon for the first time—which may perhaps be relevant for the central preoccupation with sickness, plague, religious pollution, and healing in *Oedipus Tyrannos*.

Sophocles was married and had five sons, one of whom, Iophon, became a tragedian. He was over ninety when he died. His last play, *Oedipus at Colonus*, is set in the place of his birth—Colonus, where according to legend, the polluted Oedipus came to find sanctuary in the holy grove of the Furies. This play about old age, acceptance, and redemption is a kind of sequel to *Oedipus Tyrannos*, but composed many years later. It was performed posthumously in 401 B.C.E., directed by Sophocles' grandson, also named Sophocles.

Translator's Note

Sophoclean tragedy is composed in a poetic style that is dignified, dense, and strange, but also smooth, fluent, and full of feeling. His metaphors are abundant, but not usually obscure. His characters seem like plausible inhabitants of a mythic heroic age, but at the same time are fully human. Their feelings are intense, and the plays often evoke terrible events and terrible suffering, but without bombast or a sense of melodrama. There is an aura of controlled, beautiful truth-telling in Sophocles' poetics. Virginia Woolf, in her great essay "On Not Knowing Greek," captures Sophocles' style in a marvelous image: "Sophocles gliding like a shoal of trout smoothly and quietly, apparently motionless, and then with a flicker of fins off and away."

I approached this project having completed translations of several very different texts, all, like Sophocles, in metrical verse: the tragedies of Seneca, four plays by Euripides, and *The Odyssey*. I knew I did not want to make Sophocles sound quite like any of them. Sophoclean tragedy is never as ornately rhetorical and allusive as Seneca. Sophocles was said to be further from ordinary speech than Euripides, and his plays certainly have less black humor. The language is intricate and literary, not based on an oral folk tradition like that which informs the Homeric poems—which are far more straightforward in their syntax and imagery than Sophocles. Within the limitations of my own literary and poetic capacities, I hoped to create for my English Sophocles a language that was fluent, humane, natural, and also markedly artful; sometimes conversational, but never slangy; full of puns, but not funny or unserious; always rhythmical, often rich in imagery, sometimes odd, but never stiff or unintentionally obscure.

Many modern and contemporary translators of metrical classical verse render it into prose, or stacked prose, lines laid out as verse but with no particular rhythm. As in my earlier verse translations, I wanted to use a regular meter for the dialogue passages, to echo the regular meter of the original, and to use a markedly different set of rhythms for the choral lyrics, so that the reader or listener can experience the shifts in linguistic music and emotional pitch without having to consult the notes. I kept as close as I could to the pacing of the original, but sometimes I found that my English needed to be a little longer than the Greek; the marked line numbers in this translation match the Greek rather than the English, to aid the reader who consults scholarly books or articles on the play. The original, like all Athenian drama, primarily uses iambic trimeter for the dialogue passages, a meter that was said to be the closest to normal speech; I used regular iambic pentameter, because it is the obvious literary equivalent, used within the anglophone tradition as the standard meter of dialogue in verse drama from the time of Shakespeare onwards. The original choral passages are in intricate lyric rhythms, which would have been set to music and accompanied by dancing. I did not attempt to create an exact replica of the lyric meters. Instead, I used mostly anapestic and dactylic rhythms, and a variety of line lengths, to ensure that these passages were legible and audible as very clearly distinct from the dialogue passages, and to tempt the reader, at times, to hear a melody, to clap or tap her feet to the beat.

In working on the opening scenes, it was the feet that caused me the most trouble. The feet, the hands, eyes, the plows, the ships, the harvests, the hunting, but above all, again and again, the feet: the overwhelming abundance of imagery and punning, dark double entendres that Sophocles pulls off without inducing confusion, laughter, or groans. Modern English-speaking readers are likely to imagine that puns should have no place in serious verse drama, and indeed a prominent modern editor and commentator on the Greek play, R. Dawe, repeatedly insists that Sophocles' apparent puns are mere accidents of language, not intentional wordplay; Dawe seemed to hope to save Sophocles from any imputation of bad taste. But accidental punning on this scale defies plausibility. Sophocles really does repeatedly, insistently, set the audience to solve, yet again and again, the riddle of the Sphinx, by presenting, over and over, linguistic motifs of feet, standing and falling. I hoped to honor the metaphorical and linguistic richness of the original, without making it sound ridiculous, within the relatively pun-phobic cultures of the contemporary United States and United Kingdom. Sometimes I used wordplay that I hoped would hover, as the original sometimes does, between idiomatic and mysterious. For instance, when Oedipus asks what prevented the Thebans from conducting a prompt investigation into the murder of Laius, he uses language suggesting that there must have been some kind of problem blocking their feet (*kakon . . . empodon*). I had Oedipus ask about an "impediment," a word whose root comes from the Latin for "foot" (*pes*); my pun is perhaps a notch more subtle than that of Sophocles, catering to the more delicate sensibilities of a modern anglophone listener or reader, who may more readily be offended by perceived linguistic excess. Throughout the play, I wanted to honor Sophocles' interest in riddling, dense, metaphorical language. I hoped to make the verse fluent and comprehensible, but at the same time layered, often strange, rich in surprising images and turns of phrase. I felt the language should sometimes feel enigmatic, as the original does; enigmas are a central element in the linguistic form as well as the content of the play.

Beyond style, register, wordplay, and imagery, I thought hard about the characterization of each member of the cast, including the reasonable, desperate Priest; the cautious Chorus; the two contrasting slaves, the Herdsman and the First Messenger, one eager to tell his story and one terrified of its repercussions, both old men terrified of torture and death, after long lives defined by the will of their enslavers; Creon, the family man, eager to keep private business out of the public eye; Jocasta, the pious, attentive wife whose faith in gods and in marriage is destroyed; and the commanding, quick-thinking Oedipus, whose charm, intelligence, wit, and charisma should come across as clearly as his domineering self-absorption and paranoia.

One particular challenge in translating this play was the wealth of contradictory political vocabulary that runs through this most political of Athenian tragedies—all of which implies different political systems and different political assumptions than those that will come readily to the minds of contemporary anglophone readers. "Tyrant" is not a satisfactory rendering of the various instances of *tyrannos* and its cognates, because it is far more negative than the original terms. In the title, I left the word transliterated, to make the play readily identifiable. But I could not transliterate the political terms in the text; doing so would give the false impression that all Sophocles' nonpolitical terminology is easy to translate into modern English. I was tempted to use the words "president" and "presidency," which seem to me the most common, relatively neutral English words for a person with supreme political power. But these words, in the United States at least, usually connote a very different political system, in which the executive privilege of a single individual is checked and balanced by groups of elected representatives. I compromised with a range of words such as "sovereign" and "sovereignty," or sometimes "ruler," and "power" for the cognate abstract noun *tyrannis*. This dilemma is a single instance of a challenge that is constant for every work of literary translation. Languages are always entirely knitted up into their own social and cultural contexts, and translators grapple, in every line, with the vast imaginative gap between one culture and another.

The resonances of this or any classical text with modern culture will change as our culture changes. This play is about immigrants, about what it means to be an insider or an outsider in power, about the enormous privilege wielded by an elite man who still sees himself as an outsider or underdog, about the capacity of less privileged people in society (like the enslaved herdsmen) to change their government and bring down those in power, and about what it takes for their voices to be heard or to be silenced. It prompts us to ask whether we can or even should distinguish sharply between the public and the private self. It takes place at a time of a massive medical crisis, in which families are being torn apart and children are dying. It is about family structures, and about the cultural or natural boundaries between "normal" and "abnormal" presentations of gender and sexuality. It is about paranoia and the fear of conspiracies, and about an investigation that threatens to bring down the head of state. It stages confrontations between different kinds of expertise, different kinds of privilege, different modes of intelligence, different kinds of awareness, preparation, knowledge, and blindness. It prompts questions about the proper basis for power: qualifications, or the will of the people. It probes the relationship of political theater to political effectiveness and considers whether the appearance of quick, decisive, strong, solitary action, without consultation, is sometimes or always good practice for a leader. It interrogates the question that haunts all modern democratic societies, of whether those who hold public office need to be spiritually, personally, or morally pure in their private lives, and conversely, whether any private actions are bad enough to disqualify a person from public office.

Some elements of this ancient tragedy are very far distant from the concerns and beliefs of most people alive today. It is about the workings of a god, Apollo, in whom few of us now believe. The idea that inadvertently killing one family member and marrying another would inevitably cause terrible religious pollution is alien to most modern secular understandings of how the world works. Oedipus's road rage and involuntary manslaughter of Laius are unfortunate, and his relationship with his mother is the stuff of tabloids; but people in contemporary cultures would probably not see the ignorant perpetrator as "unclean," or imagine that his presence in our society would bring plague and divine rage. We are more likely to believe that the most horrifying human actions are those that are deeply wrong from an ethical rather than a religious perspective—such as genocide or slavery or torture or child abuse.

But on another level, Sophocles' play is entirely accessible to the feelings and imaginations of contemporary readers or audiences, as Freud, the psychologist who formulated the "Oedipus complex," well understood. We can all share the nightmarish terror that the confident pursuit of greater knowledge might lead to horrible discoveries of things better left unknown. Anyone who has lived past childhood or been guilty of terrible misunderstandings knows that a person's place within a family or community may change in unexpected, perhaps shocking ways. We are all aware of people, perhaps including ourselves, who have assumed that our privileges are based on our own merit, only to discover that we have made terrible misunderstandings. We can all understand the fear that there might be some hidden horror in our past, in our parentage or history, of which we ourselves are blithely unaware.

Acknowledgments

I thank Carol Bemis at Norton for commissioning this translation. Many thanks to Pete Simon, also at Norton, for his dedicated and extremely helpful editorial feedback. Thank you to students and faculty at St. Johns College who discussed an earlier draft of this work in progress. Thank you to my colleagues Cynthia Damon and Bridget Murnaghan for very useful comments and suggestions. Thank you to the classical studies graduate students at the University of Pennsylvania, who read my draft out loud with me and discussed my choices and the specific ways the text might work in the classroom and beyond.

I also thank my partner, David, and my children, Imogen, Psyche, and Freya, for teaching me about family, community, and love. Thank you above all to the god Apollo, for preventing me from murdering or marrying any blood relatives, at least to the best of my current knowledge.

The Text of
OEDIPUS TYRANNOS

Oedipus Tyrannos

Cast

Speaking Parts:

Priest
Oedipus
Creon
Tiresias
Jocasta
Herdsman
First Messenger
Second Messenger
Chorus of fifteen male Theban elders

Nonspeaking Parts:

Children and acolytes (accompanying Priest)
Slave of Tiresias
Slaves and attendants of Oedipus
Daughters of Oedipus
Bystanders

> *The* CHORUS *is present in the orchestra.*[1] *On the stage, the* PRIEST *is gathered with acolytes and a group of young children beside the altar.*[2] OEDIPUS *comes out of the palace—through the central doors behind the stage—to address the whole crowd.*

OEDIPUS

Children! Young ones nursed by this old city
of Cadmus![3] Why are you all sitting here,
in wreaths and with those supplication branches?

---

1. "Orchestra" literally means "dancing area": the round central area of the Athenian theater used primarily for the Chorus. The actors would have been mostly on the raised wooden stage.
2. This and all subsequent stage directions, set in *italics* in the play text, have been added by the translator as a guide to the reader or director; the manuscripts of ancient plays never have stage directions.
3. Legendary founder of Thebes, whose name is closely linked to the city.

The city is all full of incense, full
of groaning, and of songs, and prayers for healing.
I thought it wrong to hear this second-hand.
Children, I came myself. I am the man
well known to everyone, named Oedipus.
Priest, as an elder you should be the one   [10]
to speak for all. What is your state of mind?
Are you afraid of something? Wanting something?
Indeed, I'd like to help with everything.
I would be cruel if I did not pity
the desperate way that you are sitting here.[4]

PRIEST

Lord of my country, Oedipus, you see us
gathered here at your altars—some so young
and weak, they cannot fly yet;[5] others heavy
with age. I am a priest of Zeus; these children
are special acolytes.[6] The other people
crowd in the marketplaces, wearing wreaths,
beside Athena's double shrine, and by   [20]
the Ismenus, the oracle of ash.[7]
See for yourself! The city reels; its head
is sunk beneath the deep and bloody waves.[8]
The land is weakening: the seeds in pods
decay; the land is dying, and the cattle
die in the fields; the laboring of women
is birthless birth. The god who carries fire,
most cruel plague, is driving through the city
and emptying our houses, while black Hades[9]
grows rich on cries of grief and lamentation.   [30]
I've come here with these children to your hearth,
not thinking you the equal of the gods,
but as the first of men, in life events
and dealings with divinities. You came
to Thebes, the town of Cadmus, and released us

4. The word for seat or sitting, *hedra*, occurs in lines 2 and 13 of the Greek text (echoed
   in this translation by "sitting . . . sitting"; note that this text's line numbers refer to the
   original Greek). It is a word associated specifically with sitting in supplication or
   prayer. The emphasis on the supplicants' physical position, sitting down, traces an
   implicit contrast with Oedipus, the one who is here and, wherever possible, standing
   on his feet.
5. The children are imagined as chicks or fledgling birds.
6. They are "special" in that they have been selected, presumably on some kind of merit.
7. Athena had twin temples at Thebes. The Ismenus was one of the two rivers of Thebes.
   The oracle of ash likely refers to the temple of Apollo, where there was an altar made of
   the ash from sacrificial victims.
8. The imagery shifts between the city as a sinking ship and as a single drowning person,
   whose head is submerged beneath the waves.
9. Hades is god of the dead.

from paying the relentless Poet's tribute,[1]
though you knew nothing special, nothing extra;
we had not told you anything. Some god
helped you lift up our lives. This we believe.
Now Oedipus, most powerful of rulers,   [40]
we are all begging you to help us somehow.
Maybe you know some way to save us; maybe
you heard some god's voice, or some person told you.
I see that people with experience
manage to bring their plans to life most often.
So come, lift up our city! You're the best
of mortals. Come, be on your guard. The city
calls you its savior now, because you were
so helpful in the past. We would not want
your rule to be remembered as the time
we stood up straight, but then fell down again.[2]   [50]
Lift up this city and make sure it's stable.
Your bird of destiny brought us good luck;[3]
be the same now. You hold the power now;
if you would go on ruling, it is better
to govern in a populated city
than emptiness. A citadel or ship
is nothing, if no people live inside it.

OEDIPUS   Poor children! I already know all this:
why you have come, and what you want. I know
that all of you are sick with plague, diseased;[4]
but no one's sickness equals mine. You each   [60]
are only suffering for your own pain,
for your own self and no one else. My being
grieves for the city, me, and you, together.
You did not wake me. I was not asleep.
I have been crying late into the night.
My mind has traveled many different paths.
I looked intently, and I found there was

---

1. The "relentless Poet" is the Sphinx, who guarded the entrance to Thebes and killed those who could not solve her riddle as "tribute." Notice that Sophocles does not name the Sphinx and never specifies her riddle. Here, she is referred to by the word commonly used for an oral poetry composer: *aoidos*. The Sphinx is imagined as a kind of poet, whose riddle is a song.
2. There are repeated metaphors in this first scene of standing and falling, echoed dramaturgically in the position of the seated supplicants, met by the upstanding Oedipus.
3. The "bird of destiny" may be any auspicious sign, since birds could stand in for any omen or mark of divine will. But perhaps it is also relevant that the Sphinx is winged.
4. The word *nosos* and its cognate verb *noseo* were used specifically of plague, including the plague of Athens (as Robin Mitchell-Boyask has argued in his *Plague and the Athenian Imagination* [Cambridge, Eng.: Cambridge UP, 2008]); they were also used of mental illness and suffering in general—and of course here there is the dramatic irony that Oedipus is, unknown to himself, "sick" with pollution.

only one cure. I did it. I have sent
Creon, Menoeceus's son, the brother   [70]
of my own wife, to Delphi, to the home
of Phoebus,[5] to find out what I can do
or say to save the city. It is late;
the measurement of day against the time
makes me concerned how he is getting on.
He has been absent longer than he should.
When he arrives, shame on me if I fail
to do it all, just as the god reveals.

      CREON *appears from the countryside direction,[6] walking toward
      the stage.*

PRIEST   Your words are timely. Just this very minute
these children pointed Creon out to me.

OEDIPUS   Apollo! Lord! I hope his bright expression   [80]
implies that he is bringing us salvation.

PRIEST   It seems his news is promising; why else
would he be wreathed so lavishly with laurel?

OEDIPUS   We'll soon find out. He's now in hearing range.
(*Shouting*) My lord! My brother! Creon! What's the word
you bring us from your journey to the god?

CREON   Good news! I mean, if everything goes right,
all this disaster will turn out just fine.

OEDIPUS   Explain yourself. What you have said so far
makes me feel neither confident nor scared.   [90]

CREON   If you want all these bystanders to hear,
I can speak now—or we can go inside.

OEDIPUS   Speak out to everyone. I feel more pain
for them than for myself and my own life.

CREON   Then I will tell you what I heard. The god
Apollo clearly says we must expel
pollution that is nurtured in this land,
not feed it till it turns incurable.[7]

OEDIPUS   What means of cleansing, what way out is there?

CREON   To impose exile, or pay death for death.
The land is feverish with this storm of blood.[8]   [100]

---

5. Apollo, who has the cult title Phoebus, is Artemis's twin brother, the god of the golden
   bow, and associated with prophecy.
6. In the Athenian theater, the side to the right of the stage was conventionally used to
   signal exits and entrances toward the countryside; the side to the left was for exits and
   entrances to the city.
7. Pollution is a neuter noun in the Greek (*miasma*): it is a thing, not a person, but Creon
   describes it in personified terms, as something that has been taken care of in Thebes,
   like a child, and may become "incurable," like a deadly disease.
8. The metaphor of a "storm of blood" echoes the blood rained down as Zeus's tears in
   The Iliad at the death of Sarpedon (*Iliad* 16.439; cf. 11.53–54); it is caused by the blood
   shared between Oedipus and his parents, and the spilled blood of Laius.

OEDIPUS   Whose blood? What death? What does he mean
  by this?

CREON   My lord, before you came here, to this city,
  the ruler of the country was named Laius.

OEDIPUS   I know, I heard about him; never saw him.

CREON   The god gives clear instructions: we must punish
  the selfsame men whose hands killed our dead king.[9]

OEDIPUS   Are they in Theban territory? Where
  can evidence be found of this old crime?

CREON   Here in this land, he says: the sought is caught,   [110]
  and what is unexamined slips away.

OEDIPUS   Was Laius killed at home or in the country?
  Was it in Thebes, or in some other land?

CREON   They say he went to seek an oracle,
  and left, but never came back home again.

OEDIPUS   Was there no fellow traveler, no witness
  or messenger with useful information?

CREON   All died but one; he ran away in fear,
  and could say just one thing of what he saw.

OEDIPUS   What kind of thing? One clue can be revealing   [120]
  if we can grasp the slender start of hope.

CREON   He said that with a multitude of hands
  the robbers killed him. More than one attacker.

OEDIPUS   How could he be so bold—unless there was
  conspiracy in Thebes, and he was bribed?[1]

CREON   It seemed that way. But after Laius died,
  we had no one to help us in our troubles.

OEDIPUS   Power had fallen![2] What impediment
  prevented you from finding out the reason?

CREON   The enigmatic Sphinx made us abandon   [130]
  puzzles, and look at what was at our feet.[3]

OEDIPUS   I will begin again and shed fresh light.
  Apollo is quite right, and so were you,
  to work so hard to help the murdered man,
  and you will see me also fight for justice,

---

9. The term "selfsame" picks up a word in the original, *autoentes*, that is usually used for killing oneself or killing a family member—a "same-killing." Creon uses the plural, as if assuming that more than one person must have been involved in the murder. The question of how many people killed Laius proves essential to the murder mystery and to the themes of the play; see the introduction.

1. Creon insists on the plurality of the attackers, but Oedipus's response assumes there was a single attacker. Oedipus quickly leaps to the idea that there must have been a conspiracy.

2. The Greek also uses the word "fall"; the Greek phrase translated "impediment" (in English, etymologically, a foot-shackle, from Latin *impedimentum*) suggests "bad thing at the feet" (*kakon . . . empodon*). The word translated "power" is *tyrannis*, "one-person government."

3. The sentence suggests both that the Sphinx forced the Thebans to focus on the immediate threat she herself posed, and that she made them abandon one riddle (the murder of Laius) in the attempt to solve another (her own, involving numbers of feet).

avenging both this country and the god.
I will myself for my own self dispel
pollution, not for distant relatives,
because whoever killed him might kill me   [140]
with that same swift avenging hand. So when
I help the dead, I benefit myself.
Now hurry, children, get up from those steps,
pick up your supplication wreaths, and someone
must gather all the Theban people. Tell them
that I will do it all, for if the god
is with us, we will have good luck—or fall.
PRIEST   Children, we can get up, because this man
has made the proclamation that we came for.
Apollo sent this oracle. May he
arrive to save us and to end the plague!   [150]

> CREON *exits.* PRIEST, *acolytes, and children rise and*
> *leave the stage by a side exit, as if for the city.* OEDIPUS
> *remains on stage, listening to the* CHORUS.[4]

CHORUS[5]
What are you, sweet word of Zeus,
that traveled from golden Delphi to glorious Thebes?
I am quaking with fear; my heart is stretched tight with the terror.
Healer of Delos, Apollo our Healer,
you fill me with awe. What debt must I pay you?
A new one or something returned
from the circling seasons of time?
Tell me, immortal Oracle, child of golden Hope.

Daughter of Zeus, I call on you first,   [160]
deathless Athena,
and your sister, the earth-shaker, Artemis,
who sits on the glorious circular throne of the market,[6]
and Phoebus Apollo, far-shooter;[7]

4. Oedipus most likely remains on stage during this choral ode; but he may leave and then reenter after the song, making a "powerful re-entrance" (P. J. Finglass, ed. and trans., *Sophocles: Oedipus the King* [Cambridge, Eng.: Cambridge UP, 2018], p. 206).
5. The Chorus members would have been singing and dancing; their words are in a different, much more complex metrical scheme from the main dialogue, as is always the case for choral odes. In this translation, the different meters are reflected by the use of iambic pentameter for dialogue sections (iambic trimeter in the original), and more varied, primarily anapestic rhythms for the choral passages. The first choral ode of a play is called the parodos. Line spaces mark breaks between one metrical unit and the next (called a "strophe" and "antistrophe" in the original, where the music and rhythm of the sections are in a symmetrical pattern).
6. It is usually Poseidon, not Artemis, who is responsible for earthquakes. Artemis was known as "glorious" (*eukleia*) in Boeotia; perhaps Sophocles has a specific cult statue of the goddess in mind. The circular throne is appropriate for the goddess of the moon.
7. Apollo, who has the cult title Phoebus, is Artemis's twin brother, the god of the golden bow.

come and appear to me, triple protectors!
If ever before you banished the flames of disaster
from earlier curses besetting the city,
come now!

Horror! My sufferings
cannot be counted, since all of us,   [170]
all of the people are sick
and no sword of the mind can save us or help us.[8]
Our famous city
is increased by nothing. The women
emerge from their labors and shrieks with no children.
Like birds on the wing, one here and one there,
you see people sent faster than furious fire
to the shore of the western god.[9]

The city is dying, the dying are numberless.
There is no pity   [180]
for children who lie underfoot and bring death.[1]
The wives and the grey-haired grandmothers
jostle each other to clutch at the edge of the altar,
screaming their desperate
prayers of pain.
The chanting is shining and with it the wailing
of mourners is piping in harmony.[2]
For their sake, golden daughter of Zeus,
look with kind eyes and protect them.

Ares,[3] a fire, is burning me now in the din and the clamor   [190]
without shields or weapons of bronze.
Turn back his onslaught,
away from the bounds
of our fatherland, down to the spacious room
of the sea goddess, Amphitrite,[4]
or into the waves of Thrace,
which welcomes no anchors.
If night has left any ruin undone,

8. This striking metaphor suggests a frustrated hope that mental effort might be able to act as a weapon to save the people of Thebes—as Oedipus's mind did when the city of Thebes was threatened by the Sphinx.
9. Hades is not normally known as the "western god," but the reference must be to him.
1. The ancient Athenians did not know about the exact means by which infectious diseases are spread, but they were certainly aware that the bodies of the sick or dying could cause others to become sick.
2. Synesthetic imagery: the sound of a chant for healing is conveyed by a verb, "shining," normally applied to bright light.
3. The god of war.
4. A sea goddess.

he does it when day comes.   [200]
Lord of the fiery lightning, Father Zeus,
blast him with thunder.

Wolf Lord, Apollo Lycaios,[5]
may the strings of your curved golden bow
scatter unstoppable arrows to help and defend us;
may Artemis blaze with the flames that she spreads
dashing through Lycian mountains.
And I call on the god
who is named after Thebes   [210]
in his circlet of gold,
the god with the wine-face, Bacchus,[6]
whose maenads whoop crowding around him,
to come with his dazzling pine-torch and burn
the god whom the gods are ashamed of.[7]

OEDIPUS

I know what you are asking. If you're willing
to listen to my words, and fix the plague,
you can get help, relief from all this pain.
I am a foreigner to this event,
and unfamiliar with what was said.[8]
The hunt would not have taken me so long   [220]
without a clue.[9] But now at last I am
a citizen, and I proclaim to you,
people of Cadmus: if you know who killed
Laius, the son of Labdacus, you must
reveal it all to me. And if the killer
is scared to blame himself,[1] his punishment

---

5. Apollo is addressed as Lycaios, a cult epithet that has often been associated with
   wolves, although the actual meaning of the title is unknown. The title, also used in
   Jocasta's prayer later in the play (line 919 in the Greek text), may be associated with
   Apollo's role as cause and healer of disease. There was a temple and cult of Apollo on
   Mount Lycaion, a remote, rocky area.
6. Bacchus = Dionysos, who is "named after Thebes" because one of his cult titles was
   "Cadmean" (*kadmeios*), in allusion to his Theban heritage, as the son of the Theban
   princess Semele. Dionysos was traditionally accompanied by wildly ecstatic women
   dressed in furs, called maenads (the mad women). The "whoop" of the maenads is their
   traditional ecstatic cry, often rendered with the onomatopoeic word "euhoe!"
7. The other gods are (according to the Chorus) ashamed of Ares, as god of destruction.
8. Oedipus applies to himself the word *xenos*, meaning "stranger," "guest," or "noncitizen": as a person from a different city-state, he was a *xenos* in Thebes, and also—he
   suggests—a metaphorical "stranger" in terms of being informed about the killing of
   Laius.
9. The Greek is ambiguous. It could suggest, "If I had been able to investigate right away,
   I would have found a clue long ago." Or it could be, "I would not have got far with the
   investigation, if there was no clue." The ambiguity underlines the crucial question of
   whether there is already evidence available to Oedipus that he could in theory "track."
1. There may be a lacuna (gap in the text) between lines 227 and 228, with a line missing
   that said something like, "the killer need not be [afraid of blaming himself]."

will not be too severe. He must leave Thebes,
unharmed, no worse than that. Or else if someone
knows that the killer came from somewhere else,[2]   [230]
he must speak up. I will make sure that man
receives his proper thanks and due reward.[3]
But if you do not speak—if anyone
pushes my words away, because he's scared
for someone close to him, or for himself—
listen to me! Whoever that man is,
I ban him from this land where I hold sway.
No one must let him in or speak to him
or share with him in sacrifice or prayer
to gods, nor let him touch the holy water.[4]   [240]
You must all push him from your homes. This man
pollutes us, as the Pythian oracle,[5]
the god, has recently revealed to me.
I fight beside the dead man and the god.
Whether the secret criminal did this
alone or with accomplices, I pray
that he wears out a poor, unlucky life
in misery.[6] And if that man has been
inside my house, and present at my hearth,
and if I know about it, I here vow   [250]
to take these curses I have made on me.
I lay it on you to fulfill all this,
for my sake, for the god, and for this land,
so ruined, barren, and unblessed by gods.
For even if the god had not compelled us,
it would not have been right for you to leave
pollution, from a well-born ruler's death.
It needs investigation. Now I have
the power that the dead man used to hold.
I also have his bed, and sow his wife
with him.[7] If he had not been so unlucky

2. Oedipus fits all the possibilities he outlines: he is a Theban and a man from a different
   city.
3. More dramatic irony, since Oedipus will give himself his due reward for revealing the
   truth.
4. The "holy water," *chernips*, is water used for purification of a crowd of worshippers; it
   was made holy by dipping a brand heated at the altar of sacrifice into the water. Oedipus is ordering that the murderer suffer the ancient equivalent of excommunication:
   he will be excluded from all types of religious ceremonies.
5. The Pythian oracle is at Delphi.
6. This sentence may be interpolated from an actor's emendation of the text; see Finglass,
   Oedipus the King, p. 252.
7. Literally, the wife is described as "together-sown," *homosporos*.

in fathering, we would have common children.[8]   [260]
But Fate has leapt upon his head.[9] And therefore
I fight for him as if he were my father,
and I will do it all to seek and catch
the selfsame man whose own hands killed the son[1]
of Labdacus, the son of Polydorus,
the son of Cadmus, offspring of Agenor
in ancient times.[2] If anybody fails
to do this, I pray gods will send to them
no crops from earth, no children from their wives;   [270]
and let them die, from this plague, or from worse.
You other Thebans who agree to this,
may Justice fight with you! May all the gods
bless you and be with you forevermore.

CHORUS
Lord, I will speak, on pain of your own curse.
I did not kill him; I don't know who did.
Apollo sent the oracle; it was
for him to say who was the perpetrator.

OEDIPUS
Yes, what you say is right. But there's no man   [280]
able to force the gods against their will.

CHORUS
Let me say what seems second best to me.

OEDIPUS
Or even third best! Tell me everything.

CHORUS
I know that Lord Tiresias excels
at seeing as our Lord Apollo sees.
My lord, investigation in these things
would gain most clear enlightenment from him.[3]

---

8. Again dramatic irony: Oedipus thinks Laius had bad luck in that he had no children; but we know that his bad luck as a father was different. "Common children" suggests, for Oedipus, "children who shared a mother," i.e., half-siblings.
9. Fate (*Tyche*) is personified and imagined as jumping onto Laius.
1. The original uses *autocheir*, literally, "same-hand," which can connote a suicide, or a person who achieves something with his or her own hands, or a person who kills a family member. Oedipus uses the word to denote the murderer, who killed Laius with his own hands; but the connotation of "family-killer" or "self-killer" adds yet more dramatic irony.
2. The patrilinear genealogy shows Oedipus demonstrating what he imagines is firm knowledge of Laius's family and paying homage to a line that he imagines has been wiped out. Agenor is the mythical father of Cadmus.
3. The Chorus repeats the word for "Lord" (*anax*) three times. The language of sight and seeing runs through the Tiresias scene, as here: "excels / at seeing" (*skopon*) and "most clear enlightenment" (*ekmathoi saphestata*: literally, "from whom one may learn most clearly").

OEDIPUS
  I have already worked this field as well.[4]
  As Creon told me to, I sent two men
  to fetch him, and he should be here by now.
CHORUS
  Good. All the rest is pointless, ancient rumors.   [290]
OEDIPUS
  What rumors? I look into everything.
CHORUS
  They say some people on the road killed him.
OEDIPUS
  I heard that too. But no one saw who did it.
CHORUS
  Well, anyone who can be touched by fear,
  who hears these threats of yours, will soon be moved.
OEDIPUS
  Words cannot scare one unafraid of deeds.
CHORUS
  The man to prove his guilt is here; they're bringing
  the prophet of the gods already—look!—
  the only human in whom truth is planted.
      Enter TIRESIAS, *blind, escorted by enslaved helpers.*
OEDIPUS
  Tiresias, you see it all: what can   [300]
  and can't be understood or spoken of
  on earth and in the sky. Though you are blind,
  you know about our city and the plague.
  My lord, you are the only one we've found
  to save us from it. If you have not heard,
  we asked Apollo, and the god replied,
  the only liberation from this plague
  is if we find the murderers of Laius,
  and kill them, or expel them from the land.
  If you have information from the birds,[5]   [310]
  or any other art of prophecy,
  do not withhold it! Save yourself and me
  and Thebes, and save the dead man from pollution.
  We're in your hands. It is the best of labors,
  to help another man as best one can.

---

4. Oedipus says he has not acted "in fallow fields," *en argois.*
5. It was traditional for diviners in antiquity to interpret the flight and behavior of birds
   as a sign of the gods' will.

TIRESIAS
It's terrible! How terrible to think,
when thinking does no good. I knew all that,
but I forgot. Or I would not have come.

OEDIPUS
What is it? How dispirited you seem!

TIRESIAS
Send me back home. If you do as I say,   [320]
we will both bear our lots more easily.

OEDIPUS
What? To deprive us of this holy word
is cruel and wrong to Thebes, your benefactor!

TIRESIAS
I see your words are heading for bad luck.
So may I not experience the same. . . .

OEDIPUS (*kneeling to beseech Tiresias*)
By the gods, don't deprive us of your knowledge!
We are your suppliants! We kneel before you!

TIRESIAS
Yes: none of you are thinking. I will never
reveal my ruin: I will not say "yours."[6]

OEDIPUS
What's that? You know, and will not speak? Do you   [330]
mean to betray us, and destroy the city?

TIRESIAS
I will not hurt myself or you. Why are you
asking these futile questions? I won't answer.

OEDIPUS
You evil monster! You'd enrage a rock!
So will you never speak? Will you keep up
this endless pose of rigid stubbornness?

TIRESIAS
You criticize my temperament, and blame me;
you do not know the one you're living with.[7]

OEDIPUS
Now you are disrespecting our own city!
Who wouldn't lose his temper at your words?   [340]

TIRESIAS
Even if I keep silent, it will happen.

6. Tiresias is speaking in deliberately riddling language, not revealing what or whose the "ruin" is.
7. There is a double meaning: Oedipus does not know the temperament or character or rage he lives with, but also does not know the "one" he lives with, i.e., Jocasta. In the Greek, "temperament," "character," or "anger," *orgē*, is a feminine noun; Tiresias says, "You do not know the [feminine] one you live with." The word *orgē* is picked up in Oedipus's response, when he asks who would not "lose his temper" (*orgizoito*).

OEDIPUS

So why not also tell me what will happen?

TIRESIAS

I would not say too much. Face up to that,
then rage your wildest, if you want to rage.

OEDIPUS

I am so seized by anger, I will not
shield you from what I think. Know this: I reckon
you helped to plant the crime, and even did it,
killing him, though not with your hands! If you
could see, I'd say the deed was yours alone.

TIRESIAS

Really? I tell you this: you must abide   [350]
by that announcement you yourself just made.
From this day on, you must not speak to us.
You are the cursed pollution of this country!

OEDIPUS

How dare you rustle up this accusation?
Do you think you can get away with it?

TIRESIAS

I have. The truth I raise is powerful.[8]

OEDIPUS

Who made you say this? Not your skill, for sure.

TIRESIAS

You did. You made me speak against my will.

OEDIPUS

What's that? Repeat it, so I'll understand.

TIRESIAS

Do you not understand? Is this a test?[9]   [360]

OEDIPUS

It doesn't make much sense. Say it again.

TIRESIAS

I say you are the murderer you seek.[1]

OEDIPUS

If you repeat that slander, you'll regret it!

TIRESIAS

Shall I say more, and make you angrier still?

8. Tiresias here uses an essential repeated verb in the play, *trepho*, "to raise up"—used for
   the raising of children or plants, and here, by extension, of Tiresias's metaphorical
   child: truth.
9. The text of this phrase ("Is this a test?") is uncertain. The manuscript reading, *e kpreirae
   legein*, suggests, "Or are you trying to speak?" which makes little sense; probably "to
   speak" has been substituted for a different original word. The general sense—"Are you
   testing me?" or "Are you trying to trick me?"—seems clear.
1. The text reads more literally, "I say you are the killer of the man whom you seek," a
   syntactical elision suggesting, on the face of it, that Oedipus is looking for Laius.

OEDIPUS

Say all you want. Your words are meaningless.

TIRESIAS

You don't know how disgustingly you live
with closest family, and you don't see
how far you're ruined.

OEDIPUS

                              Do you really think
you'll get away with saying this?

TIRESIAS

                                        If there
is any strength in truth.

OEDIPUS

                              There's none in you!   [370]
Your mind and ears are blind, just like your eyes!

TIRESIAS

You poor, unhappy man. Soon all these people
will hurl these accusations back at you.

OEDIPUS

You are the child of endless night! You'll never
hurt me, or any man who sees the light.

TIRESIAS

It is your fate to fall, but not by me.
Apollo is enough. The task is his.

OEDIPUS

Who thought of all this? Creon? Or who else?

TIRESIAS

Creon is doing nothing wrong to you:
you are the one who's hurting your own self.

OEDIPUS

Sovereignty! Riches! Skill that can surpass   [380]
the skills of others, in a life defined
by competition! What a mass of envy
is hoarded up inside all these desires!
The city gave me, as a gift, the role
of leader—but I never asked for it!
But now for this position, loyal Creon,
my friend right from the first,[2] snuck up on me,
and wants to throw me out! He has coopted
this wizard, stitcher of conspiracies!
This lying beggar! Who can only see

2. Creon is described using a phrase that suggests "my friend from the beginning," but could also suggest "my friend motivated by power": the same word, *arche*, can mean "power" or "beginning."

where profit lies! He's blind to any art.
(*To Tiresias*) Come on then, tell me, how are you a real
prophet? When she was here, that song-composer,[3]   [390]
that dog, how was it that you did not speak
a word to free these citizens from her spell—
although the riddle surely needed skill,
prophetic art, not just some passerby?
Yet you did not show up with any knowledge
from birds or gods. Instead, I came along,
"Know-Nothing Oedipus," and I stopped her!
I hit the target with intelligence,
not getting information from the birds.
This is the man you're trying to throw out,
thinking that you will stand beside the throne
of Creon. But I think that you will suffer,   [400]
you and the man who put you up to it,
when you drive out this curse. If you did not
look like an old man, you would have discovered,
by suffering, the nature of your insights!

CHORUS

We reckon, Oedipus, that he was speaking
in anger; you were too. We don't need this.
Instead, look into how we may fulfill
Apollo's oracles, as best we can.

TIRESIAS

Even if you are sovereign, still the right
to answer must be equal. I have power
in speech at least, since I am not your slave;
I am Apollo's. Do not write me down   [410]
in Creon's list of immigrants.[4] I'll speak!
You have insulted me for being blind,
but you don't know the ruin you are in,
nor where you are or who you're living with.
Do you know who you come from? You don't see
that you're an enemy to your own people,
above the earth and under it. A curse
with feet of doom will strike you, from both parents,

---

3. The Sphinx, still unnamed, is described as a *rhapsoidos*, which connotes literally a
"song-stitcher": a person who performed selections of the Homeric poems and other
traditional narrative poetry, with musical accompaniment. It is very unusual to see the
word with the feminine article; real human rhapsodes were usually men. The Sphinx
was the daughter of the Chimera (a goat-lion creature) and the dog Orthos, and niece
of the three-headed guard dog of the underworld, Cerberus.

4. The language in the original suggests an allusion to the Athenian law whereby magis-
trates (*prostatai*) had to register all legal immigrants (*metoikoi*). Tiresias is insisting
that he is a native of Thebes and not under the patronage of Creon.

and one day it will drive you from this land.
Now you see straight ahead; you will see darkness.
Your cries will resonate on every shore;   [420]
Cithaeron will be ringing with them soon,
when you know what your marriage is, and where
you smoothly sailed, to this perverted harbor.
You do not see the number of disasters
that will match you with you, and with your children.
You hurl this mud at Creon and at me,
but you will be washed out, annihilated,
crushed as no mortal person ever was.

OEDIPUS
This is intolerable! Must I keep listening
to him? You go to hell! Turn round, go back   [430]
out of my house, as fast as you can go!

TIRESIAS
I would not have come here if you'd not called me.

OEDIPUS
I didn't know you'd say such stupid things,
or I would not have brought you to my house.

TIRESIAS
I am like this: to you I may seem stupid,
but to your real birth-parents, I am wise.

OEDIPUS
What parents? Wait. Which mortal was my father?

TIRESIAS
This day will give you birth and bring you death.

OEDIPUS
Your words are all too riddling and obscure.

TIRESIAS
Aren't you the best at solving these enigmas?   [440]

OEDIPUS
You're mocking me for things that make me great!

TIRESIAS
No, but your skill itself will be your ruin.

OEDIPUS
But if I saved this city, I don't care!

TIRESIAS
I'm going now. (*To his enslaved boy*) Here, boy, take me away.

OEDIPUS
Away then! You are just a nuisance here.
Be off, and you will bother me no more!

TIRESIAS
I'll go, because I've said what I intended.
I do not fear your eyes. You can't destroy me.

This man you have been looking for so long,
Laius's murderer, that man is here.   [450]
He's called an immigrant, noncitizen,[5]
but he will be revealed a native Theban,
although he won't be glad about his fortune.[6]
Now he can see; he will go blind. Now rich,
he'll be a beggar leaning on a stick,
wandering through strange lands. He'll be revealed
the father and the brother of his children;
the son and husband of his own birth-mother;
the killer of his father, and the one
who shared his seed-place. Go in. Work it out.   [460]
If you find out it's false, call me no prophet.

Exit TIRESIAS, *led by enslaved boy.*

Exit OEDIPUS, *attended by enslaved attendants.*

CHORUS
Who did the things unspeakable, unspeakable,
with bloody hands of murder?[7]
Whom did the voice of the god,
the rock at Delphi, mean?
Now it is time for him to move his feet in flight,
faster than storm-swift horses.
The son of Zeus is after him, full-armed,
with fire and lightning bolts,   [470]
and with him come the Fates who never miss.

The word has now shone forth
from snowy Mount Parnassus
that everyone must track
the unseen man—the bull:[8] he wanders through
the wild wood, the caves,
and through the rocks, bereft, unhappy,
on unhappy feet,
fleeing the oracles from the earth's navel.[9]   [480]
But they live forever and fly all around him.

The wise interpreter of birds
has caused me terrible, terrible anxiety,
with words incredible and undeniable.

5. The sequence of binary contrasts begins with a contrast between an immigrant permanent resident (a "metic") and a citizen.
6. Fortune, *symphora*, could be either good or bad luck.
7. The Chorus members have almost blind faith in Oedipus and Tiresias and can initially
   make no sense of what they have witnessed.
8. The murderer is described as a "bull" because he is like a sacrificial animal.
9. The Earth's navel is Delphi, imagined as the center of the world's body.

I don't know what to say. I fly on hope,
not seeing the present, not seeing the future.
I didn't know, I don't know now,
of any conflict that arose between
the sons of Labdacus and Polybus's son   [490]
to use as evidence, a touchstone test,
of Oedipus's public reputation,
to find out if I ought to help the Labdacids'
in solving their mystery deaths.[1]

But Zeus and Apollo are wise; they know and can see
the mortal world. There's no true judgment   [500]
to tell if a prophet is worth more than I am.
A man may surpass
wisdom by wisdom.[2]
But when people are blaming, I never agree
until I can see if their words are correct.
After all, she with the wings in the past
appeared to him, and by the test he was seen
as the wise one, sweet to the city. Because of this,   [510]
my heart will never discover him guilty of wrong.
          Enter CREON, *from the city.*

CREON
I've come here, men of Thebes, because I learned
that Oedipus, our leader, has accused me
of dreadful things, and I won't stand for it.
If, in the present crisis, he imagines
that he has suffered any kind of harm
from me, in word or deed—then I do not   [520]
wish for long life, if I must bear this charge.
Indeed, this accusation brings for me
no simple punishment, but total ruin,
if I am called a criminal in Thebes,

---

1. The Chorus members use obscure language to avoid spelling out the dangerous possibility that they are hinting at: that their own powerful and well-respected leader, Oedipus, might be responsible for the death of Laius. They hedge by several means:
   emphasizing Oedipus's good reputation; using metaphor (the "evidence" is described in
   the original as a "touchstone"—a stone used to test the quality of a metal); avoiding the
   name of Laius (referred to in the plural as "the sons of Labdacus"); and pluralizing a
   singular event and singular victim (the "deaths" of the "Labdacids," or sons of Labdacus, rather than the single murder of Laius—the Chorus members are still unaware
   that Oedipus, too, is a Labdacid). All this deliberate obscurity marks the Chorus's
   awareness of how dangerous it would be to accuse the supreme leader of Thebes of
   murdering his predecessor. The lines are also textually corrupt, and a word or phrase is
   missing.
2. Another mysterious, carefully veiled utterance: the Chorus has half-questioned
   whether Tiresias is right, then acknowledges that there can be distinctions in human
   wisdom, then reiterates a skeptical position.

and called a criminal by you as well,
and by my family and friends.
CHORUS
                              Come now,
the insult happened, yes, but it was maybe
forced out by anger, not by conscious thought.
CREON
But was it said in public that the prophet
was swayed by my advice to tell those lies?
CHORUS
Yes, that was said; but I don't know the motive.
CREON
And was he thinking straight and looking straight,
making this accusation against me?
CHORUS
I do not know, because I do not see   [530]
what those in power over me are doing.
But he himself is coming outside now.³
        Enter OEDIPUS, *from the palace.*
OEDIPUS
You! How did you get here? Have you become
so brazen that you dare to show your face
and come to my own house, when you are clearly
the murderer of that man, and the proven,
flagrant thief who tried to steal my power?
Come on then, talk, by gods! Did you perceive
some foolishness or cowardice in me,
so you decided you would do this? Or
did you think that I wouldn't recognize
that it was you who made this treacherous plot,
sneaking against me—or when I found out,
you thought that I would fail in self-defense?
This plan of yours is stupid, isn't it?   [540]
To hunt for power, with no wealth or friends!
To get it, you need influence, and money.
CREON
Trade in your words for listening as an equal.
You need to understand before you judge.
OEDIPUS
I'm bad at listening to your clever words,
because I've found you mean and cruel toward me.
CREON
Just hear me out on this one thing, for once.

3. This line is likely an interpolation (put into the text by someone after Sophocles).

OEDIPUS

Just this one thing: don't tell me you're not evil!

CREON

If you think mindless, willful stubbornness
is something clever, you're not thinking straight.   [550]

OEDIPUS

If you think you can harm a family member
and have no punishment, you must be crazy.

CREON

Yes, I agree; what you said then is fair.
But teach me: what's this harm you say you suffered?

OEDIPUS

Did you or did you not persuade me, Creon,
that it was necessary for me to send
someone to fetch that high and mighty prophet?

CREON

Yes, and I still believe that plan was good.

OEDIPUS

So how much time has passed by now since Laius—

CREON

Did what exactly? I don't understand.

OEDIPUS

—vanished, subdued by hands that dealt him death?[4]   [560]

CREON

A long and ancient measurement of time.

OEDIPUS

So was this seer not practicing back then?

CREON

Yes, he was just as wise and just as honored.

OEDIPUS

Then at the time, did he name me at all?

CREON

No, at least not when I was standing near him.

OEDIPUS

Did you not have a search to catch the killer?

CREON

Of course we did! But we heard not a thing.

OEDIPUS

Why did this wise man not speak up back then?

CREON

I don't know. When I don't know, I stay silent.

---

4. The original uses *cheiroma*, meaning literally "handing," or metaphorically
"overpowering."

OEDIPUS
  You do know this, and you'd be smart to speak!   [570]

CREON
  Of what? If I do know, I won't deny it.

OEDIPUS
  That if he hadn't been in league with you
  he never would have said that I killed Laius.

CREON
  You know if he says that. I think it right
  to learn from you, just as you learned from me.[5]

OEDIPUS
  Go on then! But I won't be found a killer!

CREON
  All right then. Are you married to my sister?

OEDIPUS
  There's no denial possible for that![6]

CREON
  Do you rule Thebes on equal terms with her?[7]

OEDIPUS
  Yes, I take care of anything she wants.   [580]

CREON
  And am I third, the equal to you two?

OEDIPUS
  That's why you're shown up as an evil friend![8]

CREON
  I'm not! Take time to think, as I have done.
  Firstly, consider this: would anyone
  prefer to rule accompanied by fear,
  than to sleep carefree and have the exact same power?
  I, for my part, have no innate desire
  to be a leader rather than to lead;
  and anybody sane would feel the same.
  As things are now, I get it all from you,   [590]
  and never have to fear. But if I were
  myself the ruler, I would have to do

---

5. I.e., Creon hopes to question Oedipus, as Oedipus has just questioned Creon. Creon implies ignorance of what Tiresias has said.
6. Oedipus treats the question as a joke, although later in the play he will wish he could deny the marriage.
7. It is unclear whether this question implies a formal or legal division of power equally between Oedipus and Jocasta, and possibly Creon too, or a more informal arrangement by which Oedipus allows Jocasta primary influence over his decisions, rather than an official sharing of power. Oedipus's reply maintains the ambiguity: it could suggest an indulgent husband fulfilling his wife's whims, or it could suggest a more equal sharing of power. This point is important, since if Oedipus is not in fact the sole ruler of Thebes, he is not actually a *tyrannos*, a term that implies one-person rule. There is a real question about whether the city is a tyranny or an oligarchy.
8. The word for "friend," *philos*, also implies family member.

many things that I didn't want to do.
So how could I feel happier in power
than having influence at no expense?
I'm not yet so misguided as to want
anything that's not good and beneficial.
As things are now, I can greet everyone,
now everyone is glad to see me, now
people who long for you can call on me,
and they get everything like this, through me.
So why would I lose this to grasp at that?[9]
I've no desire for those priorities,[1]
nor would I join another in such actions.
Find proof yourself! Go ask the oracle   [600]
at Delphi if I've told the truth to you.
And if you catch me plotting with the prophet,
don't kill me by a single vote, but take
a double: yours and mine. Do not accuse me
by unclear evidence, in isolation.[2]
It is not right to think bad people good
or good ones bad. I say it's just the same   [610]
if you reject a good and well-loved friend,
or your own life, which you love the most of all.
In time you'll know for certain: only time
reveals an honest man, although you can
recognize someone bad in just one day.

CHORUS (*to* OEDIPUS)

A person careful not to fall, my lord,
would say he's right. Quick thinkers are not stable.[3]

OEDIPUS

A sly conspirator is plotting fast
against me, so I also must be quick
in planning countermoves. If I sit idle,   [620]
he'll do what he intends, and I will fail!

---

9. The translation here omits a line that makes little sense (line 600 in the Greek text), which is presumably a corrupt addition, an irrelevant quotation written in the margin of somebody's edition that made its way into the received text. It reads something like, "No evil mind could turn to thinking well."

1. Creon describes himself as not being a "desirer" or "lover," using a word (*erastes*) that could have erotic connotations (as in an older man's desire for an adolescent boy), but could also be less clearly sexual. Some editors have thought there might be a gap in the text, since it is odd to have a desire for "priorities," or a "view" or "opinion," rather than for the content of the opinion. If the text is correct, this is presumably a highly condensed and poetic way of saying, "I don't want to be the kind of person who thinks being in a prominent leadership position is worth it."

2. "In isolation" suggests either "by yourself" (repeating the previous line) or "in isolation from the facts."

3. The Chorus gives an allusive, periphrastic, and metaphorical commendation of Creon's speech, avoiding giving Oedipus a direct warning that he might be in trouble.

CREON
  What do you want? To drive me from the land?

OEDIPUS
  No, not at all! I want you dead, not exiled.
  . . . [4]

OEDIPUS[5]
  Whenever you reveal what envy is.

CREON[6]
  You mean you will not yield and won't believe me?
  . . . [7]

CREON
  I see you can't think straight.

OEDIPUS
                    I think of me!

CREON
  You should be thinking of me too!

OEDIPUS
                       You traitor!

CREON
  If you know nothing . . . ?

OEDIPUS
                     You must still obey me!

CREON
  Not if you're ruling badly.

OEDIPUS
                City! City!

CREON
  I share the city; it's not yours alone.   [630]

CHORUS
  Stop, lords, I see Jocasta coming out
  toward you from the house, and right on time;
  with her, you should resolve the present quarrel.
     Enter JOCASTA, *from the palace.*

JOCASTA
  You idiots! Why did you start to argue?
  Aren't you ashamed of picking private fights

---

4. Here there seems to be a gap of some lines that have fallen out of the received text, since the following line does not make sense as a response.
5. The manuscripts ascribe this line to Creon, but some scholars argue persuasively that it really belongs to Oedipus, since Oedipus is the one obsessed with envy.
6. This line is ascribed to Oedipus by the manuscripts, but again it is more likely to belong to Creon, since Oedipus is the one, in this scene and consistently in the play, who is urged to yield and be persuaded.
7. Another line at least seems to be missing here; we would expect Oedipus to speak at least one more line before Creon speaks again (as is the norm in stichomythic dialogue, when characters exchange lines). Creon's next half-line seems like a response to Oedipus's having made some further iteration of his obstinacy.

during the country's sickness?
    (*To* OEDIPUS) You go home!
(*To Creon*) And Creon, to your house as well! Don't turn
a trivial problem into something big.

CREON

Sister in blood, your husband Oedipus
imagines that abusing me is right!
He has two terrible ideas: to drive me   [640]
from my own fatherland, or to seize and kill me!

OEDIPUS

That's right! I caught him, wife, in treachery!
A wicked plot, of physical harm to me!

CREON

No! If I did a single thing you've said,
curse me, and let me die in misery!

JOCASTA

Oedipus! By the gods, believe his words!
Mostly, respect this oath, sworn by the gods,
and also me, and those who stand before you.[8]

CHORUS[9]

Sir, I beg you, be willing
to think and to do as they say.

OEDIPUS

What? Why do you want me to yield?   [650]

CHORUS

Respect him. He's never been stupid,
and now by his oath he is great.

OEDIPUS

Do you know what you want?

CHORUS

                  Yes, I do.

OEDIPUS

                        So then tell me!

CHORUS

For you never to strike at a friend or dishonor his words
when he's under a sanctified curse, and the charge is so murky!

OEDIPUS

Then you'd better know, when you're asking for this,
that you're seeking my death or my exile from Thebes.

---

8. Jocasta seems to take Creon's utterance as an oath by the gods, although he has not
   mentioned the gods explicitly. "Those who stand before you" are presumably the Chorus members.
9. The meter now shifts to lyric, a mark of high emotional tension. The original includes
   a lot of dochmaic rhythms, suggesting urgency.

CHORUS

No, by the god who is chief of all gods,   [660]
the Sun! May I die the most terrible death,
friendless and godless, if I have that thought!
But our country is dying. This wears at my heart,
and I am so unhappy, if trouble with you two
is about to be added to pain from the past.[1]

OEDIPUS

Well then, let him go, even if I must die for it—die for it!—
or else be shoved from this country by force, in dishonor.   [670]
I pity the plight you describe in your words, though I don't pity him!
That man will be hated wherever he is!

CREON

It's clear that you hate to give in, and whenever you're far gone
in anger, you're cruel. But this kind of character
most hurts the person who has it; it's fair.

OEDIPUS

Now enough! Won't you let me be? Out!

CREON

                                                    I will go—
though with no recognition from you. But these men
   know I'm equal.[2]

                                        Exit CREON, *to the city.*

CHORUS (*to* JOCASTA, *referring to Oedipus*)

Why are you waiting, my lady,
to take this man into the house?

JOCASTA

To find out what happened.   [680]

CHORUS

Suspicion arose out of words with no knowledge—
but even a false one can bite.

JOCASTA

Were these words from them both?

CHORUS

                                        Yes, they were.

JOCASTA

                                                    What was said?

---

1. The vague "pain from the past" could imply pain that actually is past (the Sphinx's tribute), or pain that has been going on for a while (the plague).
2. The original for "no recognition" suggests literally that Creon is "unknown" by Oedipus (important in a play so focused on different kinds of knowledge); the word *agnotos* could also mean "ignorant" or "harsh." The word translated "equal," *isos*, can mean "fair" or "impartial." The scholiasts (ancient commentators) suggest that the sentence means, "These men know that I am the same as I was before." For the interpretation of the line given here (*isos*="good" or "just"), see the discussion in Finglass, *Oedipus the King*, pp. 383–84.

CHORUS

   That's enough, in my view. Enough. Let it lie.
   It's over. My mind's on our country.

OEDIPUS

   You're a sensible man! Do you see what you've come to?
   You've loosened and blunted my anger!

CHORUS

   Sir, I've said this before, but be sure   [690]
   I'd seem out of my mind, I'd have no brains at all,
   if I were abandoning you,
   since you brought the fair wind that set my dear country
   up straight when it struggled and suffered.
   Now guide us to safety.

JOCASTA[3]

   O gods! My lord, whatever was the reason
   you roused all this enormous rage? Please tell me!

OEDIPUS

   I will; I honor you more highly, wife,   [700]
   than these men.[4] It was Creon, and his plots!

JOCASTA

   Explain your accusation, and this quarrel.

OEDIPUS

   He said I am the murderer of Laius!

JOCASTA

   Is that his own idea? Did someone tell him?

OEDIPUS

   He sent that wicked prophet in his place;
   he keeps his own mouth free from everything.[5]

JOCASTA

   Then now you can relax about all this!
   Listen to me, and learn. No mortal being
   has any power at all to tell the future.
   I'll show you instant proof of this. There came   [710]
   an oracle to Laius once—I'd say
   not from the god himself,[6] but his attendants—
   that he was doomed to die at his child's hands,
   whatever child he and I had together.
   In fact, the story goes, some foreign robbers

---

3. The meter now switches back to normal iambic dialogue, in the original as in the translation.
4. The Chorus members.
5. The metaphor by which Creon keeps his mouth "free" is unusual, since a "free" mouth or "free" speech, in ancient Greek as in modern English, usually suggests openly talking about illicit subjects rather than the opposite. Oedipus seems to mean that Creon keeps his mouth free from dangerous and blameworthy utterances.
6. Below the god is specified as Phoebus (Apollo).

killed him where three paths meet. Our child was born,
and only three days later, Laius bound
his ankles, and with other people's hands
he hurled him to the mountain wilderness.[7]
Apollo did not make that child the killer   [720]
of his own father, nor make Laius suffer
the dreadful death he feared from his own child.
You need not take the slightest bit of notice
of things ordained by oracles. A god
himself will easily reveal his quest.

OEDIPUS
  Wife, as I listened to you speak just now,
  how shaken and distracted was my mind!

JOCASTA
  What worry's overturned you? What do you mean?

OEDIPUS
  It's that I thought I heard you say that Laius
  was murdered at a place where three roads meet.   [730]

JOCASTA
  That was the story, yes, and it still is!

OEDIPUS
  And where is it, the place where this thing happened?

JOCASTA
  The land is Phocis, and the forked path leads
  to there from Delphi and from Daulia.[8]

OEDIPUS
  And how long is it since these things took place?

JOCASTA
  It was announced in town shortly before
  you showed up as the leader of our country.

OEDIPUS
  O Zeus, what have you planned to do to me?

JOCASTA
  What is this, Oedipus, that's on your mind?

OEDIPUS
  Don't ask me yet, but tell me about Laius.   [740]
  What did he look like, and what age was he?

JOCASTA
  Dark, though he'd started sprouting some white hair;
  his build was not dissimilar to yours.

---

7. The phrasing makes Laius active, although not with his own hands.
8. Phocis is the region in Greece that includes Delphi. The third road of the three is to or
   from Thebes, to the east. Delphi is the home of Apollo's oracle, to the west; Daulia, to
   the north, was on the edge of Boeotia.

OEDIPUS

Oh no! It seems just now I failed to see
that I was casting curses on myself!

JOCASTA

What's that, my lord? I look at you and tremble.

OEDIPUS

I'm terrified the prophet isn't blind.
But you can clarify: tell one more thing.

JOCASTA

I'll tell you anything, although I'm shaking.

OEDIPUS

Then did he go alone, or bring a large   [750]
retinue with him, as befits a leader?

JOCASTA

A group of five in all, a bodyguard
among them; Laius traveled in one wagon.[9]

OEDIPUS

No! Now all this is coming clear.
But wife, who gave you all this information?

JOCASTA

A house-slave. He alone came back alive.

OEDIPUS

Oh! Then is this man in the house right now?

JOCASTA

No. When he came from there and saw that you
were in control, and Laius dead, he begged me,
holding my hand, to send him to the fields   [760]
and shepherd pastures, very far away
from where the town could see him. And I sent him.
As much as any slave, he did deserve
to have this benefit, and more besides.

OEDIPUS

Then could he get back here to us, and quickly?

JOCASTA

Yes, but for what? Why do you want him to?

OEDIPUS

Wife, I'm afraid that I have said too much,
and that is why I want to see this man.

JOCASTA

Then he will come. But I think that I, too,
deserve to learn why you're upset, my lord.   [770]

9. There are one driver; one bodyguard (a more high-ranking attendant); and two enslaved
attendants, who are perhaps walking, not riding in the wagon.

OEDIPUS
  You will. I've reached a pitch of dread; who better
  to tell than you, when I am in this state?
  My mother, Merope, was Dorian;
  my father, Polybus, Corinthian.
  The citizens back there considered me
  important, till this incident that was
  surprising, though not worth the fuss I made:
  at dinner once, a man had too much wine,
  and claimed I was foisted falsely on my father.[1]   [780]
  I took it hard. That day, I held it in,
  but on the next, I went and asked my parents,
  and they were very angry at the insult.
  And I was glad at their response; but still,
  it always gnawed and got to me inside.
  Without my parents knowing it, I went
  to Delphi, and Apollo sent me back
  unsatisfied about the things I asked.
  But to my horror, he revealed and told
  of other dreadful curses: that I must   [790]
  have sex with my own mother, and produce
  children unbearable to human sight,
  and be the murderer of my own father.
  And when I heard these things, I ran away;
  in future, I would mark where Corinth was
  by stars,[2] and go where I might never see
  the stigma of those cursed oracles
  fulfilled. I traveled, and I reached the place
  where you say that this ruler died. And, wife,   [800]
  I'll tell the truth to you. When I had journeyed
  near to that triple crossroad, I encountered
  a man like you described, with bodyguard,
  riding a wagon drawn by colts. The driver,
  plus the old man himself, together forced me
  off-road. In anger I then struck the driver
  who'd made me turn. The old man, seeing this,
  watched till I came beside his cart, then hit

---

1. The suggestion might be that Oedipus was the son of another woman, not Merope—or
   that he was her son by another man. See Dugdale's discussion in this volume, p. 105.
2. The wording is difficult here. The received text, *ekmetroumenos*, suggests that Oedipus
   plans to measure out the area of Corinth like a surveyor, which is an odd use of language. The emendation *tekmaroumenos* suggests rather that he is "judging," "figuring,"
   or "estimating" the location, by the stars. The manuscript reading may be correct,
   since this play includes a great deal of language involving measurement, and Sophocles sometimes uses language in obscure metaphorical ways. I have translated the
   emended text, which is easier to understand.

my head with a double whip. But he received
a more than equal blow! Briefly: my hand here   [810]
struck him—I used my stick—and he rolled down
out from the wagon, and then fell down flat.
And so I killed them all. But if there was
some family connection between Laius
and him, this stranger . . . ? What man is worse off
than I am? Who more hated by the gods?
No foreigner or citizen could take me
into their homes, no one can speak to me;
they have to drive me out! And no one else
has cast these curses on me but myself!   [820]
And by my hands, I taint the dead man's bed:
the hands that killed him. So am I then born bad?
Yes! Am I godless, totally accursed?
Yes! If I have to go away, and, banished,
must never see my people, never set
foot in my fatherland, or I must join
in marriage with my mother, and must kill
my father, Polybus, who fathered me
and brought me up! So wouldn't you
be right to think some cruel god has done this
to me? No, no, I pray the holy gods,   [830]
may I not ever, ever see the day,
but disappear from human sight, before
I see that taint of fate arrive on me.

CHORUS
This makes us nervous too. But till you hear
from this eyewitness, master, don't lose hope.

OEDIPUS
Yes, this is actually my only hope:
just waiting here for him, the man, the herder.

JOCASTA
What do you want of him when he arrives?

OEDIPUS
I'll tell you. If I find he says the same
as he told you, then I'd be free from trouble.   [840]

JOCASTA
What in particular from what I said?

OEDIPUS
You said he claimed that robbers, plural, killed him.
If he still says the same in terms of numbers,
I did not kill him, since there is no way
that one man can be equal to a group.
But if he cites a single traveler,

this action then is tipping toward me.

JOCASTA

Yes, that is definitely what he said,
and there's no way that he can take it back.
The city heard all this, not only me.   [850]
And even if he switched his former story
at all, my lord, he couldn't ever prove
Laius's murder happened as it should have;
Apollo's oracle said he'd be killed
by his and my own son; but that poor boy
died long before; he never murdered Laius.
So after this, I'd never ever spare
a single glance for any oracles.[3]

OEDIPUS

Good thinking. But in any case, send someone
to get the workman.[4] Do it, don't forget!   [860]

JOCASTA

I'll hurry up and do it. Let's go in.
I won't do anything that you won't like.

            Exeunt JOCASTA *and* OEDIPUS, *into the palace.*

CHORUS

May Fate be with me!
All my words, all my deeds,
are holy and reverent!
Good actions are governed by laws whose feet step high,
who are born in the heavens above, and Olympus[5]
alone is their father. No mortal nature
poured forth or mothered them.
Oblivion never will lull them to sleep.
Great is the god in these places; he does not grow old.   [870]

Arrogance fathers sovereignty.[6] Arrogance,

---

3. This odd phrase (to "spare a glance," or "look this way or that") is unparalleled in other
   extant texts and may be a deliberately strange coinage or an unknown idiom. It clearly
   suggests not caring (about oracles), but the suggestion of sight ties in with the play's
   obsessive focus on eyes and seeing; Jocasta expresses a deliberate refusal to look in a
   certain direction.
4. This man is described with a number of different terms: as "workman" (*ergates*) here,
   and also as an "enslaved person" and messenger.
5. Mountain imagined to be the home of the most powerful gods.
6. This famous line is much debated by scholars. Some argue it should be emended to
   read "The tyrant fathers arrogance," but there is no clear reason to accept the suggestion, and the flow of thought and sound works better the other way. The word translated "arrogance" is *hybris*, which suggests any kind of violence or overstepping of
   natural boundaries. Tyrant, *tyrannos*, is a neutral term elsewhere in Sophocles, but is
   sometimes used negatively by other authors in this period. The word translated
   "fathers," *phuteuei*, could suggest either animal or human or plant growth. Here, as
   throughout the ode, it is unclear whether the Chorus is referring directly to Oedipus
   (and questioning his legitimacy and his piety) or making vague generalizations.

if filled too full of too much,
against what's right and good,
attains the highest cornices[7] and then
topples down headlong to necessity,
where it can find no footing.
But I pray to the god not to end
the wrestling that's good for the city.   [880]
I'll never stop having a god as my savior.

But if someone is using their hands or their words
to step higher than others,
and, fearless of Justice,
shows no due respect to the seats of the gods,
may evil Fate take them
to pay back the curse of their pride
if they profit from ill-gotten gains,
if they do not hold back from unspeakable words,   [890]
if they stupidly touch the untouchable things.
What man in the midst of such actions could ever
ward off the weapons of gods from his soul?
If behavior like this becomes honored,
then why should I dance in the chorus?[8]

No longer will I go to honor the navel
of earth, the untouchable,
nor to the temple at Abae,   [900]
nor to Olympia,[9]
if these things are not tangible truths
fitted fast for all mortals.
Do not forget this, Zeus, master of all!
May your power eternal remember it always.
Indeed, now the oracles told about Laius
are wiped and destroyed
and Apollo is nowhere shown bright in his glory.
Religion is ruined!   [910]

7. The text here is doubtful, and "cornices" is an emendation proposed because the received text is metrically wrong; the word for "cornice," *geisa*, is unusual, so might have been missed by scribes. The image suggests someone making a strange ascent up a high and elaborately decorated building—perhaps the backdrop of the stage, the front of the palace, was painted as if with cornices on the roof. Aristotle in the *Poetics* says that Sophocles was the first tragedian to use painted scenery.
8. This seems to be a metadramatic moment: the Chorus members are asking why they should participate in this tragic chorus, which is part of a religious ritual in honor of the god Dionysos, if those who act impiously can get away with it, and even accrue honor.
9. Abae also had a sanctuary of Apollo. There was a temple to Zeus at Olympia; Olympia was also, like Delphi, a center for prophecy.

Enter JOCASTA, *with enslaved attendants, carrying suppliant
branches; she addresses the* CHORUS.

JOCASTA

My lords of Thebes, the thought occurred to me
to come toward the temple with these wreaths
and incense in my arms, since Oedipus
is lifting up his heart too high; he's swayed
by every kind of grief. He does not judge
new facts by old ones, like a man of sense.
He's vulnerable to every word of fear.
I made no progress giving him advice,
so I have come as suppliant to you,
Apollo Lycian, our nearest god,[1]   [920]
to pray that you provide us some release
and bless us. As things are, we all are frightened
seeing the pilot of our ship struck down.

Enter FIRST MESSENGER, *from the countryside.*

FIRST MESSENGER

Strangers, I want to know where I can find
the palace of your ruler, Oedipus.
Please tell me if you know where he may be.

CHORUS

Stranger, this is his house; he is inside.
This is his wife and mother of his children.[2]

FIRST MESSENGER

I wish her luck and happiness forever,
as Oedipus's true and perfect wife.[3]   [930]

JOCASTA

Stranger, the same to you; your kindly words
deserve a blessing. Tell us now why you
have come. What is your news? What do you want?

FIRST MESSENGER

Luck for your home and for your husband, lady.

JOCASTA

But please explain your visit. Who has sent you?

FIRST MESSENGER

I came from Corinth. I'll soon tell my news.
You'll like it, surely, but it might upset you.

---

1. Apollo is the nearest god both because his altar is in front of the palace, and because he
   is most closely associated with oracles and prophecies. On "Lycian" see note 5, p. 10.
2. A momentary double entendre, since Jocasta is Oedipus's wife and mother *tout court*,
   as well as his wife and the mother of his children.
3. The First Messenger may be implying Jocasta is truly his wife because she has his
   children; marriages were imagined to be sealed by offspring.

JOCASTA
    What double power does this message have?
FIRST MESSENGER
    The Isthmians[4] will soon establish him
    as ruler there; that's what the people say.   [940]
JOCASTA
    Then is old Polybus no longer ruler?
FIRST MESSENGER
    No, he is held inside the grave by death.
JOCASTA
    What did you say? That Polybus is dead?[5]
FIRST MESSENGER
    If I am lying, I deserve to die.
JOCASTA (*to one of her enslaved attendants*)
    Slave! To your master, hurry, tell him this!
    Look where you stand now, oracles of gods!
    Years ago, Oedipus was full of fear
    and ran from this man so he would not kill him.
    But now he's dead by chance, not killed by him.
        Enter OEDIPUS, *from the palace.*
OEDIPUS
    My darling wife Jocasta, why have you   [950]
    called me to come here from inside the house?
JOCASTA
    Listen to this man. As you do, consider
    what those fine holy oracles have come to.
OEDIPUS
    Who is this man? And what's he got to tell me?
JOCASTA
    He's a Corinthian. He came to tell us
    your father, Polybus, is dead and gone.
OEDIPUS
    What is this, stranger? You must be my witness!
FIRST MESSENGER
    If I must first sum up the message clearly,
    know this: the man has gone the way of death.[6]
OEDIPUS
    Because of treachery? Or some disease?   [960]

---

4. Corinth was built on an isthmus, so the Isthmians are the Corinthians.
5. A couple of words are missing from this line in the original.
6. Despite claiming a desire to speak clearly, the First Messenger uses notably convoluted
    language, perhaps in his desire not to cause grief or offense that might be dangerous
    for him.

FIRST MESSENGER
A featherweight tips old limbs down to rest.[7]

OEDIPUS
The poor man died of sickness, so it seems.

FIRST MESSENGER
Well, he had measured out a lengthy lifespan.

OEDIPUS
Terrible! Why then, wife, should anyone
consult the hearth of prophecy,[8] or birds
that cry above us, which foretold that I
would kill my father? Now he's dead and lies
beneath the earth; I'm here; I have not touched
a sword—unless he died of missing me!   [970]
In that sense, I'm the reason that he died.
So Polybus has taken down to Hades
those oracles, and rendered them worth nothing.

JOCASTA
Did I not tell you all this long ago?

OEDIPUS
You did. But I was led astray by fear.

JOCASTA
So now you need take none of this to heart.

OEDIPUS
How could I not still fear my mother's bed?

JOCASTA
Why should a person fear, when chance rules all,
and nobody has any clear foreknowledge?
It's best to live at random, best you can.
Don't be afraid of marrying your mother.   [980]
Many a mortal in his dreams has slept
beside his mother. But whoever treats
these things as nothing lives most easily.

OEDIPUS
You would be right in all of this—if only
she were not still alive. But as she is,
I can't be sure if what you say is right.

JOCASTA
Your father's tomb must be an eye of comfort.[9]

---

7. There is an implicit metaphor of scales weighing the difference between life and death; this scale tips easily for those who are very old.
8. Delphi is imagined as the hearth of the world since it is supposedly at the center of the earth.
9. Literally, "a great eye." The word "eye" is used in Greek as an endearment, as we might call somebody the "apple of my eye." But the usage here is unparalleled in extant Greek: it is never used of a tomb rather than of a living person.

OEDIPUS
Yes, but I am afraid of her, alive.
FIRST MESSENGER
Really? Who is this woman you are scared of?
OEDIPUS
Merope, sir, who lived with Polybus.   [990]
FIRST MESSENGER
What makes that woman frightening to you?
OEDIPUS
Stranger, the dreadful god-sent oracle.
FIRST MESSENGER
A secret one? Or may a person hear it?
OEDIPUS
You can. Apollo told me I was fated
to have sex with my mother, my own mother,
and shed my father's blood with my own hands.
That's why I have been exiled for so long
from Corinth, my home town. It worked out well,
but still, it's sweet to see one's parents' eyes.
FIRST MESSENGER
What? Did that fear keep you away from Corinth?   [1000]
OEDIPUS
Yes sir, I did not want to kill my father.
FIRST MESSENGER
Then why, my lord, have I not set you free
from this anxiety? I wish you well.
OEDIPUS
If you did that, you'd get fair recompense.
FIRST MESSENGER
Indeed, that's why I came here: so that when
you came home, I would benefit somehow.
OEDIPUS
I'll never get together with my parents.
FIRST MESSENGER
My child! You clearly don't know what you're doing.
OEDIPUS
What's that, old man? Instruct me, by the gods!
FIRST MESSENGER
If that's the reason that you won't go home . . .   [1010]
OEDIPUS
I'm scared Apollo's words may turn out true.
FIRST MESSENGER
You're scared of the pollution from your parents?
OEDIPUS
That's it, old man. That fear is always with me.

FIRST MESSENGER
   But do you realize you're scared for nothing?
OEDIPUS
   How so, if I'm their child, and they my parents?
FIRST MESSENGER
   Because he, Polybus, is not your kin!
OEDIPUS
   What do you mean? Did he not father me?
FIRST MESSENGER
   No, he did not! No more than I myself did!   [1020]
OEDIPUS
   What was his reason, then, to call me "son"?
FIRST MESSENGER
   Listen: he got you as a gift from me.
OEDIPUS
   He loved me—though I came from someone else?
FIRST MESSENGER
   Because before that, he had had no child.
OEDIPUS
   You gave me to him: did you buy or find me?
FIRST MESSENGER
   I found you on the folds of Mount Cithaeron.
OEDIPUS
   Why were you walking in that area?
FIRST MESSENGER
   I was in charge of mountain flocks up there.
OEDIPUS
   You were a homeless man for hire? A shepherd?[1]
FIRST MESSENGER
   My child, I was your savior at that time.   [1030]
OEDIPUS
   You picked me up; then what was wrong with me?[2]
FIRST MESSENGER
   Your ankles and your feet could testify.
OEDIPUS
   No! What old trouble are you bringing up?
FIRST MESSENGER
   Your feet were pierced and I set you free.
OEDIPUS
   I brought a dreadful shame out of my cradle.

---

1. Oedipus's question suggests a snobbish contempt for the First Messenger's lowly station, which is corrected by the response.
2. Oedipus assumes that the First Messenger must have saved him from some physical ailment.

FIRST MESSENGER
  You got your name because this happened to you.[3]
OEDIPUS
  Gods! Did my mother or my father do it?
FIRST MESSENGER
  The man I got you from would surely know.
OEDIPUS
  So someone gave you me? You didn't find me?
FIRST MESSENGER
  Another shepherd handed you to me.   [1040]
OEDIPUS
  Who was it? Could you recognize and show him?
FIRST MESSENGER
  I think they called him one of Laius's slaves.
OEDIPUS
  You mean the man who used to rule in Thebes?
FIRST MESSENGER
  Yes, certainly. This man was that man's herdsman.
OEDIPUS
  Is this man still alive? So I could see him?
FIRST MESSENGER
  Your Theban countrymen would know that best.
OEDIPUS (*to bystanders and enslaved attendants*)
  Does any one of you here know this herder?
  The one he mentioned? Have you seen him here,
  or in the countryside? If so, speak up!
  It's time to find the truth about all this.   [1050]
CHORUS
  I think he means the same man from the country,
  the one that you were looking for just now.
  Jocasta would be able to explain.[4]
OEDIPUS
  Wife, do you know the man whom recently
  we summoned here? Is he the one he means?
JOCASTA
  Why mention him? Just turn away, forget
  that all these empty words were ever spoken.
OEDIPUS
  There's no way I could get such evidence
  as this, and not reveal my origins!

---

3. The name "Oedipus" could suggest either "Know-Foot" (from the verb *oida*, "know,"
and *pous*, "foot") or "Swell-Foot" (from the verb *oideo*, "to swell"). The Messenger is
suggesting the latter etymology. See introduction, pp. vii–xx above.
4. It is not explained how the Chorus would know this.

JOCASTA

No, by the gods, if you value your life,   [1060]
don't make this search! My sickness is enough.

OEDIPUS

Don't worry! If I am, on Mother's side,
third-generation slave, you're still a queen!⁵

JOCASTA

Listen to me, I beg you! Don't do this!

OEDIPUS

No, I won't listen! I must learn the truth.

JOCASTA

I'm saying this with your own good in mind.

OEDIPUS

Then this "own good" has long been harming me.

JOCASTA

You're cursed, poor man. You don't know who you are.

OEDIPUS

Won't someone go and bring that herdsman here?
Let her enjoy her wealthy family!⁶   [1070]

JOCASTA

Oh, you poor man! That's all I have to say,
and it's the last thing that I'll ever say.

                                        Exit JOCASTA.

CHORUS

Why on earth, Oedipus, has your wife rushed
away, in desperate grief? I am afraid
some trouble will be breaking from her silence.

OEDIPUS

Then let it break! Let her do as she pleases!
But as for me, I want to see the source
of my own birth, however small and lowly.
She's full of pride, as women are, and maybe
she is ashamed of my bad family.⁷
But I account myself the son of Fate,   [1080]
who gives good things, and I'll not be ashamed.
She is my mother, and my kindred are
the months that made me small and made me big.
So born, I'd never turn to someone else,
the kind who wouldn't learn my origins.

---

5. A third-generation slave means one whose grandparent was enslaved. Oedipus assumes that Jocasta is worried he will turn out to have slave heritage.

6. Oedipus assumes that Jocasta, who comes from a rich royal household, is motivated by snobbery, rejecting him because, as an exposed foundling child, he may be the son of enslaved or poor people.

7. There is irony in Oedipus using the phrase "bad family" (*dusgeneia*, literally, "bad birthing").

CHORUS

If I am a prophet
with judgment and knowledge,
I swear by Olympus that you, Mount Cithaeron,
at moonlight tomorrow will be raised up in glory   [1090]
as ancestor, mother, and nursemaid of Oedipus,
and we will be dancing for you in our chorus
because you bring blessings
for rulers of ours.
Hallelujah, Apollo![8]
May this be your will.
But who was your mother, child? Which of the long-lived
nymphs on the mountain had met with your father,
Pan?[9] Or who slept with Apollo, with Loxias?[1]   [1100]
All of the countryside pastures are dear to him.
Or was it Hermes, the lord of Cyllene,
or Bacchus, the god who
inhabits the mountaintops,
who took you as foundling from one of the flashing-eyed
nymphs whom he often
is playing with?[2]

The HERDSMAN *enters and approaches.*

OEDIPUS

Gentlemen, I have never met this man,   [1110]
but if I had to guess, I'd say I see
that herdsman we've been looking for. He matches
this man in his advanced old age, and also
I recognize the men escorting him
as my own house-slaves. But I guess you would
know more than me; you've seen the man before.

CHORUS

Yes certainly, I know him. He served Laius,
an honest man, if any herdsman can be.

OEDIPUS (*to the* FIRST MESSENGER)

I'll ask you first, is this the man you mean,   [1120]

---

8. The Greek cry is *ie*, an exclamation to a god used in times of extreme emotion; it
formed an epithet for the god, as here, so that Apollo is addressed as *ieie*, a god to whom
we call *ie*.
9. Pan is a god of wild places and the countryside. Nymphs are goddesses closely associated with wild places, either mountains, waters, caves, or trees.
1. Loxias is a cult title of Apollo, associated with his role as provider of oracles. The Chorus imagines that Apollo might be the father of Oedipus, by some unknown mother.
2. Hermes is another god associated with the countryside and with ambiguous signs; he was
born on Mount Cyllene in Arcadia. Bacchus=Dionysos (see note 6, p. 10), another god of
the wild associated with the nymphs. The word translated "flashing-eyed" is written in
most manuscripts as "Heliconian" (*Helikonidon*), as if suggesting that these nymphs come
from a different mountain; but this reading is unmetrical, and it is strange to associate
the nymphs with a different mountain from the one on which Oedipus was abandoned.

from Corinth?

FIRST MESSENGER
              Yes, he is the one you see.

OEDIPUS (*to the* HERDSMAN)
    Now you, old man, look here and answer all
    my questions. Did you once belong to Laius?

HERDSMAN
    Yes, not a bought slave; raised up in that house.

OEDIPUS
    What was your line of work or way of life?

HERDSMAN
    Most of my life was following the herds.

OEDIPUS
    And in what places did you mostly shelter?

HERDSMAN
    Either Cithaeron or else thereabouts.

OEDIPUS
    So did you meet this man there? Do you know him?

HERDSMAN
    How would I? Doing what? Who do you mean?

OEDIPUS
    This man here. Did you ever interact?   [1130]

HERDSMAN
    Well, not so I could call to mind right now.

FIRST MESSENGER
    It's not surprising, master. But I will
    remind him. I know well he does remember
    when on Cithaeron's land he drove two flocks
    and I drove one. I was his neighbor
    for three whole six-month seasons, from the spring
    till Arkturus was rising.[3] Then at winter
    I drove my flocks to my own fold, while he
    drove his to Laius's stables. Am I telling
    the truth or not, in saying all this happened?   [1140]

HERDSMAN
    You're right, though all of this was long ago.

FIRST MESSENGER
    So come on, tell us, do you know you gave
    a child to me, to bring up as my own?

HERDSMAN
    What is this? Why do you ask about this story?

---

3. A line is missing in this sentence. The Bear-Watcher, Arkturus, is the brightest star in
   the constellation Boöetes; its rise marks the beginning of winter in this region.

FIRST MESSENGER (*gesturing to* OEDIPUS)
 This man, my friend, is him. He was that baby.
HERDSMAN
 To hell with you! Why won't you shut your mouth?
OEDIPUS
 Stop that, old man, don't scold him! It is you
 whose words deserve a scolding, not this man.
HERDSMAN
 What wrong have I done, master, best of masters?
OEDIPUS
 You failed to speak about the child when questioned.   [1150]
HERDSMAN
 He's talking with no knowledge: futile labor!
OEDIPUS
 If you won't talk to help me, pain will make you.
HERDSMAN
 No, by the gods, I'm old! Please do not hurt me.
OEDIPUS
 Somebody, quickly twist his arms behind him.
HERDSMAN
 No, why? Poor me! What do you want to learn?
OEDIPUS
 Did you give him the child he asked about?
HERDSMAN
 Yes, and I wish I'd died that very day.
OEDIPUS
 You'll come to that, if you won't talk as needed.
HERDSMAN
 But if I speak, I'm ruined all the more.
OEDIPUS
 It seems this man is set on wasting time!   [1160]
HERDSMAN
 I'm not! I said I gave him, long ago.
OEDIPUS
 Where did you get him? Your house? Someone else?
HERDSMAN
 He wasn't mine. He came from someone else.
OEDIPUS
 Which of these citizens? And from which house?
HERDSMAN
 No, by the gods, no, master! Ask no more.
OEDIPUS
 You're done for if you will not answer me.

HERDSMAN
Well, it was one of the babies born to Laius.[4]

OEDIPUS
A slave, or born to him as his own kin?

HERDSMAN
I'm on the point of danger in my story—

OEDIPUS
And I in hearing it. But I must hear.   [1170]

HERDSMAN
They said it was his son. But she, inside,
your wife, would be the best at telling this.

OEDIPUS
Did she give him to you?

HERDSMAN
                                She did, my lord.

OEDIPUS
To do what?

HERDSMAN
                    So that I might kill the child.

OEDIPUS
Her baby?

HERDSMAN
                    She was scared of prophecies.

OEDIPUS
What were they?

HERDSMAN
                    That the child would kill his parents.

OEDIPUS
Then why did you give it to this old man?

HERDSMAN
In pity, master. I thought he could take it
to his own country. But he saved the child
for utmost ruin. And if you are him,   [1180]
as he says—know that you were born accursed.

OEDIPUS
Oh, oh! Everything now comes clear.
O light, I look at you for the last time!
Now I'm revealed as who I am: the child
of parents who should not have had a child.
I lived with those who should not be together,
and I killed those whom it was wrong to kill.

---

4. The phrasing could cover both those born biologically to Laius and those born to
people enslaved in Laius's household and, hence, his property.

CHORUS

O generations of mortals,
I count you as equal to nothing,
even when you are alive.
Who indeed, what man, ever wins
more good fortune than just enough   [1190]
to give an appearance, a show,
then slip down?
You, poor Oedipus, you! I hold the god of your story,[5]
yours, yours as example,
and I count no mortal happy.

You shot your arrow far beyond[6]
and mastered good fortune, good blessings,
in everything.
Yes, by Zeus, you destroyed
the girl with the twisted talons
who sang riddling omens![7] You stood   [1200]
against our deaths, as a tower for my land.
From that time onward you were called my king,[8]
and you have received the greatest of honors,
ruling in this, the greatest of cities,
in Thebes.

But now, who now have you heard of
more deeply unhappy, in troubles more savage,[9]
who lives with such terrible change in his life?[1]
O famous, infamous Oedipus!
The same mighty harbor

---

5. The phrase "god of your story" in the original is *daimon*: literally, a divine force or deity
   that controls individual destinies. The word translated "good fortune" in line 1190 is
   cognate, *eudaimonia*: it suggests a life blessed throughout by a benevolent deity.
6. The image of Oedipus as a far-shooting archer, who "shot" successfully in solving the
   riddle of the Sphinx, associates the mortal man with the god Apollo, who is frequently
   given the epithet "far-shooting" (see note 7, p. 8). There is a momentary hint that Oedipus may have shot not just superlatively far, but perhaps too far.
7. As usual in this play, the Chorus avoids mentioning the Sphinx by name; she is herself
   a riddle.
8. "King" in Greek is *basileus*, a word that, as noted in the introduction (p. x), seems to
   contradict Oedipus's self-presentation as a *tyrannos*, a nonhereditary monarch. Bernard
   Knox ("Why Is Oedipus called *Tyrannos*?," *Classical Journal* 50.3 [December 1954]:
   97–102) suggests that the term is used here because now the Chorus members realize
   that their ruler is in fact the heir to the throne by kinship. Others argue that the various political terms are not so sharply distinguished.
9. The language of wildness or savagery (*agrios*) marks the way that Oedipus's geographical and social position has changed, from being at the center and pinnacle of social life
   in the city to being an outcast, to a world beyond cultivated fields, in the mountains
   and deserts and uninhabited areas of earth.
1. The text of line 1205 is corrupt. My translation is based on the tentative suggestion of
   Finglass following Kassel (Finglass, *Oedipus the King*, p. 533).

was enough for both you and your father,
as slaves of the bedroom,
to fall in, the same.[2]
How on earth could those furrows
—your father's!—how could they
bear you for so long in silence, poor man?[3]   [1210]

Time can see everything; time found you out,
though you did not want it. Time brings to justice
your long-ago parented parenting; marriage un-marriage.
Child of Laius,
I wish, how I wish
that I never had seen you.
How intensely I mourn you
and pour from my mouth
a cry of deep grief.[4] To tell truth,
from you I took breath and through you   [1220]
I rocked to sleep my eyes.
         Enter SECOND MESSENGER *from the palace.*
Lords, who are always honored in this country,[5]
I have to tell you, show you, make you feel
such grief—if you are still concerned about
the house of Labdacus, like family.[6]
No river, I believe—not River Ister
nor Phasis,[7] with their purity—could wash
this house of all the evil that it holds,
which it will soon be bringing out to light:
deliberate actions, not unwilling ones.[8]   [1230]

2. Jocasta's vagina or womb is the metaphorical harbor into which both father and son
   have sailed or "fallen"; falling on or into is a common metaphor for sex. The word translated "slave of the bedroom," *thalamepolos*, literally, "bedroom-server," is a standard term
   for a female domestic attendant or enslaved woman in Homer, and it can also be used
   for male eunuchs. Here the word is usually explained as meaning "bridegroom," but
   this usage would be entirely unparalleled. Sophocles is more likely making a striking
   extension of a word usually applied to low-class or enslaved people to apply to the elite
   Laius and Oedipus in their bedroom service.
3. The metaphor switches so that Jocasta's body is now a plowed field, whose "furrows"
   have been sown by both father and son.
4. The text here is corrupt; I follow the text as printed in Finglass.
5. The Chorus members, the old elite of Thebans, are now almost the default rulers,
   because the royal family is destroyed.
6. The text is debated. The word translated "like family," *eggenos*, is taken by the ancient
   commentators (the scholiasts) to be metaphorical, connoting "truly," like a true-born
   child. The word is emended by some scholars to *eugenos*, "nobly," on the grounds that
   the Chorus members are not actually part of Oedipus's family. I have kept the manuscript reading, because Sophocles is very likely playing on what it means to act in a
   familial way, in accordance with birth or *genos*, and exploring the muddled distinction
   between Oedipus's birth family and his ostensibly adoptive Theban family.
7. The Ister is the ancient name for the Danube; the Phasis is the modern-day Rioni.
8. The line insists on a distinction between the earlier parricide/incest and the more
   recent deliberate self-blinding.

Self-chosen pains are those that hurt the most.
CHORUS
  What we already knew was cause enough
  for grieving. What new message are you bringing?
SECOND MESSENGER
  The news is very quick to say and quick
  to learn: the godlike Queen Jocasta's dead.
CHORUS
  Poor woman! Why on earth? What was the cause?
SECOND MESSENGER
  She killed herself. You do not have to bear
  the worst of it, because you did not see it.
  But still, as far as memory can serve,
  you'll grasp how terribly the woman suffered.   [1240]
  When she, in fury,[9] came inside the hall,
  at once she dashed toward her marriage bed,
  her fingers ripping out her hair. She slammed
  the doors shut from the inside, and she called
  on Laius, Laius long since dead already,
  remembering the seed from long ago
  that killed him and left her who gave it birth
  with curse of children: children manufactured
  by his own children. She cried at the bed,
  where she—reduplicated pain!—had borne
  husband by husband, children by her child.   [1250]
  How, after that, she died, I do not know.
  Oedipus burst in shouting, and he made it
  impossible to watch her suffering.
  Instead, we looked at him, as he rushed round:
  he dashed to ask us for a sword, and where
  his wife, not wife, where could he find his mother,
  the field of double harvest, of himself
  and of his children?[1] But, as he was raving,
  some spirit must have shown him where she was;
  it wasn't any of us bystanders.
  Screaming terribly, as if he was   [1260]
  guided by someone, at the double doors

---

9. The word *orgē* is applied earlier to Jocasta in a play on words by Tiresias (see note 7, p. 14). Commentators and dictionaries claim that this word is here being used in a unique sense, unparalleled in extant Greek, to mean "passion" rather than "fury," apparently because most commentators are unable to imagine why Jocasta might be angry. But the text says that she is angry, and she has good reason to be so, given that her whole life has been ruined. Whereas the central object of Oedipus's violent rage turns on his own perceptions (his eyes) and the god Apollo, Jocasta's rage centers on her marriage and her marriage bed, the locus of elite female status.
1. The Messenger treats Oedipus's words partway between quoted and indirect speech.

he leapt, and from their sockets bent and twisted
those doors, and fell inside the room,[2] and there
we saw his wife, the woman, hanging from
a twisted noose. And he, when he saw her,
let out a dreadful groan, in misery.
He loosed the rope that she was hanging from;
and once she lay, poor woman, on the ground,
what happened then was terrible to see.
He ripped the spikes of beaten gold she wore
out of her clothing,[3] and he held them up,
then struck the sockets of his own round eyes,   [1270]
shouting about how they would not see her,
nor what bad things he did and underwent,
how for the future, they would see in darkness
those he should not have seen; they would not know
those he should not have known. With words like these
he used the spikes to pummel at his eyes,
not once but many times, and as he did so,
his bloody eyeballs drenched his cheeks; they flowed
continually, not ever letting up.[4]   [1280]
The former happiness was truly happy,
but now, today: moans, ruin, death, and shame,
whatever evil can be named is here.

CHORUS
Poor man! Has he now found relief from pain?

SECOND MESSENGER
He's yelling, "Someone open up the doors!
Show all the Thebans one who killed his father,
his mother's . . ." I can't quote those blasphemies.
He said that he would fling himself from Thebes,   [1290]
not stay, a curse upon the house, as he
himself had prayed. But he is weak and needs
a guide. He is more sick than he can bear.
He'll show you too: the latches of the doors
are opening, and soon you'll see a sight

---

2. These concrete details suggest an echo between the woman inside the room and the room itself; she, like it, has a "double" entry, in that she has been penetrated by both father and son; Oedipus has "fallen" into her before.
3. Elite Greek women usually wore an ankle-length gown, a *chiton*, fastened at the shoulders with two long spikes, *fibulae*. I have used the word "spike" rather than "brooch" or "pin," because *fibulae* were often long, substantial pieces of sharpened metal. Designed to be strong enough to hold up a heavy weight of cloth, they were sturdy enough to pierce through the eyeball.
4. The translation here omits four lines that are likely interpolated, since they are full of metrical and linguistic problems. The lines read: "The dripping globs of gore; and with all that / black rain of hail, of blood, was being wetted. / These evils broke from two, not one; they came / commingled suffering, for man and woman."

that even one who hated him would pity.

The palace doors open. OEDIPUS *comes out, his mask altered
to represent his bloody, empty eye sockets.*

CHORUS

What[5] terrible pain for a person to see,
most terrible pain I have ever encountered.
What madness, poor man, came upon you? What spirit   [1300]
leapt further than furthest
onto your spirit-accursed fate?
The sorrow! The pity! My eyes cannot meet yours,
although there's so much that I'd like to be asking you,
so much to learn and so much to look at.
You make me shudder.

OEDIPUS

Oh, oh, oh! I am undone.
What land can I go to? The pity, the pain!
Where are my words being carried? They fly all around.   [1310]
Spirit, O Spirit![6] How far you have leapt!

CHORUS

To horror that cannot be looked at or heard.

OEDIPUS

Darkness! My dark cloud,
attacking, repelling,
not to be spoken of, not to be governed,
blown by a wind of disaster!
Gods, no!
No, again no! What a sting from these sharp points,
what a sting from the terrible memories!

CHORUS

No wonder that in such disaster
you suffer twice over, you feel the pain twice.   [1320]

OEDIPUS

My friend,
you are still with me, my trusted attendant.
You have stayed to take care of me now I am blind.
Aaah!
I'm not unaware, I can still recognize
your voice through my darkness.

CHORUS

You did terrible things! How could you do it,
to snuff out your eyesight? What spirit inspired you?

---

5. The meter shifts to lyric.
6. In the original, the "Spirit" is *daimon*, an unspecified divine force.

OEDIPUS

   Apollo, my friends, these things were Apollo,
   who brought to fulfillment my pain and my ruin.   [1330]
   But nobody struck me but me: self-handed,
   I did it, to my own unhappy self.
   Why should I see
   when my sight could see nothing joyful?

CHORUS

   It was so, as you say.

OEDIPUS

   What could I look at and what could I love,
   what word could I hear with pleasure, my friends?
   Take me away, as fast as you can,   [1340]
   take me, my friends: I am ruin!
   I am the most cursed and of all human beings
   most hated by gods.

CHORUS

   Your mind and your misery—equally pitiful!
   How I wish that I had never known you.

OEDIPUS

   Damn him, that wandering herdsman, whoever he was,   [1350]
   who took me from that savage bond on my feet
   and protected and saved me from death;
   he did me no good!
   If I had died then I would not be
   the cause of such pain to myself and my loved ones.

CHORUS

   I wish the same.

OEDIPUS

   I would not have come as my own father's killer,
   or have people name me the bridegroom
   of those I was born from.
   Now I am godless, the child of unholy ones,   [1360]
   joint parent with those whose poor child I was.
   Now if any ruin outranks any ruin,
   it comes to the portion of Oedipus.[7]

CHORUS

   I[8] don't know how to say your plans were good;
   better that you were dead, than living blind.

OEDIPUS

   Don't teach me or advise me that my actions

---

7. Oedipus suggests that the most "outranking" or "more senior" (*presbuteron*) trouble or
ruin belongs to him, and has come to him by lot (*elache*), like many political offices in
classical Athens. He imagines his situation as an elevation to the top ranks of pollution.
8. The meter switches back to regular iambic here.

were anything but best. I do not know   [1370]
how, with what kind of eyes, I ever could
look at my father, when I go to Hades,
or my poor mother. What I've done to them,
those two, deserves much more than death by hanging.
And how could I desire to see the sight
of my own children, given where they came from?
Never, with my own eyes; not ever, ever.
Nor would I see the city or the towers
or holy statues of the gods, from which
I myself banned myself, I who was raised
the one most privileged in Thebes, the one   [1380]
in total misery: since I myself
declared that everyone must drive away
the one who is unholy, whom the gods
have shown to be unhallowed, from the line
of Laius.[9] When I had uncovered such
a stain, my stain, would I look with straight gaze
at them? Of course not. If there were some way
to block the stream of hearing through my ears,[1]
I wouldn't have held back from shutting up
my whole poor ruined body, so I'd be
blind and deaf both. It is sweet to live   [1390]
inside the mind's house, far away from pain.
O Mount Cithaeron! Why did you take me in?
Why did you not just seize me and destroy me
immediately, so I would never ever
have shown myself to people and revealed
my origins? O Polybus and Corinth,
supposedly my old ancestral home,
you brought me up as if I were so fine,
but I was festering inside. And now
my wrongful nature, wrongful origins,[2]
have been found out. That place where three roads meet!
That hidden grove, that thicket, narrow place
of triple paths! You drank, from my own hands,   [1400]
my blood, my father's blood! Do you remember
me? What I did? And what I did next, after
I came here? Marriages! Marriages![3] You were

9. The gods have revealed the paradox, that the polluted man comes from the royal family.
1. The orifices of the body are the "doors" by which the public world impinges on the private self.
2. The word for "wrongful" or "bad," *kakos*, can also connote lower-class.
3. The original is plural; this could be plural standing in for singular, or it could refer to Jocasta's two marriages, or it could be that Oedipus is imagining his marriage as inherently plural (generative of plural, mixed, incestuous family roles).

source of my birth, you gave me life, then sent
the same seed back again, and you revealed
fathers as brothers, children, kindred bloodshed,
brides, wives, and mothers, and whatever actions
cause deepest shame among humanity.
What's wrong to do is wrong to speak about.
Hide me outside, as fast as possible, [1410]
by gods! Or kill me, or throw me away
into the sea, where you will never see me
ever again. Come on, don't shrink from touching
a miserable man. Do what I say!
Do not be scared. No one, no human being,
could bear my sufferings, but I alone.
   Enter CREON, *from the city.*

CHORUS
Look! Here is Creon, just the man you need
for what you're asking; he can make decisions
and act, since he alone has now been left
as guardian of Thebes,[4] instead of you.

OEDIPUS
Oh no! How can I answer what he says?
How can I show him that I can be trusted, [1420]
when earlier, I treated him so badly?

CREON
No, Oedipus, I did not come to laugh,
nor blame you for bad actions in the past.
But if you can no longer hold in honor
the generations of humanity,
at any rate you should respect the flame
that nourishes all things, our Lord the Sun,
and not display pollution out in public,[5]
which neither earth, the holy rain, nor light
will find acceptable. (*To his enslaved attendants*) Now
   hurry, quickly!
get him inside the house! It is not holy
for anyone outside the family
to see or hear a family's disasters. [1430]

OEDIPUS
By gods, you've far exceeded all my hopes—
the highest man descending to the lowest.

4. The Chorus characterizes Creon not as the monarch or ruler or sovereign (not *tyrannos*
or *basileus*), but as "guardian," *phylax*, as if he occupies a caretaking role.
5. Creon contradicts Oedipus's claim that he can touch anybody, since the burden of his
sufferings is borne by him alone; according to Creon, Oedipus is tainted by deadly pollution, and should hide himself from the natural and divine as well as human worlds.

Please do this, for your own sake, not for mine.
CREON
    What do you need? What are you asking for?
OEDIPUS
    Fling me away, as fast as possible,
    out of this land, to somewhere nobody
    can speak to me or see me anymore.
CREON
    I would have, certainly, if I had not
    wanted to find out from god, before all else,
    what must be done.
OEDIPUS
                But what he said already
    was totally transparent! That the killer   [1440]
    of his own father, the unholy one,
    must die—and that is me.
CREON
                    That's what was said.
    But since we stand in such a point of crisis,
    it's best to learn from him what must be done.
OEDIPUS
    You'll find out, for a wretched man like me?
CREON
    Yes, now at last you might trust in the god.
OEDIPUS
    I'll lean on you and beg you this: the woman,
    bury her as you wish, inside the house—
    it's right that you do this for your own people.[6]
    But as for me, let this, my fathers' home,
    never be forced to meet me living here;   [1450]
    let me live in the mountains, on my own
    Cithaeron, which my mother and my father
    appointed for me, living, as my tomb
    and caretaker, where I may die a death
    caused by the two who have already killed me.
    I know this much at least, that I will not
    die of disease or any other thing.
    I'd never have been saved from death, if not
    for terrible disaster of some kind.
    But let my fate go anywhere it will!
    Creon, you need not worry for my sons,
    since they are men, so they will never lack   [1460]

6. Jocasta, Creon's sister, is still part of his family; Oedipus, an in-law by a tainted, unholy marriage, is not.

the means to live, wherever they may be.
But pity my poor daughters! They have never
known me to separate my dinner table
from them; whatever food I touched, they shared.
Please care for them. And most of all, allow me
to touch them with my own hands, and to give them
my cries of grief about our sufferings.
Master, please!⁷
You're noble in your birth. If I could touch them
with my own hands, it would seem like I had them,
just as I had them back when I could see.   [1470]
What am I saying?⁸
Gods, am I really hearing my two darlings
crying? Has Creon pitied me and sent
my dearest, favorite children here to me?
Have I guessed right?

CREON

Yes, I did this for you; I knew what joy
they used to give you, and would give you now.

OEDIPUS

Bless you for bringing them!⁹ And may the spirit
take better care of you than he did me.
Children, where are you? Come to me, come here,   [1480]
to me—into your brother's arms and hands,
ambassadors, whose public service¹ was
to make your father, your own father's eyes,
which used to be so clear, see as they do.
Children, I didn't see, I didn't know,
but I have been revealed to be your father
by that same place from which I too was plowed.
I cannot look at you, but I am crying
for both of you, considering how bitter
the life that other people will compel you
to live will be, from this time going forward.
What gatherings of citizens will have you?

---

7. This is a short (one-foot) line in the original, marking the intense emotion.
8. Another short line in the original, again only a third of normal metrical length.
9. Literally, "for this road," an idiomatic way of expressing any arrival or trip, but with an extra resonance in a play where roads and crossroads have been so significant.
1. The odd language by which hands are "ambassadors" echoes the original verb, *prouxenesan* (*proxeno*), which literally connotes a person performing the office of a *proxenos*, a visiting dignitary from another city who is a public guest and friend of the state. The verb can be used to signify simply "perform" or "do," but the metaphor may be alive; Oedipus imagines his own hands and other body parts as separate people. As Finglass notes (*Oedipus the King*, p. 607), there may also be "a particular irony" in the image, since Oedipus has moved so disastrously from one city to another. The earlier image, by which the body is a house, has now given way to a different image, by which the body is a conglomeration of people inhabiting different city-states.

What festivals? You will be brought to tears   [1490]
and come back home, not see the celebration.
And when you reach the proper age for marriage—
children, who will there be, who'd cast his lot
to get such insults? Names to ruin both
your parents and you too!² What suffering
is missing from the list? Your father killed
his father! And he plowed the one who bore him,
the place in which he had himself been sown,
and he got you from sources that were equal
to where he had come out from his own self.
This is the kind of insult you'll receive.
So who will marry you? There's no one, children;   [1500]
it's clear, you must be ruined: dry and barren,
no marriages. Son of Menoeceus,³
since you alone are left to these two girls
as father—now that we two who produced them
are dead and gone—don't let them become homeless,⁴
husbandless beggars; they're your family.
Pity them! You can see their situation,
with nothing but what you can share with them.
So please say yes, and touch me, trueborn lord!   [1510]
Children, if you were old enough to listen,
there's so much I would tell you. As it is,
I ask you only this: live as you can.
I pray that you will have a better life
than that of your own father.

CREON
                              Now enough!
You must stop crying. Go inside the house.

OEDIPUS
I must obey, although it brings no joy.

CREON
Yes, everything is good at its right time.   [1520]

OEDIPUS
Do you know on what terms I go away?

CREON
You'll tell me and I'll listen. Then I'll know.

OEDIPUS
Send me away in exile from the land.

---

2. The text in this sentence is problematic; I have rendered what seems to be the general
sense.
3. Creon.
4. The text of this line is problematic; the transmitted text is unmetrical, and the verb as
translated here ("let them") is a guess.

CREON
You're asking me for what a god must give.
OEDIPUS
But I'm the man most hated by the gods.
CREON
Then you'll soon get it.[5]
OEDIPUS
                    Do you mean it?
CREON
                                Yes.
I don't like saying things I do not mean.
OEDIPUS
Then take me from this place now, right away!
CREON
Go now. But let your children go.
OEDIPUS
            No, no!
Don't take these girls from me!
CREON
                You must give up
your wish to rule in everything. The power
you had has not stayed with you through your life.
CHORUS
Inhabitants[6] of Thebes, our fatherland,
look here! This Oedipus, who solved the famous
riddle, and was most powerful, who never
glanced at the citizens' envy, or at fortune,
has now collided with this great tsunami
of ruin. So all mortals ought to look
toward this final day, and call no person
happy, who has not traveled all through life
without experiencing any pain.   [1530]

5. I.e., the gift of exile.
6 . These last lines are probably not by Sophocles but by a later interpolator, because they
   are riddled with linguistic difficulties; see further discussion in Finglass, *Oedipus the
   King*, pp. 615–17. Some commentators have also objected on the grounds that the sen-
   timents expressed here are hokey, although simplistic moralizing is fairly common at
   the end of Athenian tragedy.

COMPARATIVE SOURCES

Note on the Comparative Sources Selected

The comparative ancient sources provide insight into the wide range of different ancient approaches to the myth of Oedipus, and thereby enable readers to see what is distinctive about Sophocles' approach. The first selection, from *The Odyssey*—which was composed much earlier than Sophocles' play, and would have been well known to the dramatist and his audience—describes the suicide by hanging of Oedipus's mother, here called Epicaste. The passage suggests a different version of the myth, since Oedipus is described as ruling Thebes even after the terrible discoveries; there is no suggestion here of exile or self-blinding.

Euripides' play based on this myth, *Oedipus*, was created after Sophocles' version. Only fragments survive, but they are enough to show some radical differences in the treatment of the story, such as the greater prominence given to the Sphinx. Jocasta clearly had a particularly important role, unsurprisingly given Euripides' special interest in complicated female characters; the fragments suggest that Euripides got good mileage out of the creepiness of the incestuous marriage. Oedipus was, in this version, blinded forcibly rather than by his own hands.

Thucydides' *History of the Peloponnesian War* includes a detailed account of the plague at Athens of 430 B.C.E., which may be in the background of the description in *Oedipus Tyrannos* of the plague at Thebes.

Sophocles' own much later play about the Oedipus myth, *Oedipus at Colonus*, provides a very different image of the blind protagonist and his children, as the exiled, polluted hero rejects and curses his son Polyneices and is eventually welcomed into the Athenian sanctuary by Theseus. In the lyric passage included here, the Chorus members question Oedipus about the murder of Laius and the choice to blind himself, and Oedipus emphasizes that he acted in ignorance.

Included next is a passage from the philosopher Aristotle's *Nichomachean Ethics*, which clarifies what, according to Aristotle, "acting in ignorance" or "involuntary action" might mean. Aristotle does not discuss the case of Oedipus, but his analysis is helpful for considering how near-contemporaries of Sophocles might have seen the moral dilemmas raised by the myth and by the play. Aristotle does not invoke the (modern) concepts of fate and free will, which are often projected back onto the play. Also included are some short selections from Aristotle's *Poetics*, in which he analyzes and praises the plot structure of Sophocles' play. These selections are particularly interesting for the ways that Aristotle justifies the plot's implausibilities.

Two later works of mythography, by Hyginus and Pseudo-Apollodorus, offer useful prose retellings of the myth that probably draw on earlier traditions, and they give a sense of the whole story arc. Even though these sources are much later than Sophocles' play, many elements of the stories would have been much older, and known to the tragedian and his audience.

Next is the final section from another ancient verse tragedy based on the Oedipus story: that of Seneca, the great Roman philosopher, essayist, and tragedian who lived in the first century C.E. As this segment shows, Seneca's version of the myth is gorier than Sophocles', has more thrilling rhetorical bombast, and is much more explicitly concerned with the correct response to an already overdetermined tradition and with "fate" (a topic of deep interest to Roman stoic philosophers). As this passage also shows, Seneca has Jocasta stab herself with Oedipus's sword in front of him in the final moments of the play—in contrast to the more decorous offstage self-hanging of Sophocles' Jocasta.

Finally, I include the closing scene of a modern verse tragedy based on *Oedipus Tyrannos*: *The Darker Face of the Earth* transposes the action to a nineteenth-century U.S. slave plantation. Rita Dove follows Sophocles' plot closely, but juxtaposes the Sophoclean horrors of pollution, parricide, and incest with the differently horrifying trauma of slavery.

HOMER

[The Story of Oedipus's Mother]†

This passage from Book 11 of *The Odyssey*, the "Book of the Dead," is
narrated by Odysseus, who has traveled to the land of the dead and summoned them to him by digging a ditch filled with blood. Epicaste is one of
a series of famous mythological women whom he sees. This version of the
myth, which far predates Sophocles and would have been well known to
him, does not seem to imply that Oedipus blinds himself, nor that he is
driven into exile: he rules Thebes after making his terrible discoveries.

I saw
fine Epicaste, Oedipus's mother,
who did a dreadful thing in ignorance:
she married her own son. He killed his father,
and married her. The gods revealed the truth
to humans; through their deadly plans, he ruled
the Cadmeans in Thebes, despite his pain.
But Epicaste crossed the gates of Hades;
she tied a noose and hung it from the ceiling,
and hanged herself for sorrow, leaving him
the agonies a mother's Furies bring.

EURIPIDES

From Oedipus‡

Euripides' play *Oedipus* was composed and produced after Sophocles',
around 415–10 B.C.E. Euripides' version, which now exists only in fragments, included a description of the Sphinx and her riddle (in contrast
to Sophocles' reticence about the details of the riddle), and his Oedipus was forcibly blinded by servants of Laius while he was known as
the son of Polybus—before the revelations about his actual parentage.
Euripides' Jocasta lived on after the discoveries and was probably a
more substantial character than the Sophoclean version.

† From *The Odyssey*, trans. Emily Wilson (New York and London: Norton, 2018), 11.271–81.
  Copyright © 2018 by Emily Wilson. Reprinted by permission of W. W. Norton & Com-
  pany, Inc. The original is translated from *Homeri Opera*, ed. T. W. Allen, vol. 3, 2nd ed.
  (Oxford: Clarendon P, 1917).
‡ Translated and with notes by the editor of this Norton Critical Edition from Euripides,
  Selected Fragmentary Plays, vol. 2, ed. Christopher Collard, Martin J. Cropp, and
  J. Gibert (Warminster, Wiltshire, Eng.: Aris & Phillips, 1995), pp. 114, 116, 118, 120,
  122. For many of the lines, as is common for fragments of plays, we do not know the
  speaker. The number of the fragment is cited in bold before each.

539a. Although Apollo forbade it, [Laius] had a son.[1]
540. . . . Hairy foliage . . .
Curling her tail under lionfeet
down she sat tucking her swift-flying
. . . in time . . .
. . . leafy foliage . . .
. . . hold her wing to the sunbeams.
If the beast held her back to the horses of Helios[2]
she looked all golden; if she turned to clouds,
dark, like the rainbow Iris, shining back her gleam.[3]
541.

SERVANT OF LAIUS
We press the son of Polybus to the ground
and blind him, putting out his eyes.
542.
Gold and bright silver aren't the only things
with value; goodness also is a currency
for every human, which they all should use.
543.

[OEDIPUS?]
Children and wife are a man's sovereign power.[4]
. . .
Indeed, I say it's an equal disaster
for a man to lose his children, or his country, or his wealth,
or his loyal wife, since wealth alone . . .
. . . Certainly it is better for a man to have a sensible wife.
544. The most difficult thing of all to fight is a woman [or "wife"].
545.

JOCASTA
Every sensible wife is her husband's slave;
a reckless one will stupidly despise him.
545a.

JOCASTA
Beauty is useless for a married woman,
but prudent self-restraint helps many of us.
You see, every loyal wife who's melted with her man
knows how be restrained. This is the first thing:
even if her husband's very ugly, she
must think he's handsome, if she's got a brain.
It's not the eye that judges, but the mind.

---

1. This was the first line of the play, which probably, like many Euripidean plays, included a prologue giving the backstory and a taster of the plot.
2. The Sun, imagined as a god who rides across the sky in a chariot drawn by horses.
3. This is clearly a description of the Sphinx.
4. The word rendered "sovereign power" is *tyrannis*.

Whenever he is talking, she should think
he's speaking well, even if he's saying nothing,
and when she works, the goal of all her labor
must be to please her husband. If he suffers,
it's sweet if she can share his grumpy face,
sharing her husband's suffering and joy.
So now, I will be sick to share your sickness,
and share your troubles with you. It will be
not in the slightest bit annoying for me.
546.
[CHORUS?]
Every wife is inferior to her husband,
even if the worst man
marries an admirable woman.
547.
There's one desire, but more than one pleasure from it.
Some desire bad things, some desire good.
548.
One has to watch the mind! The mind!
What use are good looks, if you lack good sense?
549.
Certainly one day brings many changes.
550.
Greater joy comes from surprises.
551.
[JOCASTA]
Envy, which ruins the mind of many,
destroyed him and me along with him.
552.
Is it more useful
to be smart but a coward
or brave but a fool?
The former keeps quiet and lazy;
the latter defends himself, but he is stupid.
Both contain sickness.
553.
It's stupid for a man to tell the world his business.
It's smart to keep it hidden.
554.
The god has given us many transformations
of life and many changes in our fortune.
554a.
If any unjust man comes and sits at the altar,
I myself, dismissing law, would bring him
to justice, and I wouldn't fear the gods.

A bad man always ought to get bad treatment.
554b.
O citadel of the Cecropian land,[5]
O wide sky!
555.
Justice sees even in darkness.
556.
The song-making reed, which the Black River grows,
the nightingale, clever at blowing her pipes . . .
557.
. . . without joints . . .

THUCYDIDES

From The History of the Peloponnesian War 2.47–54[†]

Thucydides, a general in the Peloponnesian War, wrote his history of the war at the end of the fifth century B.C.E., well after Sophocles' play. But his account of the plague in Athens of 430 B.C.E., and its social repercussions, evokes something of the context for the drama and the relevance of the mythic plague for the audience, whether we think *Oedipus Tyrannos* was composed around 430 or around the time of the later plague of 425. In Thucydides' account, as in the play, plague has serious social, political, and theological repercussions.

47. * * * Early in the summer [of 430 B.C.E.], the Peloponnesians and two-thirds of their allies invaded Attica, just as in the previous year, led by the Spartan king Archidamus, the son of Zeuxidamus. They settled in and started destroying the land. After only a few days, plague first broke out in Attica among the Athenians. It was rumored that outbreaks appeared earlier in various places, around Lemnos and elsewhere, but such an enormous epidemic that killed so many people has not been recorded anywhere.

In the beginning, the doctors were helpless to take care of people, because they had no idea what was happening; they themselves died in the greatest numbers, because they spent most time with the sick. All other human skills were equally useless. They tried prayers in the temples, divination, and other religious practices, but none of them did any good, and finally they gave up on them, overcome by the disaster.

---

5. Attica, more specifically Athens. Cecrops was the mythical first king of Attica.
† Translated and abridged by the editor of this Norton Critical Edition from *Thucydides: Book II*, ed. E. C. Marchant (London and New York: Macmillan, 1891; rpt. 1961).

48. Apparently it began in the part of Ethiopia north of Egypt, and then spread to Egypt and Libya and most of the land of the Persian emperor. Then it suddenly fell on the city of the Athenians, and at first affected the people in the port of Piraeus, which is why they said that the Peloponnesians had poisoned the reservoirs—there were no wells there yet. Later it also reached the upper part of the city, and far more people started dying. Others—doctors and private individuals—should speak about its probable causes and the reasons they think could have prompted such a massive change. I will simply say what it was like, so that if it happens again, people can read my account and have better evidence to recognize it. I'll tell what I know from having suffered the plague myself, and witnessed other people suffering from it.

49. As everyone agrees, that year had been especially free from other kinds of sickness. If anybody was already sick, it turned into plague. Others, who had been healthy, were struck for no apparent reason, first by strong hot flashes in the head, reddened and inflamed eyes, and internal parts such as throat and tongue turned bloody, and they started breathing a bad, smelly breath. After that, there was sneezing and hoarseness, and shortly the pain reached the chest, and there was a terrible cough. * * *

[Thucydides continues with a detailed account of many more symptoms, describing how the disease progressed and killed its victims; the excerpt continues as he describes the social consequences of the outbreak.]

51. The plague came in many different strange forms as it affected different individuals, but those were its general characteristics. At that time, the other usual afflictions did not affect them; all sicknesses turned into plague. Some died of neglect, some who were well taken care of also died. There was no single cure that could be used to help them; what was useful for one patient harmed another. A strong body seemed no more immune to it than a weak one; it seized every type of body, even those who were taking excellent care of their health. The worst part of this disaster was the depression whenever anyone realized they were sick; they immediately despaired and turned away in their minds, and did not keep any resistance against it. One person fell through nursing another, and they died like sheep. This caused the greatest number of deaths. When they were too frightened to want to take care of each other, they died in isolation, and many homes were emptied for lack of someone to care for the sick. If they did go in, they died, and especially those with a claim to special goodness. Through their sense of shame, they took no care for themselves in going to visit their friends, even when the patients' own family members were finally worn out with the groans of the dying, and overcome by the scale of

the disaster. But for the most part, those who had themselves survived the disease showed most pity for the dying and the suffering,
because they knew the prognosis and they themselves had now no
fear of the plague, because it didn't take the same person twice, at
least not fatally. . . .

* * *

52. The existing trouble was made even worse by the movement of
people from countryside to city center, especially for those moving
in. There was not enough housing; they lived in stifling huts during
the summer, so it was chaos, they died, and the corpses lay on top
of each other and the half-dead reeled in the streets and around all
the fountains, desperate for water. The temples in which they shel-
tered were full of corpses, of people who had died there. Indeed,
as the disaster grew worse and worse and people did not know what
was going to happen to them, they stopped bothering about anything, even temples and holy rites. All the norms of burial were
overturned, the usual customs of funeral rites; now each person
buried their dead as best they could. Many people lacked resources
because so many of their family had already died, so they had
humiliating burials. Some nipped in front of somebody else's funeral
pyre and added their own corpse on top and ignited it; others flung
the corpse they were carrying on top of some already burning pyre,
and went away.

53. The plague began creating greater lawlessness in other areas
too. It made it easier for people to dare do things that were once done
secretly and not on a whim, because they saw the sharp change from
people who were fortunate, then suddenly dead, and those who had
had nothing at once inherited their property. So they thought they
should spend quickly and live for pleasure, thinking of their bodies
and their wealth as equally ephemeral. Nobody was eager to stick to
so-called noble behavior, thinking it unclear if they'd die before
they achieved it. Immediate gratification and an eye to the main
chance were considered good and useful. No fear of the gods or
human law constrained them, because they thought it was all the
same whether they worshipped the gods or not, seeing everybody
dying equally; law-breakers did not expect to be alive until the time
of their trial, to be punished; they thought they had already been
condemned to a greater punishment, and before it fell on them, it
was right to enjoy life.

SOPHOCLES

From Oedipus at Colonus†

Sophocles' play *Oedipus at Colonus* was composed decades after the *Tyrannos*, in 406, shortly before the playwright's death. The blind Oedipus has arrived with his daughters at the sacred shrine of the Eumenides (the Furies), outside Athens. The Chorus, a group of native inhabitants, have advised him how to purify himself for inadvertently trespassing on the sacred ground of the shrine. While they wait for the arrival of Theseus, king of Athens, who will decide whether or not to welcome the refugee Oedipus into the city, the Chorus members ask Oedipus about his past history. The passage is composed in lyric meter and would presumably have been sung; the style is poetic and densely metaphorical, and the Chorus speak in allusive terms, as if reluctant to name the horrors of Oedipus's life in a holy place. Oedipus here denies all moral and legal responsibility for his actions.

* * *

CHORUS
    Stranger, it's dreadful to wake up an ancient horror
    that has now for a long time been lying asleep.
    But I'm longing to ask you—
OEDIPUS
    What?
CHORUS
    About that impossible, miserable agony
    that was revealed, that lived with you.
OEDIPUS
    No! By your own hospitality,
    don't open the humiliations I have suffered.
CHORUS
    It's big, it never ceases being told;
    stranger, I want to hear the story straight.
OEDIPUS
    Aargh! No!
CHORUS
    Please! Please!
OEDIPUS
    Ah, no! No!

† Translated by the editor of this Norton Critical Edition from lines 510–49 of *Oedipus Colonus* in *Sophocles: Fabulae*, Oxford Classical Texts, ed. H. Lloyd-Jones and N. G. Wilson (Oxford: Oxford UP, 1990), pp. 378–80.

CHORUS
Do this for me, as I've done what you wanted.

OEDIPUS
I have borne the worst of horrors, strangers,
I've borne them unwillingly,
let the god know it;
none of them were chosen by myself.

CHORUS
What? How?

OEDIPUS
The city bound me to an evil bed—
and I knew nothing—
to a ruin of a marriage.

CHORUS
Did you—I heard this—fill
a cursed marriage bed
by your own mother?

OEDIPUS
Stranger, it's death to hear.
But these two are my daughters, by—

CHORUS
What do you mean?

OEDIPUS
Two children, two curses.

CHORUS
Zeus!

OEDIPUS
Produced by the same mother, a shared labor pain.

CHORUS
So they are your daughters and also—

OEDIPUS
Sisters; we share a father.

CHORUS
Oh, no!

OEDIPUS
Yes. So many horrors come again.

CHORUS
You suffered.

OEDIPUS
I suffered things I can't forget.

CHORUS
You did—

OEDIPUS
I did nothing.

CHORUS
  Really?
OEDIPUS
  I took a gift; I wish I'd never had
  the miserable blessing I got from the city.
CHORUS
  Poor man! What then? You murdered . . . ?
OEDIPUS
  What is this? What do you want to find out?
CHORUS
  Your father's . . . ?
OEDIPUS
                    Ah! Ah! You've struck me a second time, plague
                        upon plague.
CHORUS
  You killed . . . ?
OEDIPUS
                    I killed. But I have—
CHORUS
  What?
OEDIPUS
          —extenuating circumstances.
CHORUS
                                            What?
OEDIPUS
                                            I'll tell you.
The people whom I killed would have killed me!
I'm clean by law: I came to it in ignorance.

                        ❊   ❊   ❊

ARISTOTLE

Nicomachean Ethics 3.13–119 (1110b17–1111a21)†

Aristotle (384–22 B.C.E.) lived almost a century after Sophocles. He was
a philosopher, a student of Plato. He is concerned in this work with
defining the good life, *eudaimonia*, which must, he argues, imply being
a good person, which in turn must imply having good emotions and
voluntarily doing good things. In this section, the start of Book 3, he
defines voluntary action by distinguishing it from things done under

---

† Translated and with notes by the editor of this Norton Critical Edition from *Aristotle:
  Nicomachean Ethics* (Teubner, 1878), pp. 44–46.

compulsion and things done in ignorance; only voluntary action is worthy of praise. The passage is included for insight into how near-contemporaries of Sophocles might have seen the question of whether Oedipus could be blamed for any of his actions, and the degree to which they should be seen as involuntary.

Something done in ignorance is never voluntary, but it is involuntary only if it is regretted and painful [to the person who did it]. A person who acts in ignorance but doesn't feel bad about their action certainly didn't act voluntarily—because they didn't know—but also not involuntarily—because they didn't feel bad. So there are two types of involuntary action: when the agent regrets it, it's involuntary; when the agent doesn't regret it, we can call it not voluntary. It is different, so it's better for it to have its own term. And acting through ignorance seems different from acting in ignorance. For when someone is drunk or angry, they don't seem to act through ignorance, but through one of those things mentioned: they don't know, but they're not unknowing. Certainly, all wicked people are ignorant of what they should do and what they should avoid, and because of this type of error, they're unjust and generally bad. But "involuntary" doesn't mean whether someone doesn't know what's beneficial, because it's not ignorance in the choice that is the cause of the involuntariness; instead, that's the cause of the person's wickedness. Nor is it general ignorance, for which people are blamed. Rather, it means ignorance about specific facts dealing with the objects and circumstances of the action, because one pities and commiserates in such cases. The person who acts without knowing any of these types of facts acts involuntarily.

Perhaps it is useful to specify the nature and number of relevant facts. They are: who acts; what they do; about what or in what they're acting [the circumstances or objects of the action]; and sometimes also with what, such as the instrument, and the motive, such as saving somebody; and how, for instance, gently or intensely.

Nobody sane could be ignorant of all these things, and obviously nobody sane could fail to know the agent of the action; how could he fail to know himself? But the agent might not know what he is doing; for instance, people say something "slipped out" while they were talking, or they might not know that saying something was forbidden, as Aeschylus said of the Mysteries,[1] or they might say they let it off when they were trying to demonstrate it, like the man with the catapult. Someone might think their son was an enemy, as

---

1. The poet Aeschylus, Sophocles' older contemporary, was accused of violating the secrets of the Mysteries (a ritual in honor of Demeter) through a passage in one of his plays, but he was acquitted.

Merope does,[2] or think a sharpened spear had a blunting button on it, or that a heavy stone was actually pumice. Someone could give medicine to try to cure a person, but kill them. Someone might mean to grip, as in arm's-length wrestling, but strike. In all these cases, there is ignorance of the circumstances of the action, so someone who does not know any of these things seems to have acted involuntarily, especially when the unknown facts are especially important ones. The most important facts seem to be the circumstances and goal of the action. That is the kind of ignorance that is called involuntary, but it is still necessary for the action to be painful and regretted [afterwards by the agent].

An involuntary action is done under compulsion or through ignorance, so it would seem that voluntary action is one whose origin lies in the agent, and the agent knows the facts relevant to the action. Perhaps it's not right to say that acts done in anger or passion are involuntary. First, because then no nonhuman animal acts voluntarily, and nor do children. Then, are none of our actions voluntary if they're done in passion or anger, or are good actions done willingly, and shameful ones involuntarily? Wouldn't that be silly, when the same person is responsible? Perhaps it is strange to call the things one should aim for involuntary. It is necessary to be angry about certain things, and to desire certain things, such as health and learning, and some involuntary things seem painful, and things that satisfy our desires seem pleasant. Next: what difference is there, qua involuntary action, between mistakes made by conscious reasoning, and those made in anger? Both should be avoided, and irrational feelings seem no less human, so actions done in anger or passion also belong to the person who does them. It is weird to categorize those as involuntary.

Poetics 10–11, 13[†]

[A good plot is] not only an imitation of a complete action, but also of frightening and pitiable events, and this is best generated when the events happen through each other, but contrary to expectation: it's most impressive if this happens naturally and by chance, because also chance events are most surprising when they seem to have happened on purpose, as when the statue of Mityos in Argos killed the man responsible for the death of Mityos, when it

2. This Merope, a mythological character, was the subject of a lost play by Euripides called *Cresphontes*. She is not the Merope who was queen of Corinth and Oedipus's adoptive mother.
† Translated by the editor of this Norton Critical Edition from *Aristotle: Poetics* (Teubner, 1893), pp. 13–17.

fell on him while he was watching a spectacle. That type of thing doesn't seem random. So it's necessary that plots of that type are best.

Plots can be simple or complex; actions also, of which plots are imitations, are the same way. By "simple" I mean an action where the change of fortune happens alone, without reversal or recognition, and by "complex," those in which the change happens with recognition or reversal, or both. Those things have to happen from the arrangement of the plot, so that what happens next should come either necessarily or probably out of the events that precede. There is a big difference between things that happen after one another, and things that happen because of one another.

Reversal is the change of events to the opposite, according to what I've said, and this, as I've mentioned, should be by probable or necessary means, as in *Oedipus*, the man coming to comfort Oedipus and free him from fear about his mother, reveals who he is and does the opposite.

* * * Recognition is, as the name implies, a change from ignorance to knowledge, either toward love or enmity, between characters assigned [by the plot/the poet] to good or bad fortune. The best recognition is when it happens along with reversal, as in *Oedipus*.

* * *

[13] Now we must consider what goals the work of tragedy should have, and what poets should avoid when they put their plots together, and where they should get them. Since the arrangement of the best tragedy isn't simple but complex, and it's the imitation of things that arouse pity and fear—that's the proper goal of this type of imitative art—it is clear first that poets shouldn't show decent men undergoing a change from good fortune to bad, because that's not frightening or pitiable, but disgusting. Nor bad people going from bad fortune to good, because that's the most untragic of all, because it has none of the elements it should, and it is not feel-good, let alone pitiable or frightening. Nor should tragedies show a very bad man falling from good fortune to bad; that kind of story structure is feel-good, but not pitiful or scary, because pity is for undeserved misfortune, and fear is for someone like ourselves; pity for someone who does not deserve bad luck, fear for a person similar to us, so the plot I just cited is not pitiful or scary.

What remains is a protagonist in between these. He is the kind of person who is not exceptional for goodness, falling into misfortune not through wickedness and criminality, but through some kind of error. It's one of those characters who are very fortunate and have a very good reputation, like Oedipus or Thyestes[1] or the famous men from families like that. A good plot has to be simple rather than, as some say, double, and should change not from bad fortune to good, but the opposite, from good fortune to bad, not through wickedness but through a major error, done by the kind of person I have cited, or better rather than worse than that. Facts provide evidence, because at first, poets used to cite random plots, but now the best tragedies are formed from few [mythical] households, for instance those about Alcmeon, Oedipus, Orestes, Meleager, Thyestes, Telephus, and the other characters who happened to experience or do terrible things.

* * *

Fear and pity can be generated by spectacle, but they also emerge from the arrangement of events itself, which is superior and the mark of a better poet. For the story can be told without seeing the play, so that somebody hearing the events that happened can shiver and feel pity from the story—as someone would feel just hearing the story of Oedipus.

[Aristotle distinguishes different types of action that are liable to generate pity or fear and then discusses whether it is better for the playwright to represent these actions as having been done voluntarily or involuntarily.]

It is possible for the action to be done, as ancient poets handled it, by knowing agents who recognize each other—as Euripides made Medea kill her children [in the knowledge that they were her children]. Or characters can act, but not know that they are doing something terrible, but then later recognize their kinship, as in Sophocles' *Oedipus*. This case is outside the play, but it can be inside the tragedy, as in Astydamas's *Alcmeon*, or the *Wounded Odysseus* of Telegon.[2]

* * *

* * * Stories should not be composed from irrational elements; for the most part, a poet should exclude the irrational, or keep it outside the plot, as in *Oedipus* there is the fact that he does not know that Laius is dead, but that is outside the play.

---

1. Thyestes was a mythical king of Olympia who murdered his half-brother Chrysippus, usurped the throne of Mycenae, and slept with the wife of his brother, Atreus. In revenge, Atreus killed Thyestes' children and fed them to him. The family was a popular subject for tragedy.
2. Lost plays.

HYGINUS

Fables 66–67†

Gaius Julius Hyginus was a Roman author who lived around 64 B.C.E.–17 C.E. His prose collection of mythic stories drew on many sources that are now lost; for instance, he was probably familiar with the Aeschylus trilogy on Laius and Oedipus, and Euripides' version of Oedipus. Hyginus's version of the myth is different from Sophocles'— for instance, in the circumstances of Oedipus's murder of Laius, the oracle about how to stop the plague, and the way the secret comes out.

Laius

Laius, son of Labdacus, was given an oracle from Apollo to beware of death from the hand of his son. So when Jocasta, daughter of Menoeceus, his wife, gave birth, he ordered the baby to be exposed. Periboea, wife of King Polybus, found and rescued the exposed baby, while she was washing clothes beside the sea. Polybus found out, but because they had no children, they raised him as their own, and because his feet were pierced, they named him Oedipus.

Oedipus

After Oedipus, the son of Laius and Jocasta, grew up, he was stronger than any of the others and through envy of him, his peers accused him of being not really the son of Polybus; an additional reason was that Polybus was so gentle, while Oedipus was hotheaded. So he set off for Delphi to find out about his parents. Meanwhile, it had been revealed to Laius through signs that his death at the hand of his son was near. So while he too was going to Delphi, Oedipus met him. Laius's bodyguards ordered Oedipus to give way to the king, but he wouldn't. The king drove on his horses and the wheel ran over Oedipus's foot. Oedipus was angry and, in ignorance, dragged his own father from his chariot and killed him. After the death of Laius, Creon, son of Menoeceus, took the throne. Meanwhile the Sphinx, daughter of Typhon, was sent to Boeotia, and she was destroying the Thebans' fields. She set a challenge for Creon the king: if anybody could solve the riddle she posed, she'd leave; but if the person failed to solve the riddle, she'd eat him up; and she would never leave the territory otherwise [i.e., unless the riddle was solved]. When all Greece had heard about this, the king

---

† Translated by the editor of this Norton Critical Edition from *Hyginus: Fabulae*, Bibliotheca Scriptorum Graecorum et Romanorum Teubneriana, 2nd ed., ed. P. K. Marshall (Munich: K. G. Saur Verlag, 2002), pp. 65–67.

said that he promised to give the throne and his sister Jocasta in
marriage to any man who solved the riddle of the Sphinx. After
many men had come, in desire for the throne, and been eaten by
the Sphinx, Oedipus, the son of Laius, came and solved the riddle.
The Sphinx threw herself to her death. Oedipus accepted his
father's throne and Jocasta, his mother, as his wife, without knowing it; from their union came Eteocles and Polyneices, Antigone
and Ismene. Meanwhile, crop failure and starvation fell on Thebes
because of Oedipus's crimes, and when Tiresias was asked why
Thebes was suffering from this plague, he answered, if any of the
dragon's teeth people survived,[1] and died for his fatherland, he
would free it from the plague. Then Menoeceus, father of Jocasta,
threw himself from the walls. While this was happening at Thebes,
Polybus died in Corinth; when this news came, Oedipus began by
taking it badly, because he thought his father was dead. But Periboea revealed the truth about his adoption. Likewise Menoetes, the
old man who had exposed him, recognized him from the scars on
his feet and ankles as the son of Laius. When Oedipus realized this
and saw that he had done all those terrible crimes, he took the
spikes from his mother's dress and put out his eyes, and handed the
throne to his sons to rule in alternate years, and went in exile from
Thebes, with his daughter Antigone as his guide.

PSEUDO-APOLLODORUS

Library 3.5–6†

The *Library*, a text of unknown authorship once attributed to an Athenian named Apollodorus, is a compendium in Greek of ancient myths,
composed in the first or second century C.E. The author draws on
mythic traditions from ancient, now lost sources. This version of the
Oedipus story is different from that of Sophocles in certain ways, such
as the specifics of Laius's murder. Unlike Sophocles, the author spells
out the specifics of the riddle of the Sphinx and the various oracles.

After the death of Amphion, Laius took the throne. He married the
daughter of Menoeceus, whom some people call Jocasta, and others
Epicaste, although the god had sent an oracle that he should not

---

1. Thebes had been founded by Cadmus, who killed a dragon that guarded the local
   spring. He was instructed to sow half the dragon's teeth in the ground; armed men
   sprang up (the Sparti—Sown Men), who immediately started killing each other. One
   of the survivors, Echion, became king of Thebes after Cadmus; Oedipus was his
   great-nephew.
† Translated and with notes by the editor of this Norton Critical Edition from Apollodorus, *The Library*, vol. I: *Books 1–3.9*, ed. J. G. Frazer, Loeb Classical Library 121
   (Cambridge, MA: Harvard UP, 1921).

become a father, since the son he fathered would be a parricide. Laius got drunk and slept with his wife. He used spikes[1] to pierce the ankles of the child that was produced, and gave it to a herdsman to expose. But that herdsman exposed it on Cithaeron, and the cowherds of Polybus, the king of Corinth, found the baby and brought it to the king's wife, Periboea. She took him and adopted him, and as she took care of his ankles, she named him Oedipus, giving him that name because his feet [*pous*] were swollen [*anoidesai*].[2]

When the child was grown up, he was stronger than his age-mates; because of their jealousy, he was teased for being illegitimate. He asked Periboea about it, but could get no information. So he went to Delphi to find out about his parents. The god told him not to travel to his fatherland, because he would kill his father and have sex with his mother. Hearing this, and thinking he was the child of his supposed parents, he left Corinth. But when riding a chariot through Phocis, he met Laius, also driving a chariot, on a narrow road. Polyphontes, Laius's herald, ordered him to get out of the way; because he refused and there was a delay, the herald killed one of his two horses. Oedipus got angry and killed both Polyphontes and Laius, and then reached Thebes.

Damastratus, the king of the Plataeans, buried Laius, and Creon, the son of Menoeceus, took control of the kingdom. But while Creon was king, a disaster fell upon Thebes. Hera sent a Sphinx, who was the daughter of Echidne and Typon, and had a woman's face, the torso, feet and tail of a lion, and the wings of a bird. She sat on Mount Phicion, asking the Thebans this riddle which she had learned from the Muses: "What has one voice, four feet, two feet and three feet?" There was at the same time an oracle that the Thebans would get rid of the Sphinx when they solved the riddle, so they kept getting together to figure out what it meant, but when they found no answer, she snatched one of them and ate him up. Many died, including finally Haemon, Creon's son. So Creon announced that he would give the kingdom, and the wife of Laius, to anybody who solved the riddle. Oedipus heard that and solved it, saying that the riddle posed by the Sphinx referred to a human being, who is born as a baby, cradled in arms, who is four-footed, and then becomes two-footed, and when a person is old, they take on a third foot, which is a stick. The Sphinx threw herself off the acropolis, and Oedipus took the kingdom and married his mother, in ignorance, and had sons by her—Polyneices and Eteocles—and daughters, Ismene and Antigone. Some people say that he had the children with Euryganeia, daughter of Hyperphas.

---

1. Pins to fasten clothing, like those with which Sophocles' Oedipus blinds himself.
2. This line suggests the etymology from "swell" (*oideo*) and "foot" (*pous*).

Later, when the secrets were revealed, Jocasta hanged herself with a noose, and Oedipus blinded his eyes and was exiled from Thebes. He laid curses on his sons who had watched him expelled him from the city and did not help him. He came with Antigone to Colonus, where the shrine of the Eumenides is, and sat as a suppliant, and was welcomed by Theseus. Shortly afterwards, he died.

SENECA

From Oedipus†

Seneca, c. 4–65 C.E., a Roman philosopher, speechwriter, essayist, teacher, and advisor to the emperor Nero, wrote several tragedies based on Greek mythological themes, including an *Oedipus*. Seneca's tragedies may have been designed for recitation by one or more actors rather than full dramatic performance, although they are certainly stageable. Seneca's *Oedipus* is gorier than Sophocles' version; it includes, for instance, an extensive scene in which the prophet Tiresias enacts a bloody sacrifice. Seneca's Oedipus, even at the beginning of the play, is far less self-confident and more fearful than Sophocles' version of the character. Included here is the whole final sequence of the play, in which Oedipus discovers the truth about his parentage and blinds himself. One notable difference from Sophocles is that Oedipus's children are not featured.

* * *

OEDIPUS How cruel Fate attacks me on all sides!
   Well, come then, tell me how my father died.
OLD MAN The old man passed away in gentle sleep.
OEDIPUS My father is dead and no one murdered him.
   Proof! I now can hold clean hands to heaven,   790
   I need not be afraid of my own actions.
   But wait—the worst part of the oracle remains.
OLD MAN Your father's royal power keeps you immune.
OEDIPUS I will inherit my father's throne—but I still
   fear my mother.
OLD MAN Why should you be afraid of a parent, who only
   wants you home again?
OEDIPUS   My duty as a son makes me run from her.
OLD MAN You abandon her now she is widowed?
OEDIPUS   That is what I am
   scared of.

† From *Seneca: Six Tragedies*, trans. Emily Wilson (Oxford: Oxford UP, 2010), pp. 62–69. © Emily Wilson 2010. Reprinted by permission of the licensor through PLSclear. Notes were added by the editor for this Norton Critical Edition.

OLD MAN   Tell me what fear lies buried in your mind.
  I am used to keeping royal secrets hidden.
OEDIPUS   I shudder at marriage to Mother, foretold by Delphi.   800
OLD MAN   That is no reason for fear! You need not worry:
  Merope was not really your true mother.
OEDIPUS   Why should she raise a child that was not hers?
OLD MAN   Royal lines need heirs to keep them safe.
OEDIPUS   Tell me, how did you hear their family secret?
OLD MAN   I gave you as a baby to your mother.
OEDIPUS   You gave me to her, but who gave me to you?
OLD MAN   A shepherd on Cithaeron's snowy ridge.
OEDIPUS   How did you happen to be in that place?
OLD MAN   I used to tend my long-horned sheep up there.   810
OEDIPUS   Now for the proof. How is my body marked?
OLD MAN   Your feet were scarred by being pierced with iron.
  You got your name from your swollen, damaged feet.
OEDIPUS   Who gave my body to you as a gift?
OLD MAN   He was chief shepherd of the royal flock.
  He had many shepherds under him.
OEDIPUS   Tell me his name.
OLD MAN   I cannot. Old folks' minds
  get tired and the memory grows dull.
OEDIPUS   Well, could you recognize him if you saw him?
OLD MAN   Perhaps I could. Frequently, even now,   820
  a trivial detail calls old memories back.
OEDIPUS   Let shepherds bring their whole flock to the altars.
  Servants! Go, hurry up and fetch the man
  who is in charge of all the royal herd.
JOCASTA   No! The truth was hidden—on purpose or by chance;
  in either case, let ancient secrets stay concealed forever.
  Truth often harms the one who digs it up.
OEDIPUS   What is there to be scared of? What could be worse
      than this?
JOCASTA   You need to understand, this quest is something big:
  the country's health and that of the royal house   830
  are in the balance. Stop, do not go on:
  you need not make the moves; fate will reveal itself.
OEDIPUS   In times of happiness, no point in shaking things up.
  But in a time of crisis, the safest thing is change.
JOCASTA   Do you want a grander father than a king?
  Be careful not to find one you regret.
OEDIPUS   I need certainty, even if I regret
  the family I find.—Look, here is Phorbas,[1] the old shepherd man

---

1. In Sophocles, this character is not named.

who used to have control of the royal sheep.
Old man, do you remember his name or face?   840
OLD MAN   His face smiles to my mind . . . I am not sure.
His appearance seems familiar, but I do not know.
OEDIPUS   Did you serve Laius, when he was the king,
driving his rich flocks under Mount Cithaeron?
PHORBAS   Yes, Mount Cithaeron always had good grazing.
In summertime our flocks fed in those meadows.
OLD MAN   Do you know me?
PHORBAS   My memory hesitates.
OEDIPUS   Did you once give a baby to this man?
Speak! Do you hesitate? Why are you pale?
Why search about for words? Truth hates delay.   850
PHORBAS   These things are hidden by long lapse of time.
OEDIPUS   Speak! Or let torture force you to the truth.[2]
PHORBAS   I gave the child to him, a useless gift:
that baby could not live to enjoy the light.
OLD MAN   Hush! He is alive and will, I hope, live long.
OEDIPUS   Why do you say that baby must have died?
PHORBAS   An iron pin had been driven through his feet
to bind his legs up, and the wound was swollen;
foul pus infected the child's little body.
OEDIPUS   What more do you want? Now fate is drawing near—   860
Who was the baby?
PHORBAS   Loyalty forbids—
OEDIPUS   Servants! Bring fire. Burning will change his mind.
PHORBAS   Is truth discovered by the path of blood?
Master, have mercy.
OEDIPUS   If you think me cruel
and violent, the cure is near at hand:
tell me the truth. Who was the baby? Who were its parents?
PHORBAS   The mother of the child was your own wife.
OEDIPUS   Gape open, earth! Lord of the Underworld,
master of shadows, seize and return me to lowest Hell,
reverse my birth and let me be unborn.   870
Thebans! Heap stones on my accursed head,
slaughter me; let fathers, sons, and wives,
and brothers take up arms against me,
let this sick people take fire-brands from funeral pyres,
and hurl the flames at me. The guilt of my times is mine:
I wander hateful to the gods, a blasphemy.
The day I first breathed unformed infant breath,
already I deserved to die. Now, match your sins,

---

2. Enslaved people were routinely tortured to force testimony.

dare an achievement worthy of your crimes.
Go on, make haste into the royal house: 880
congratulate your mother on her children!
CHORUS   If I had the power
   to shape Fate to my will,
   I would let the gentle breezes
   guide my sails, and my yardarms
   would never shudder under whirlwind blasts.
   May soft and gentle winds
   guide my fearless boat,
   never turn it from its course.
   May life carry me on   890
   down the middle path.
     Frightened of the Cretan king
   the mad boy[3] sought the stars,
   trusting new technology
   competing with real birds
   and hoping to control
   wings all too false.
   He robbed the sea of its name.
   But the clever old man
   Daedalus, kept a middle course,   900
   and stopped in the middle of the clouds,
   waiting for his winged child
   (as a bird flees from the threat
   of the hawk, then gathers together
   her brood, scattered by fear)
   until the boy, in the sea,
   waved his drowning arms
   tangled by the ropes of his bold flight.
   All excess hangs
   in doubt.   910

Act Five

CHORUS   But what is this? The gates are creaking;
   look, a servant of the king
   is beating his head in mourning.
   Tell us the news you bring.
MESSENGER   When Oedipus understood the words of fate

3. I.e., the mythical character Icarus, son of the engineer Daedalus. Daedalus built an ingenious labyrinth for Minos, king of Crete, but Minos then trapped him and Icarus in a tower. Daedalus built wings so they could fly to freedom; but Icarus flew too close to the sun, melted the wax gluing his wings together, and fell to his death in the Icarian Sea.

and realized his awful heritage, he cursed himself:
'Guilty!' he cried, and thinking of death, he rushed
into his hated home, fast as he could.
Just as the Libyan lion rages in the fields,
shaking its yellow mane and threatening;   920
his face is dark with anger, his eyes wild,
he roars and groans, cold sweat runs over his body,
he froths at the mouth and hurls out threats,
and his enormous buried pain spills out.
He was full of wild imaginings and plans
to fit his fate. 'Why put off punishment?
Bring swords and drive them through my guilty heart,
or burn me with hot fire, stone me to death.
Is there a tigress or a bird of prey
to tear my chest apart? Cithaeron, you contain   930
such wickedness already: set against me
beasts from the forest or bloodthirsty hounds—
or send again Agave.[4] My soul, why fear death?
Only death can save me from my guilt.'
   He set his tainted hand upon the hilt
and drew his sword. 'But no! Can you absolve
such evil with so short a punishment,
a single blow? Death can pay for your father—
But your mother? What about the children,
disgustingly conceived? How can you atone   940
for your country, mourning and ruined by your crimes?
You cannot be redeemed! In Oedipus alone
the laws of Nature are perverted, even birth
is strange. Then let my punishment be novel too.
May I live and die, and live and die,
constantly reborn, to feel again
new punishments. Use your head, poor fool:
suffer for many years unprecedented pain.
Have a long death. I must think of a way
to wander, distant from the dead and from the living.   950
I want to die, but must not meet my father.
Why do I hesitate?' Look now, a sudden stream
gushes down his face, his cheeks are wet with tears.
'But is it enough to weep? Do my eyes pour
only this thin liquid? Drive them from their homes,
to follow their own tears. Are you satisfied yet,
gods of marriage? Gouge them from their sockets!'

4. Agave killed her son Pentheus, king of Thebes, in a frenzy inspired by Dionysos, on Mt. Cithaeron.

He raged, his cheeks showed a ferocious fire,
his eyes could scarcely stay inside his head;
his face was wild and full of feeling, angry, savage,   960
as if he had gone mad. He lets out a terrible scream,
and plunges his hands at his face. But his goggling eyes
pop out, trying to meet his thrust of their own accord.
They want to meet the source of their destruction.
Greedily his nails dig into his eyeballs,
ripping and tearing out the jelly from the roots.
His hands stay stuck in the empty spaces, glued there,
and buried deep inside, he scrabbles with his nails
at the deep empty caverns where his eyes once were.
He rages more and more, too much, achieving nothing.   970
   There is no danger now of light; he lifts his head,
scanning the vault of heaven with empty sockets,
testing his new night. Fragments still hang
from his clumsily excavated eyes. He rips them off,
and cries in triumph to the gods: 'Now spare my homeland,
I implore you! Now I have done right, I have accepted
my proper punishment. I found at last a night
appropriate for my marriage.' A horrible dripping
covers his mangled face, bloody with ripped veins.
CHORUS   Fate is driving us: give in to fate.   980
No amount of worrying can change
the threads of fate's fixed spindle.
All that human beings suffer,
all we do, comes from on high.
The decrees determined by the spindle
of Lachesis[5] will never be reversed.
The path of everything is always fixed,
our first day tells our last.
Even God cannot turn back
the things which rush by in the web of cause.   990
No prayer can change the swift-revolving pattern
fixed for each life. Many people find
fear itself can harm; while they fear fate,
they find themselves encountering their fate.

Epilogue

CHORUS   Listen! The gates! He struggles to approach,
blind and with no guide to help him walk,
on his dark way.

---

5. Lachesis is one of the three mythical Fates who spin the threads of human life.

OEDIPUS   Good! It is done. I have paid my debt to my father.
I am happy with the darkness. What god blesses me,
pouring this dark cloud upon my head?   1000
Who forgave my sins? I escaped day's knowing eyes.
Father-killer, you owe nothing to your hands.
The light ran from you. This face suits Oedipus.

CHORUS   Look, Jocasta skitters out, leaping and wild,
a madwoman, like Agave, frenzied mother,
who grabbed her own son's head, but then at last
realized what she had done. Seeing poor Oedipus
she hesitates: she wants him and she fears him.
Shame gives way to grief, but her words get stuck.

JOCASTA   What can I call you? 'Son'? No? But you are my son.   1010
Ashamed? Talk to me, son! No? Why do you turn away
hiding your empty eyes?

OEDIPUS   Who wants to spoil my darkness?
Who gives back my eyes? It is my mother's voice.
My work is wasted. Such monsters as we are
must never meet again. Let the seas divide us,
and lands far distant, and if under here
there hangs another earth, with other stars
and another, exiled sun—let one of us go there.

JOCASTA   It is the fault of fate; fate cannot make one guilty.

OEDIPUS   Do not speak to me, I will not listen.   1020
I beg you, by the remnants of my body,
by the unlucky children of my blood,
by all the good and evil names we share.

JOCASTA   Why are you numb, my soul? And why resist
sharing his punishment? You ruined woman,
through you all human laws are muddled and confused.
Die by the sword, release your wicked life.
Even if the father of the gods, shaking the world,
should hurl his curving thunderbolts at me,
I could never pay for all my sins.   1030
Evil mother! I want death. I need to find
a way to die.—Come, use your hands to help
your mother, if you killed your father; this is your last job.
    No, I ought to grab his sword; my husband died
by this same blade.—Why not call him the right name?
He is my father-in-law. Should I use this weapon
to pierce my heart, or push it deep into my naked throat?
Where should I strike? How can I not know? Of course!
Strike my all-too-fertile womb, which bore a husband-child.

CHORUS   She falls down dead. She died by her own hand,   1040
the sword is driven out by so much blood.

OEDIPUS   Prophet, guardian, god of truth, I blame you.
  I only owed the fates my father's death;
  now I am a double parent-killer, worse than I feared:
  I killed my mother. She died for my crime.
  Apollo, you lied! My sins outdid my fate.
     Totter along your darkened path, and use
  your hands to feel the way for your faltering feet,
  the trembling kings of your nocturnal life.
  Hurry! though your footsteps slip, go, rush away!   1050
  But stop! Be careful, do not fall upon your mother.
     People weary with disease, heavy with plague,
  half-dead already, look, I am leaving you.
  Lift up your heads. Now gentler skies are yours,
  after I go. Those who are dying, whose lives
  are wandering below, may now breathe in
  the breath of life. Go on now, help the dying;
  I take the deadly plague away with me.
  Harmful Fate and dreadful spasms of Disease,
  Black Plague, Wasting and Ravening Pain,   1060
  come with me! Come! I am glad to have such guides.

RITA DOVE

From The Darker Face of the Earth[†]

Rita Dove (b. 1952) is a wide-ranging, prolific, and prize-winning Afri-
can American poet, essayist, and playwright. She was U.S. poet laure-
ate from 1993 to 1995. Her play, *The Darker Face of the Earth*, uses the
plot of Sophocles' *Oedipus Tyrannos*, but sets it on a slave plantation in
the pre–Civil War American South. Dove's Oedipus character, Augustus (the title of a Roman emperor, or, as he says, "the name of a king"),
is an enslaved young black man who is highly intelligent, highly educated, and aware of the French and American Revolutions and slave
rebellions in Haiti and on the slave ship *La Amistad*. He organizes the
enslaved people on the plantation to rebellion; the plotting is overheard
by Hector, an old slave whom Augustus kills to silence him. Augustus
also begins an affair with the white mistress of the plantation, Amalia.
In talking to the other enslaved people, he comes to believe that he is
the son of Amalia's husband, Louis, who must, he thinks, have raped
one of the enslaved women. Augustus is sent by the other slaves to kill
Louis and Amalia, and he stabs Louis. But in the passage included here,
the last sequence of the play, Augustus discovers that he is actually

---

† From *The Darker Face of the Earth*, 3rd ed. (Ashland, OR: Story Line P, 2000),
pp. 142–50. © 1994, 1996, 2000 by Rita Dove. Reprinted by permission of the publisher, Story Line Press. Notes are by the editor of this Norton Critical Edition.

Amalia's son from a consensual relationship with Hector. Dove's version of the discovery raises profound questions about whether incest and parricide really are the most horrible secrets that could be uncovered, by setting them against the manifold horrors and abuses of slavery.

* * *

AUGUSTUS *heads for* AMALIA'S *room; lights come up on* AMALIA, *who has stepped into the hall.*

AMALIA   Augustus, there you are! What's happening?
I called Ticey, but she won't come!

AUGUSTUS (*Backing her into the room.*)
I thought you didn't care
what happened out there.

AMALIA   Why are they shouting?
Why doesn't Jones make them stop?

AUGUSTUS   I reckon the dead don't make good overseers.
Your slaves are rebelling, Missy.
Liberté, Égalité, Fraternité![1]

AMALIA (*Stares at him uncomprehendingly, then runs to the window.*)
Rebelling? My slaves?
Augustus, make them stop!
They'll listen to you!

AUGUSTUS   Like I listened to you?
You led me into your parlour
like a dog on a leash. Sit, dog!
Heel! Care for a sherry? A fairy tale?

AMALIA   No, you were different!
You were—

AUGUSTUS (*Grabs her.*)
No more conversation!
Where is my mother?

AMALIA   Your mother? How would I know a thing like that?

AUGUSTUS   Your husband confessed.

AMALIA (*Aware of danger on all sides, seeking escape.*)
What could Louis have to confess?

AUGUSTUS   A shrewd piece of planning,
to destroy him with his own son
after you had failed to destroy
the son himself!
But you had to be patient.
Twenty years you had to wait
before you could buy me back.

---

1. Freedom, Equality, Brotherhood!: slogan of the French Revolution.

AMALIA   Louis, your father? You must be joking!
AUGUSTUS   Shall I help you remember?
  You supplied the basket yourself—
AMALIA   Basket?
AUGUSTUS   —lined in blue satin, trimmed with rosettes—
AMALIA   *Red* rosettes?
AUGUSTUS   Monsieur LaFarge agreed
  to sell his own baby—but that wasn't enough,
  was it? You wanted the child dead.
  So you slipped a pair of riding spurs
  into the sewing basket.
  And you know the kind of scars
  spurs leave, Missy. Like crowns . . .
  or exploding suns.
AMALIA   My God.
AUGUSTUS   The woman who patched me up
  kept that basket as a reminder.
AMALIA   No . . .
AUGUSTUS (*Shakes her.*)
  What did you do with my mother?
  Who is she?
  Slaps her.
  Tell me!
AMALIA (*Wrenches free to face him; her voice trembling.*)
  So you want to know who your mother is?
  You think, if I tell you,
  the sad tale of your life
  will find its storybook ending?
  Well then, this will be my last story—
  and when I have finished,
  you will wish you had never
  stroked my hair or kissed my mouth.
  You will wish you had no eyes to see
  or ears to hear. You will wish
  you had never been born.
AUGUSTUS   I've heard grown men scream,
  watched as the branding iron
  sank into their flesh. I've seen
  pregnant women slit open like melon,
  runaways staked to the ground
  and whipped until
  they floated in their own blood and piss.
  Don't think you can frighten me, Missy:
  Nothing your lips can tell

can be worse than what
these eyes have seen.
AMALIA   Bravo! What a speech!
But you've seen nothing.
Backs up to appraise him, smiling, slightly delirious.
That same expression! How could I forget?
My lover then stood as tall as you now.
AUGUSTUS   Your lover?
PHEBE *bursts in.*
PHEBE   They're coming, Augustus!
They're coming to see if you did
what you were told! Oh, Augustus—
you were supposed to kill her!
AUGUSTUS (*Shaking himself into action, threatening* AMALIA.)
My mother, who is my mother?
Out with it!
AMALIA   Phebe, you tell him.
You were there.
Everyone was there—
under my window,
waiting for news . . .
PHEBE   That . . . was the night
we all came to wait out the birth.
AUGUSTUS   What birth?
AMALIA   Hector on the porch.
AUGUSTUS   What about Hector?
*More shouts outside; compelled by the urgency of the growing revo-
lution,* PHEBE *tries to distract* AUGUSTUS.
PHEBE   There's no time!
AUGUSTUS (*Grabs* AMALIA *as if to slit her throat.*)
What about Hector?
AMALIA   Chick in a basket, going to market!
They said you died, poor thing.
That's why Hector went to the swamp.
AUGUSTUS *stares desperately at her.* PHEBE *turns, thunderstruck.*
AUGUSTUS Hector?
AMALIA   But you didn't die. You're here . . .
Reaches for him; he draws back.
PHEBE (*Looks from* AMALIA *to* AUGUSTUS, *horror growing, recites
tonelessly.*)
Stepped on a pin, the pin bent,
and that's the way the story went.
AMALIA (*Sadly, in a small voice.*)
Silk for my prince, and a canopy of roses!

You were so tiny—so sweet and tiny.
I didn't know about the spurs.
PHEBE   You sold your own child.
Hector's child.
AUGUSTUS   Hector . . .
The knife slips from his fingers.
AMALIA   I was trying to save you!
AUGUSTUS   Save me?
AMALIA (*Extremely agitated.*)
I felt like they had hacked out my heart.
But I wouldn't let them see me cry.
AUGUSTUS (*Wrestling with the horror.*)
You? My mother?
AMALIA (*Clutching herself.*)
It was like missing an arm or a leg
that pains and throbs, even though
you can look right where it was
and see there's nothing left.
She stops abruptly.
AUGUSTUS   My own mother gave me away.
But I found my way back . . .
a worm crawling into its hole.
AMALIA   For weeks afterwards
my breasts ached with milk.
AUGUSTUS (*Sinking to his knees.*)
Better I had bled to death in that basket.
*A great shout goes up as the insurrectionists gain entry to the main
house.* AMALIA *takes advantage of the ensuing distraction to pick
up the knife.*
PHEBE   Augustus!
AUGUSTUS (*Passive.*)
The Day of Redemption is here.
PHEBE   They'll kill you, Augustus!
AUGUSTUS   Time to be free.
AMALIA   Poor baby! I thought
I could keep you from harm—
and here you are,
right in harm's way.
PHEBE *gasps;* AMALIA *stabs herself as* AUGUSTUS, *alerted by* PHEBE'S
*gasp, jumps up, too late to stop her. The room turns red as the out-
buildings go up in flames.*
AUGUSTUS   Amalia!
Catching her as she falls.
No . . .
Calling out in anguish.

Eshu Elewa ogo gbogbo![2]
The chanting of the rebelling SLAVES *grows louder.*
PHEBE Oh, Augustus . . .
AUGUSTUS (*Lays* AMALIA's *body down, gently.*)
 I had the sun and the moon
 once. And the stars
 with their cool gaze.
 Now it's dark.
PHEBE It's alright. You'll be alright now.
AUGUSTUS (*Staring as if trying to make out something in the distance.*)
 Who's there? How she stares,
 like a cat at midnight!
PHEBE Nobody's there, Augustus.
AUGUSTUS Don't you see her?
PHEBE *shakes her head, terrified.*
 Look, she's hidden behind a tree.
PHEBE Oh, Augus—
AUGUSTUS Shh! You'll frighten her. There's another one—
 he's been flogged and pickled in brine.
 That skinny boy ate dirt; that's why he staggers.
 So many of them, limping, with brands
 on their cheeks! Oh, I can't bear it!
PHEBE Come along, now.
AUGUSTUS (*Calling out to the "ghosts."*)
 I came to save you!
The SLAVES *burst in, brandishing bayonets and torches.*
BENJAMIN He did it.
SLAVES Selah! We're free!
The SLAVES *lift* AUGUSTUS *onto their shoulders. The* SLAVE WOMAN/
NARRATOR *stands at the door, holding a torch, taking in the scene.*
SLAVES Freedom, freedom, freedom . . .
The "Freedom!" chant grows louder and more persistent as the
SLAVES *parade out of the room,* AUGUSTUS *on their shoulders;*
PHEBE *follows them, sobbing.* SCYLLA *takes the torch from the*
SLAVE WOMAN/NARRATOR *and sets fire to the window's billowing*
curtains as she slowly straightens up to her full height.
Blackout.
The End.

2. Eshu and Elewa (Eleguá) are Yoruba spirits, Orishas. Eshu is associated with wildness, Elewa with crossroads, and both are tricksters. "Ogo gbogbo" means "all glory" in Yoruba. These Orishas, often invoked earlier in the play by Hector, take the place of the Greek Apollo.

CRITICISM

Note on the Criticism Selected

The scholarly bibliography on Sophocles is immense and potentially overwhelming for students. I have chosen essays from this wealth of material that will, I hope, help orient a first-time reader of the play within its social, historical, literary, and dramatic contexts. Most of the essays chosen are very recent, to offer a sense of current scholarly thought.

The oldest piece, Froma Zeitlin's "Thebes: Theater of Self and Society in Athenian Drama," is included here because it has been so foundational for a generation of scholarship on ancient Athenian tragedy, and because it provides a clear, thoughtful road map for thinking about how Sophocles' mythical Thebes might be presented as like and unlike his contemporary Athens. Three of the more recent pieces—by Eric Dugdale, Joshua Sosin, and Edith Hall—provide detailed insights into social and historical context. Sosin discusses the Athenian homicide law, providing a new interpretation of the legal and ethical implications, within a fifth-century context, of the murder of Laius. Dugdale discusses Athenian practices of naming, adoption, and family structures. Hall reminds us that ancient Athens was a slave-owning society and that the plots of Athenian tragedy, produced by and for enslavers, often hinge on the intimate, dangerous knowledge that enslaved people may have about the lives of their enslavers.

The other four essays deal in different ways with crucial themes of the play. Martha Nussbaum's piece weaves together an account of Freud's famous psychological theory of the "Oedipus complex" with an account of how ancient Greek thinkers had quite different attitudes toward dreams, and quite different assumptions about the most common forms of buried fear, centering less on sex than on precarities of status and fortune. Kirk Ormand's essay on Jocasta's silent death, offstage, analyzes the gendered imagery by which her body is represented in the play and considers the relationship of things seen to things unseen, and of words spoken and words unspoken. Language and interpretation are the central topic of Michael Kicey's "Road to Nowhere," which foregrounds the problematization of interpretation in the play and teases out how this issue may relate to the imagery of movement, falling, and walking. Teresa Danze's essay argues that the tragedy is centrally concerned with a theme that is part of the theatrical experience of its spectators and also essential to its ethics and politics: that of pity for those who suffer.

FROMA I. ZEITLIN

From Thebes: Theater of Self and Society in Athenian Drama[†]

I. *The Topos of Thebes*

The city I am calling Thebes occupies a very small territory, no larger than the extent of the stage in the theater of Dionysos under the shadow of the Akropolis at Athens. In keeping with the conventions of Attic tragedy, no special scenery or stage set identifies it and no particular props are necessary for its representation. The typical facade of the *skēnē*, the stage building, which normally stands for the front of a house or palace, serves just as well for Thebes as for any other location where dramas are supposed to take place.

And yet we know the city once the play has begun, or better, we ought to recognize the place—not only from its being named as Thebes or as the city of Kadmos, not only from references to its walls with the seven gates which are its most distinctive architectural feature, but from what over and over again the tragic poets cause to transpire there as they treat the different myths that share a common terrain in Thebes. We think immediately of the saga of the house of Laios which situates Oidipous at its center and extends beyond him to the dramas of his children—his sons, Eteokles and Polyneikes, and his daughters, Antigone and Ismene. But there is also the prior story of Kadmos, the Spartoi, or Sown Men, and the founding of the city through autochthony (birth from the earth) and fratricide, as the Sown Men fight one another to their mutual destruction with the exception of five who survive to inaugurate the history of the city. And, third, we must include the myth of the god Dionysos himself, the son of Zeus and Semele, reputedly born at Thebes, who returns home to claim recognition of his divinity and to establish the cult of his worship in his native city.

In proposing that there is some conceptual category in the Athenian theater named "Thebes" and that some underlying "unity of place" organizes these disparate stories and their treatment in the work of all three Athenian tragic poets, I am, in effect, suggesting that we look at Thebes as a *topos* in both senses of the word: as a designated place, a geographical locale, and figuratively, as a

† From *Greek Tragedy and Political Theory*, ed. J. Peter Euben (Berkeley: U of California P, 1986), pp. 101–41, as it appeared revised in *Nothing to Do with Dionysos?: Athenian Drama in Its Social Context*, ed. John J. Winkler and Froma I. Zeitlin (Princeton: Princeton UP, 1990), pp. 130–67. Reprinted by permission of Princeton University Press and the author. Some of the author's notes have been omitted.

recurrent concept or formula, or what we call a "commonplace." That is, through the specific myths associated with Thebes on the Athenian stage, certain clusters of ideas, themes, and problems recur which can be identified as proper to Thebes—or rather to Athenian tragedy's representation of Thebes as a mise-en-scène. Additionally, certain formal structures underlie the variety of different plots—similar types of scenes, character portrayals, semantic fields, and so on. All these elements attest to a certain unifying tendency which allows each myth and each version of that myth its own autonomy, but brings them all together as a coherent and complex ensemble. This wide-angle lens which brings the background into sharper focus can extend our conceptions of what constitute formal conventions in the theater and can show how these might interact together at their different levels for a larger design. Better still, this same lens can also illuminate the ideological uses of Athenian theater as it portrays a city onstage that is meant to be dramatically "other" than itself. Thebes, I will argue, provides the negative model to Athens' manifest image of itself with regard to its notions of the proper management of city, society, and self. As the site of displacement, therefore, Thebes consistently supplies the radical tragic terrain where there can be no escape from the tragic in the resolution of conflict or in the institutional provision of a civic future beyond the world of the play. There the most serious questions can be raised concerning the fundamental relations of man to his universe, particularly with respect to the nature of rule over others and of rule over self, as well as those pertaining to the conduct of the body politic.

* * *

OIDIPOUS AT THEBES

In one sense, we might describe the career of Oidipous as a search for a home—or more precisely, a place where he might be at home, where he might truly belong. Viewed from this perspective, Oidipous immediately presents us with an extraordinary paradox. For once Oidipous discovers that he has found his true home in Thebes, he also discovers to his or our horror that he has been only too much "at home." The strange territory to which he had come when, to contravene the oracle of Apollo at Delphi, he had turned away from the road to Corinth in favor of the road to Thebes, proves to be none other than the place where he was born. Thus his subsequent sojourn in the city turns out to be not his first, as all had thought, but his second. Here the dramatic tradition diverges: in two extant plays reference is made to his death at Thebes at some indeterminate time (Aiskhylos, *Seven* 914–1004, Sophokles,

Ant. 899–902), but later theatrical works keep him alive in order to expel him once again from Thebes, this time never to find his way back.[1]

The moment of this last exile is not fixed. Sophokles prepares the way when, at the end of *Oidipous Tyrannos,* Oidipous longs to go at once into exile (*Oid. Tyr.* 1436–50, 1518–19), fulfilling the edict he had imposed upon the unknown murderer before he knew that the other he sought was in truth himself (*Oid. Tyr.* 224–54; cf. 815–24). But in *Oidipous at Kolonos* he tells us that in fact he had first remained in Thebes. Only much later, he says, long after his grief and anger had modulated into acceptance and when his truest desire was to stay at home, did Kreon and his sons cruelly expel him against his will and sentence him to years of homeless wandering (*Oid. Kol.* 425–44, 765–71, 1354–59). Euripides' *Phoinissai* marks yet another shift in the temporal ordering of events in Oidipous' life. Here, where the drama presents the sequel to Oidipous' story in the next generation, the aged father is still present in Thebes, where he is kept inside the house like a "hidden ghost," "a pale shadow of a dream" (*Phoi.* 63–66, 1539–45). But he is not to remain there. At the end of this panoramic play, when Oidipous has lived to see the curses he had laid upon his sons accomplished in their death at each other's hands, Kreon belatedly drives him out to embark on the path that will lead him, as he seems to know in advance, to the town of Kolonos and to a death there far away from Thebes (*Phoi.* 1705–7).[2] Sophokles in his version also, of course, brings the aged king to the same precinct in Attika and sets the stage there for the last act of his story, which is entirely concerned with finding a permanent home for Oidipous—first as suppliant stranger, and then as a hero for the city once he vanishes into the sacred tomb. But Oidipous cannot reach this last resting place until he first confronts Thebes again and successfully resists the temptation he is offered to return home.

The true terms of that offer, however, tell us why he will refuse. No one who comes from Thebes to fetch him has the power or desire to promise him a place at home in the house or inside the city, despite pretenses to the contrary. Rather they will offer him only a site betwixt and between, on the border of the city's territory, where he will be home and not home, returned and not returned (*Oid. Kol.* 299–400, 784–86; cf. 1342–43). For Oidipous the man, who demands the dignity of his human status, the supplications of Kreon, the

---

1. I omit here discussion of the epic tradition.
2. It is generally agreed that Euripides' drama precedes that of Sophokles, although the passages in the *Phoinissai* relevant to the place of Oidipous' exile have sometimes been suspected of interpolation.

current ruler, and of Polyneikes, Oidipous' son, are a sham, since they desire only to gain domination over his person and this for their own political ends. On ritual grounds, it may also be true, as Kreon claims, that the patricide can never be repatriated (*Oid. Kol.* 406–7). But in a larger sense, Thebes' spatial designation of Oidipous' position in its land at this late date only spells out more explicitly the underlying rules of the system in this city whose own ambiguities are matched by those of its most exemplary native son.

Thebes is the place, I will argue, that makes problematic every inclusion and exclusion, every conjunction and disjunction, every relation between near and far, high and low, inside and outside, stranger and kin. Thus the person of Oidipous perhaps crystallizes in purest form the city of Thebes itself. And by that same logic, Thebes is therefore the only possible place for his birth. In Sophokles' last play, Oidipous will finally break the symbiotic relation between himself and his city when he takes his stand upon the new territory of Athens to which both his destiny and his choice have assigned him. But in the prior stages of his life story, what happens to the figure of Oidipous is emblematic of the larger concerns associated with Thebes. When he fluctuates between a fixed imprisonment in the house and an unstable wandering too far from home, or when, in a different vein, he alternates between a condition of self-referential autonomy and involvement in too dense a network of relations, Oidipous personifies in himself the characteristics that Thebes manifests in all its dramatic variants, through all its other myths, and through the extant work of all the tragic poets of Athens.

* * *

II. *Thebes as the Anti-Athens*

What then does Thebes as a topos represent for Athens on the dramatic stage in the theater of Dionysos? My answer is brief. I propose that Thebes functions in the theater as an anti-Athens, an other place. If we say that theater in general functions as an "other scene" where the city puts itself and its values into question by projecting itself upon the stage to confront the present with the past through its ancient myths, then Thebes, I suggest, is the "other scene" of the "other scene" that is the theater itself. Thebes, we might say, is the quintessential "other scene," as Oidipous is the paradigm of tragic man and Dionysos is the god of the theater. There Athens acts out questions crucial to the *polis*, the self, the family, and society, but these are displaced upon a city that is imagined as the mirror opposite of Athens.

The dramatic relation of Athens is twofold. First, within the theater, Athens is not the tragic space. Rather, it is the scene where
theater can and does "escape" the tragic, and where reconciliation
and transformation are made possible. Thebes and Athens are, in
fact, specifically contrasted to one another in several plays, such as
Sophokles' *Oidipous at Kolonos* * * *. But Thebes is also the obverse
side of Athens, the shadow self, we might say, of the idealized city
on whose other terrain the tragic action may be pushed to its furthest limits of contradiction and impasse. As such, it also furnishes
the territory for exploring the most radical implications of the tragic without any risk to its own self-image.

In other words, Thebes, the other, provides Athens, the self,
with a place where it can play with and discharge both terror of
and attraction to the irreconcilable, the inexpiable, and the unre-
deemable, where it can experiment with the dangerous heights of
self-assertion that transgression of fixed boundaries inevitably
entails, where the city's political claims to primacy may be exposed
and held up to question. Events in Thebes and the characters
who enact them both fascinate and repel the Athenian audience,
finally instructing the spectators as to how their city might refrain
from imitating the other's negative example. There where Thebes
holds the stage, both Dionysos and Oidipous, from opposite cor-
ners (of the "irrational" and "rational"), tempt the self to play
roles that can only lead to disaster. And both Dionysos and Oidipous end by confounding identity, their own and others', establishing hopeless antitheses and hopeless mixtures. They do this
at different moments in the mythic history of Thebes and by different dramatic means throughout the history of the Athenian
theater.

* * *

For the tragic poets Thebes represents the paradigm of the closed
system that vigorously protects its psychological, social, and political boundaries, even as its towering walls and circular ramparts
close off and protect its physical space. Once we grasp the import
of autochthony and incest as the underlying patterns at Thebes, we
can diagnose the malaise of this city, which has no means of establishing a viable system of relations and differences, either within
the city or without, or between the self and any other. Unable to
incorporate outsiders into its system and locked into the priority of
blood relations of the *genos*, Thebes endlessly shuttles between the
extremes of rigid inclusions and exclusions on the one hand and
radical confusions of difference on the other. * * *

* * *

A typical Theban scenario shows us a king who at first governs, as he imagines, wholly in the city's interests, relying solely on his powers of reason and judgment to maintain civic order. But the pressure of events reveals him as one who has confused the relationship between ruler and city, identifying the state, in fact, with himself. In each case, the true imperative is the desire to rule, to exercise single hegemony over others and to claim all power for himself.[3] Yet once confronted with the limitations he has never acknowledged, this ruler discovers that he cannot rule himself, cannot maintain an unequivocal identity. And in this surrender to hidden constraints, he must surrender the political kingship he has craved. That Thebes is the paradigmatic home of tyrants, as even Oidipous is liable to become when at home, can be attributed perhaps to the fact that incest and patricide are seen as the typical tyrannical crimes (cf. Plato, Rep. 9. 571b4–d3).[4] But the desire on the political level to rule alone in autonomy is also equivalent in the family domain to the desire for an autonomous self-engendering, which the acts of patricide and incest imply. Such a desire finally crosses the last boundary in demanding equivalence for the self with the gods and taking their power for its own. Thebes therefore shows us the self playing for the highest stakes, only to succumb inevitably to the triple force of the restrictions that *polis,* family, and gods impose. * * *

* * *

REPEATING THE PAST

Thebes is opposed to time as it passes through subsequent phases which ordinarily would lead to change, reconciliation, development, and transformation, whether through a genetic model or through the formation of new institutions in the city. In Thebes the linear advance of the narrative events turns out in the end to be circular, as closed back upon itself as the circular walls that are the city's most distinctive architectural feature in space. Time in Thebes returns always and again to its point of departure, since it can never

3. The desire for *kratos* and *arkhē* is a prominent motif in every Theban play. Both Oidipous in *Oid. Tyr.* (628–30) and Kreon in *Antigone* (733–39) are brought to the point where they openly declare that they must rule at any cost and that the city belongs, in fact, to the ruler. Kreon in *Oid. Tyr.* stresses in his argument with Oidipous the precise opposite, that he has no desire to rule and is content to wield only informal power (*Oid. Tyr.* 583–602). But once he comes to regency in Thebes, after the sons of Oidipous both die in their bid for power, he offers the same rationale in his argument with Haimon. Although Kreon's play precedes that of Oidipous in the Sophoklean corpus, the point is that whoever fills the role of king (or regent) succumbs to the same political error.
4. The phrasing of Eteokles' rebuke to the unruly women in the *Seven against Thebes* is very suggestive in this regard: Obedience to rule (*Peitharkhia*), they say, is Good Luck's mother (*tēs Eupraxias mētēr*), wedded to Salvation (*gynē Sōtēros; Seven* 224–25). The son of Oidipous says more than he knows.

generate new structures and new progeny that can escape the paradigmatic patterns of the beginning. What this means is that Thebes is a place where the past inevitably rules, continually repeating and renewing itself so that each new generation, each new episode in the story, looks backward to its ruin even as it offers a new variation on the theme. This is the city, after all, where Laios was bidden to die without issue, a prophecy that indeed finally comes to pass in the third generation.

From this perspective, we may say that Thebes is a world that obeys the law of the Eternal Return in contrast to one where history can unfold into differential narrative for the future, a history supported by the paradigm of its founding myths as a point of origin but not subject to the tyranny of their domination over all its representative figures and events. The autocratic prestige of both autochthony and incest in Thebes claims power over each character in turn. More specifically, failure to inaugurate a viable line of time for the individual actor produces two negative patterns for the self—doubling of one figure with another at the same moment of time, whether father and son or brother and brother, and compulsive repetition of actions from the past.

* * *

On the narrative level, the structure of Sophokles' *Oidipous Tyrannos* itself brilliantly demonstrates the general principle. Every advance Oidipous makes toward uncovering the identity of Laios's murderer, every new figure who enters upon the stage in the forward movement of the plot, only leads him further in a retrograde direction, until, with the last and critical entry of the old herdsman, he returns to the very moment of his birth as the infant with the pierced feet who was given over to that very herdsman to carry off to Mount Kithairon. With this revelation of his origins, Oidipous simultaneously realizes another regression—namely, that he had returned to seed the mother's womb from which he was engendered. Is not incest, after all, the quintessential act of return? Is not incest the paradigmatic act that destroys time by collapsing the necessary temporal distinctions between generations?

From this point of view, the riddle of the Sphinx can be read in two ways. On the one hand, the riddle suppresses the dimension of time, since the enigma resides in the fact that it makes synchronic the three phases of human life by uniting them under the single form (or voice) that is Man. As such, Oidipous' unique ability on the intellectual level to solve the riddle is commensurate on the familial level with his singular acts of patricide and incest. On the other hand, the full interpretation of the riddle would seem to require that man must properly be defined in his diachronic dimension. Man is to be measured by the sum total of his life, which can only be known as he passes through time. Hence, each of his multiple aspects (four-footed, two-footed, and three-footed) will be construed as a sequential phase of orderly human development.[5] For Oidipous at Thebes, time is out of joint, not only because he has effaced generational difference, but because his act of reversing time in returning to seed the womb from which he was born is predicated on the earlier act of patricide that speeded up the temporal process by giving him his father's place too soon.

EDITH HALL

Suffering under the Sun
[The Knowledge of the Slave][†]

* * *

Tragedy is replete with characters of slave status who perform various functions. Almost always nameless, frequently mute, they attend upon royalty, carry out menial tasks such as the arrangement of Clytemnestra's carpet in [Aeschylus'] *Agamemnon* (908–9), or the binding of other slaves on the orders of Menelaus in Euripides' *Andromache* (425–6). The so-called 'messenger,' whose function is to report violent incidents taking place within or away from the household, is often a slave. It is most intriguing that tragedy should have granted such lowly figures these privileged speeches, especially since slaves could not even give evidence in Athenian courts. And although modern audiences can find these speeches tediously static, the frequency with which the scenes they describe appear on vases is an indication of their ancient popularity.

Indeed slaves, although formally powerless, can wield enormous power in the world of tragedy through their access to dangerous knowledge. The Theban shepherd in *Oedipus Tyrannus* was born a slave into the Theban royal household, rather than bought in from outside (1123). This man with no name, identified variously as 'shepherd,' 'peasant' and 'slave,' is the only living person other than Tiresias who knows and has long known the truth concerning Oedipus. Parallels are drawn between the slave and the prophet,

---

5. For a discussion of the two contrasting aspects which the riddle can suggest, see also J.-P. Vernant, "From Oedipus to Periander: Lameness, Tyranny, Incest in Legend and History," *Arethusa* 15 (1982): 24–26.

† From "Confrontations" in *Greek Tragedy: Suffering under the Sun* (Oxford: Oxford UP, 2010), pp. 119–21. © Edith Hall 2010. Reprinted by permission of the licensor through PLSclear. The author's notes have been omitted.

who are both reluctant to answer their summonses to the palace. Tiresias was sent for twice, and Oedipus was surprised at how long it took for him to arrive (289): the slave who witnessed the murder of Laius was also summoned twice (see 118, 838, 861), and when he finally arrives, Oedipus remarks in similar language on how long it took him to arrive (1112).

The ageing slave refuses to concede that he gave the baby Oedipus to the Corinthian messenger. Refuses, that is, until he is threatened with the torture to which all slaves were subject by jurisdiction in the law-courts of Athens. Indeed, slave evidence was regarded as virtually inadmissible unless extracted under torture; lying, seen as unbecoming in the free citizen (Sophocles, *Women of Trachis* 453–4), was seen as a natural feature of the slave. Oedipus first threatens the Theban man with pain (1152), and then actually orders his attendants to twist the old man's arms behind his back, in preparation for torture (1154). Finally the victim breaks, and the truth is extracted from him. Thus perhaps the most famous recognition in tragedy, Oedipus' recognition of himself, results directly from the knowledge of a slave.

Many critics have objected to the coincidences which meant that so much dangerous knowledge resided in a single man, in particular that the same slave who was asked to expose the baby survived to be the only living witness of Laius' murder. 'This Theban is the man who took the infant Oedipus to "trackless Cithaeron," who witnessed the murder in the pass, who saw Oedipus married to Jocasta. In other words, astonishingly, wildly improbably, he has been keeping company with Oedipus all of Oedipus' life.' But such criticisms neglect the social structures which meant that slaves, especially those regarded as particularly trustworthy through having been born into the house, must often have known more about their masters and their families than their masters can have known themselves. Is it really so unlikely that a man sufficiently trusted by Jocasta to have been entrusted by her with the exposure of the infant would also have been selected to accompany Laius on his mission to Delphi? The invention of this extraordinary slave-character, whose knowledge kills Jocasta, reflects at an aesthetic level the ancient awareness that the dehumanized slaves who lived cheek by jowl with the free, and were privy to their secrets, sometimes had knowledge with literally lethal potential. * * *

ERIC DUGDALE

From Who Named Me? Identity and Status in Sophocles' *Oedipus Tyrannus*[†]

Much has been written about Oedipus' paradoxical identity, but one aspect that has been relatively neglected is the social dimension to its construction. This article argues that questions of legitimacy, citizenship, and social status are raised at critical points in the play. My interest in the topic was first piqued by Oedipus' famous speech in which he declares that he is * * * "a child of Fortune" in line 1080. What would this expression have meant to an Athenian audience of the fifth century, I found myself wondering? From the context, it would seem to be a response to the revelation by the Messenger that he is a foundling. In this speech, Oedipus shows awareness of the social stigma attached to those without a proven pedigree at the same time as he seeks to neutralize its effect on public perception.

Although the exact date of the play's composition is unknown, it most likely belongs to the early 420s B.C.E. We can be sure that Pericles had already enacted his citizenship law of 451/450, which stipulated that both parents had to be Athenians in order for the offspring to enjoy the rights of citizenship (*Ath. Pol.* 26.3). Already before the passage of this law, *nothoi* or extramarital children had been excluded from citizenship, probably since the time of Solon. And yet Pericles secured from the Athenian assembly an exemption from his own law for his illegitimate and metroxenic son, also called Pericles, when his legitimate sons Xanthippus and Paralus died in the great plague. Furthermore, there is plenty of evidence from classical Athens that suggests that it was often difficult to distinguish between citizens, metics, and slaves. It is not surprising, then, that identities were often blurred and contested * * *.

What, then, is the position in which Oedipus finds himself as he addresses the uncertainties surrounding his identity? Is his confidence justified when he declares that, though Jocasta may be ashamed at his low birth (* * * 1079), he will not be dishonored as a result (* * * 1081)? And what does he mean by this statement: is he claiming that he will not lose social standing * * *, or that he will not lose his citizen rights * * *, or both?

† From *American Journal of Philology* 136 (2015): 421–45. © 2015 by Johns Hopkins University Press. Reprinted by permission of Johns Hopkins University Press. The author's notes have been omitted.

In addressing these questions, we must acknowledge at the outset that we cannot simply map onto a play set at Thebes in the mythical past the social and legislative realities of fifth-century Athens. At the same time, Athenian tragedy's habit of going away to Thebes rarely involves as radical a displacement as we might expect. In what follows, I will argue that the play reflects the anxieties surrounding identity and status of the society in which it was conceived, and that an understanding of Athenian practices helps us appreciate the implications of the various details that the play provides as clues to Oedipus' identity.

Oedipus at Corinth

We begin at Corinth. Oedipus was raised as the son of King Polybus and his lawful wife Queen Merope, as Oedipus himself makes clear in retelling his life-story to Jocasta (774–77):

* * *

My father was Polybus of Corinth,
and my mother Merope, a Dorian; and I was brought up
as the greatest of the citizens, till this thing
happened to me

What Oedipus' account underscores is that the people of Corinth as a whole believed him to be the legitimate son of Polybus and Merope, and that this conferred on him not only citizenship but also preeminence among the citizens as heir apparent. Thus at Corinth his citizenship and status are predicated upon his relationship with Polybus and Merope, as is emphasized by the use of the temporal clause introduced by πρίν.

The Drunkard's Allegation

The loose words of a drunken sot dropped carelessly at a dinner party mount the first challenge to Oedipus' legitimacy. The words that Oedipus uses in narrating the event provide important clues as to the implications of the allegation (779–84):

* * *

At dinner a man who had over-imbibed
drunkenly alleged that I had been passed off on my father as
  his child.
I was angry, and for the rest of that day
was barely able to restrain myself. But the next day I went up to
my mother and father and questioned them. Upset at the insult,
they took it out on the man who had let the remark fly.

The allegation that the drunkard makes is that Oedipus is a coun-
terfeit (*plastos*, 780) son to Polybus—in other words, that he is a supposititious child, an infant that was actually conceived by another
woman but then smuggled in and passed off as the child of Polybus.
The wording of the allegation as reported by Oedipus (* * * 780)
suggests that the scheme was carried out without the connivance of
Polybus. Most translators gloss over this important detail by translating the clause loosely as "claimed that I was not my father's son,"
or something similar. Jebb (1966, 87) in his commentary gets it
right when he fleshes out the meaning as follows: "'falsely called a
son,' * * * 'for my father,' i.e. to deceive him." Ahl (1991, 143) spells
this out further: "A *plastos . . . patri* is an infant imported by the
mother and 'passed off on his father.'" This seems to be the version
of events that we find in the opening scene of Euripides' *Phoenis-
sae*, where Jocasta describes how the foundling Oedipus was given
by Polybus' horse herders to Merope, who suckled the infant * * *
and convinced her husband that she had given birth to him (28–31).
In Sophocles' play, however, the drunkard's version proves only
partly true.

Polybus' Role

We get a more accurate report later in the play from the Corinthian
Messenger, who was himself present at the scene of the foundling's
rescue. The Messenger provides an important detail: it was Polybus
himself who received the infant straight from his hands (* * * 1022).
So Polybus knowingly and willingly received the foundling Oedipus
into his *oikos*[1] and raised him as his son; he was not duped by
Merope into believing that the infant Oedipus was his biological
offspring. In Greek society, the legitimacy of a child was attested
not at birth but in festivities that occurred a few days later. Childbirth was a private affair, witnessed by a midwife and other females
but rarely by the husband or other males. * * * Given the high infant
mortality rate during childbirth and the practice of exposing
unwanted neonates, the first few days offered the father an interval
to determine the viability of the infant and the desirability of raising it before he recognized it as his legitimate offspring at ceremonies that took place a few days after birth * * *. The Corinthian
Messenger's description in line 1022 of Polybus receiving the infant
Oedipus from his hands reminds us of the act of taking up an
infant into his arms which constituted a father's acknowledgment
of paternity.

---

1. Household—*Editor's note.*

   Thus the evidence of the play suggests that Oedipus was an
exposed foundling who was raised by Polybus and Merope as their
legitimate son when they proved unable to conceive biological
children. Certainly an exposed infant would have been an obvious
choice for procuring a baby discreetly. This is in fact how the Messenger describes the incident in line 1024: the act of a husband
whose childlessness had driven him to this. As a side point, it is
worth noting that Oedipus' question at 1025 implies that found-
lings might be trafficked; such infants would likely be of slave or
of unknown origin. When the Messenger explains that Polybus
did not beget him, Oedipus asks (1021): * * * "Then why on
earth did he call me his son?" Again, Oedipus makes it clear that
Polybus acknowledged him as his son. His wording * * * reminds
us of the importance of the naming ceremony in the process of
legitimation. * * *

Who Named Oedipus?

Contrary evidence is indeed supplied in Sophocles' play, albeit in
modified form—not before a jury, but with Oedipus himself conducting the investigation. The Messenger and the Shepherd provide the eyewitness testimony and the pierced feet of Oedipus the
physical evidence against Oedipus' blood kinship with Polybus. In
pointing at Oedipus' feet as evidence corroborating his story, the
Messenger adds a further proof: Oedipus' name attests to that incident (1036): * * * "So you were given the name which you now have
from that occurrence." Oedipus' next question is infused with
urgency (1037): * * * "By the gods, by my mother or by my father?
Tell me!" Oedipus' impassioned question comes at the crux of his
relentless investigation into his identity. But what does it mean?
Most commentators take it as referring back to the piercing of his
feet, mentioned by the Messenger three lines earlier, or more generally to his exposure on the mountainside.

                              *   *   *

However, a number of factors militate against this interpretation.
Far from being an instance of "etymological moralizing" that Oedipus would choose to ignore, the Messenger's explanation of Oedipus'
name is crucial to Oedipus' quest to discover his own identity.
Although such word-play may seem frivolous to modern ears, to
ancient Greeks such etymologies often conveyed deeper truths, and
sometimes provide the solution to riddling prophecies. Furthermore, Sophocles' drama signals the importance of Oedipus' name
through a tapestry of etymological allusions. But in this scene the
issue of Oedipus' name carries even more weight.

Rather than reading Oedipus' question elliptically, I believe we should take it at face value, as a response to what immediately preceded it. Oedipus asks who named him, his mother or his father.

* * *

The play never gives a direct answer to the question. But it seems likely that the original audience would have understood Oedipus' question as part of his ongoing quest to determine his identity. If his father named him, then this would imply that his father at least recognized him as his son, whether legitimate or illegitimate. If his mother named him, then this would suggest that he is a "fatherless" child, a scenario that he confronts later in the scene when he says to Jocasta (1062–63):

* * *

> Do not worry! Even if I prove to be the offspring of three
> generations of female slaves, you will not be shown to be
> low-born.

Here Oedipus is tracing his ancestry in matrilineal terms since, in this worst case scenario, his paternal ancestry has been called into question. He makes the same point implicitly at line 1080 in describing himself as the child of *Tychē*; he refers to *Tychē* metaphorically as his mother, but makes no reference to any father.

The question that Oedipus asks at 1037 (who named me?) has already been answered obliquely by Jocasta when, earlier in the play, she retold the oracle received by Laius that he was fated to be killed by his own son (717–19):

* * *

> But the birth of the infant was not
> three days past when Laius bound his ankles
> and cast him out by the hands of others on the trackless
>   mountain.

In Jocasta's account, the infant remains nameless. Clearly it is a dramatic necessity that Jocasta not know the name of her exposed son, and thus it is also necessarily the case that it was not she who gave Oedipus his name. But her account also gives us an important indication that it was not Laius either. Jocasta is very specific in indicating that Laius had his son exposed within three days of his birth. To an Athenian audience, this telling detail would indicate that Laius rejected the infant before the ceremonies * * * that marked the first stage in the process of a child's recognition and induction into the community.

When Oedipus later interrogates the Shepherd, he asks him who handed over the infant for exposure (1162). It was Jocasta, the infant's mother, the Shepherd reluctantly replies (1173). In contrast to the scene at Corinth, where Polybus takes the infant into his hands and welcomes him into his *oikos*, Laius has him cast out onto the mountainside by the hands of others (* * * 719). Instead of acknowledging him as his legitimate son through ceremonies and gifts, Laius takes the added precaution of piercing the infant's feet, thereby making his death more certain by rendering him unattractive for adoption through physical deformity. In so doing, however, he inadvertently gives the child the defining physical characteristic that gives rise to his name and ultimately serves as the proof of his identity as the son of Laius. Thus, in a truly Sophoclean paradox, Laius unwittingly gave Oedipus his name through the very act that was intended to render him nameless. We may speculate that it was Polybus who presided over Oedipus' naming ceremony, but his name will ultimately serve as proof that Oedipus is not in fact Polybus' son.

Oedipus' Journey: Emigrant or Returnee?

Thus, Oedipus' name is one of a number of clues that seem to point in the direction of illegitimacy, although the audience is aware from the start that the truth is quite different. Oedipus' quest to prove that he is the legitimate son of Polybus and Merope, though seemingly a blind alley, provides the impetus that takes him on the journey to Delphi and Thebes and leads to his discovery of his true identity. This counterpoint of appearance and reality explains the tensions inherent in Oedipus' story and its riddling wording. Oedipus' story contains at once the seeds of vindication and of shame, of satisfaction and of disquietude. At Corinth, Oedipus interrogates his presumed father and mother (782–83) in order to get to the bottom of the allegation that he is not their true son. We are not told what they said in reply—only that they reacted vehemently to the insult (783–84). It seems that their response satisfied Oedipus (* * * 785)—and yet the issue continued to trouble him (* * * 785–86).

Oedipus' decision to consult the Delphic oracle is a strategy typical in a case of disputed legitimacy, especially of a royal heir. Normally, one would expect the consultation and reporting of an oracular response to constitute a very public claim to divine validation; Oedipus, however, undertakes the consultation in secret (787–88), a detail that suggests that he is less sure that the outcome will be favorable, even as the audience knows that his legitimacy is certain. * * *

Oedipus' reaction to the oracle is similarly ambiguous. His departure from the kingdom that he was expected to inherit seems to be an admission of illegitimacy, although it is predicated on his mistaken belief that Polybus and Merope are his biological parents. Thus, Sophocles casts the shadow of illegitimacy over much of the play. Its pall sets in motion the chain of events that leads to Oedipus' discovery of a yet more terrible truth and heightens the play's irony. Seen from the perspective of the audience, aware of the paradoxical interplay between appearance and reality, Oedipus' journey can be seen to head in two different directions. On the one hand, it follows a course away from home, mirroring the journey into voluntary exile of illegitimate young men * * *. On the other hand, it follows a course towards home, mirroring the heroic journey of a young man such as Theseus,[2] who sets out from the land of his exile on a quest that leads him to his fatherland, where he discovers the tokens that prove his identity as rightful heir to the throne. Here, too, the resemblance is more apparent than real. At its most important turns, Oedipus' story is a perversion of the heroic journey: en route, Oedipus encounters and kills not just a mythical monster, the Sphinx, but also his own father; when he reaches his fatherland, the bride that he wins as the victor's prize is his own mother.

The play entertains a variety of possible identities for Oedipus once it is established that he is not the biological son of Polybus and Merope: that he is their supposititious son, that he is a foundling of low birth, even that he is the descendant of slaves. All of these possibilities carry the social stigma of *dysgeneia*, which can refer equally to illegitimacy and to birth into low social class; but none of them must needs bring about Oedipus' fall from power, since his kingship at Thebes is predicated not on his pedigree but on his achievements. The only possibility that can lead to his downfall is the one that Oedipus still refuses to entertain and that the audience knows to be true: that he is the legitimate and high-born son of Laius and Jocasta. The case of Oedipus constitutes the ultimate paradox. It transgresses the very language upon which social values rest: he is at once of good descent (as member of the royal family) and of bad descent (as member of the cursed house of Labdacus and participant in maternal incest). He is at once the ultimate insider (as member of the endogamous Theban royal family and legitimate heir to the throne) and also the ultimate outsider (as one whose unspeakable deeds will make him a pariah).

2. Mythical king of Athens—*Editor's note.*

Oedipus at Thebes: The Naturalized Citizen

Sophocles explores the issue of Oedipus' paradoxical identity through three polarities. One is the axis of nature versus nurture * * *. But there are two further polarities that contribute to the construction of identity and shed light on Oedipus' status in Thebes at the moment of recognition. One is the polarity of citizen versus alien, the other the polarity of legitimacy versus illegitimacy. I have sought to demonstrate that the specter of illegitimacy raised its ugly head while Oedipus was at Corinth. It posed a threat not only to his social status but also to his claim to the throne of Corinth. But this specter proves to be illusory: Oedipus' continued legitimacy as heir apparent is corroborated by the Messenger who reports that, upon the death of Polybus, the citizens of Corinth have appointed Oedipus king (939–42). Whether they did so in the knowledge that he was not Polybus' biological son is not clear, since we are not told whether the circumstances of his adoption were a secret closely guarded by his rescuers or were known by others. We can be sure, however, that his status at Thebes and his claim to the Theban throne are not dependent on his ancestry. The honors that he was accorded by the citizens of Thebes were conferred on him for what he did, not for who he was.

The play presents Oedipus as an immigrant to Thebes who was granted citizenship in recognition of his good services to the city. This is made clear at several points over the course of the play. In the prologue, the Priest presents Oedipus as an immigrant savior who delivered the city from the terrible tribute that was being exacted (35–36). He repeatedly indicates that they now turn to him because of the capabilities that he has demonstrated in past difficulties (33–39, 44–53), citing his intellectual acuity, ingenuity, decision-making, experience, and the prosperity that has marked his reign. The Chorus reaffirms the causal link between the honors and kingship bestowed on Oedipus and his service to the country in delivering it from the Sphinx (1197–1203, 1525). When Oedipus responds to the citizens' appeal for help by issuing a proclamation against the murderer of Laius, he draws a contrast between his alien status at the time of the murder and his current citizen status that legitimates his proclamation (219–20, 222–23):

* * *

I shall speak these words as a stranger to the story,
and a stranger to the deed . . .
But as things are, since I have become a citizen with the rest,
    though late,
I utter to all Cadmeans this proclamation:

Dawe correctly infers the implications of Oedipus' statement (1982, 117): "Only now that Oedipus enjoys full citizen status has he the right to initiate criminal proceedings." Implicit in Oedipus' wording is the recognition that he is a citizen not by birth but by special appointment * * *.

It is worth mentioning that grants of citizenship to individual foreigners for services rendered to the city did occur during the fifth century, both at Athens and elsewhere. At Athens, a naturalized citizen had the right to hold office and occasionally did so. Although Sophocles' play is not set in democratic Athens, Oedipus is nevertheless portrayed as having been appointed as king by the will of the people (1202–3), and there is an intimation that his rule is dependent on their continued support (54). To an Athenian audience living in a cosmopolitan town such as Athens with its large population of resident aliens, the conferral of citizenship on an apparent foreigner such as Oedipus and his rise to prominence would not have seemed strange. Furthermore, the conferral of citizenship on a foreigner did not invalidate his claim to citizenship in his native *polis*. In sum, Oedipus' preeminent status at Thebes is founded not on his lineage but on his timely service to the city. In this sense, Oedipus is indeed a child of Fortune.

Oedipus as "Child of Fortune"

The speech in which Oedipus declares himself a child of Fortune (1076–85) is famous, but there is no consensus as to what it means, and most commentators have settled for a paraphrase. I would like to characterize Oedipus' role in this scene as one of a number of attempts to take control by interpreting the past, present, and future. Oedipus' words reflect an awareness of the social stigma attached to those without a proven pedigree at the same time as they seek to neutralize its effect on public perception.

Oedipus' status as leader at Thebes appears to depend on how he can manage the eventualities of life. He responds to the precarious position in which he now finds himself with the poise and assurance characteristic of great leaders. At a time when his very identity seems uncertain, his pronouncements are defiantly confident * * *.

As king, Oedipus is used to taking the lead. We have already witnessed his power of anticipation earlier in the play when he reveals that he has already sent Creon to Delphi (69–72) and that he has summoned Tiresias (287–89). But in this scene, Jocasta has stolen the initiative * * *. Her mood has affected the Chorus leader, who worries about unspecified future [evils] (1075). The Chorus leader turns to the king (1073) to provide a correct interpretation of the situation. Thus the primary motivation for his pronouncements in this speech, as in the opening scene of the play (1–13, 58–77), is a desire to reassure his unsettled subjects. In this he proves successful; in the third stasimon[3] (1086–1109), the Chorus reaffirms its loyalty to the king and adopts his positive interpretation of the situation over Jocasta's voice of doom that had previously unsettled it.

As well as fitting the immediate context of Oedipus' speech, this reading makes sense of the words of the speech itself. The Chorus is afraid that evils may burst forth after Jocasta's reticence (1074–75). Oedipus responds directly to their fears (1076): "Burst forth what may!" He is not the devious politician who papers over problems; his method is to address them head on. He does not side-step the possibility that he may be the son of low-born parents. Instead, he makes this possibility explicit in 1079. In describing himself as [child of Fate] (1080), he is not suggesting that he is a son of [Fate] rather than of mortal parents, the kind of fanciful substitution that the Chorus makes in its catalogue of potential divine fathers when it speculates whether it was Pan, Apollo, Hermes, or Dionysus who begat Oedipus on Mount Cithaeron (1098–1109). Rather, he is presenting himself not only as a foundling (perhaps the most literal meaning of the expression "son of [Fate]") but also as an opportunist, a person who seizes the moment and turns seeming disadvantage to his advantage. This is a realistic portrayal of the type of person who does well in the world; [fate] may be a force beyond human control, but the successful leader is one who not only reckons with the effects of [fate] in weighing up the best course of action, but who also uses [fate] to his advantage. As the Priest notes in the opening scene, it is because they judge him preeminent in dealing with the vicissitudes of life that he and his fellow Thebs have sought out Oedipus' help (31–34).

Oedipus describes his connection with [Fate] in relational terms: he is the child of [Fate] and she is his mother, as is emphasized by repetition (1080–82). Oedipus is not just uttering a commonplace like our "soldier of fortune." [Fate (*Tychē*)] is a neutral term, and his future is uncertain; but by declaring himself the child of [Fate], he privileges one face of [fate] over the other * * *. Though unpredictable, she is not frightening.

This is more than wishful thinking. It reflects an attempt by Oedipus to predict and manage his own destiny just as he appears to be passively accepting whatever [fate] may bring him. * * *

* * *

* * * Oedipus here presents as empirical calculation of the future his personal opinion, in the hope that it will thereby become a reality.

3. Section of the choral song—*Editor's note.*

This is natural given his position as *tyrannos* whose word is law. The surprise that Oedipus expresses in the opening scene at Creon's delay (73–75) belongs to a ruler who is used to his word being converted into action and who himself acts decisively. In a moment of extreme uncertainty, he uses very bold language in this speech. Not only does he call himself a child of fortune, but he also places himself * * * emphatically at the source of this declaration * * *. In a very real sense, he is attempting to construct his own identity.

This interest in self-presentation is continued in the next clause. Why the reference to months? * * * Moons mark seasons that signify change—one need only think of the ancient belief, still held by many around the world, that the sap or life-giving juice rises in trees during the waxing of the moon. Oedipus, in describing the moons as "kindred" (* * * 1082), presents change in a benevolent light. Moons or months may represent change, but they have prescribed or marked (* * * 1083) him out to be small and great. * * * It is interesting to note that Oedipus has arranged the trajectory of his life, as prescribed by his kinsmen months, as first small * * * and then great * * *. The Chorus, taking its new-found optimism from Oedipus, describes the immediate future in terms of the full moon: * * * "tomorrow's full moon shall exalt you as the fellow-native and nurse and mother of Oedipus," 1089–91. * * * But change is a double-edged sword, and Oedipus' waning will occur within the space of this day.

The structure of the speech also supports a prescriptive interpretation of Oedipus' words. In lines 1080–85, he uses the logical structure of a syllogism to superimpose onto the uncertain a structure of certainty. Thus the thrust of Oedipus' speech moves the hearer from the uncertainty of the opening * * * in 1076 to an affirmation of certitude, underscored by the logical construction of the final sentence in lines 1084–85.

The choral stasimon that immediately follows this speech (1086–1109) picks up on Oedipus' purpose. The attempt by the Chorus to predict the uncertain future is even more explicit than that of Oedipus (1086–95):

* * *

If indeed I am a prophet
and wise in my judgment,
by Olympus,
O Cithaeron, you shall not fail to know
that tomorrow's full moon will exalt you as the fellow-native,
nurse and mother of Oedipus,
and that you are honored by us with dances
for the kindnesses that you rendered
to my ruler.

That the tone of the Chorus has changed from one of bewildered fear of future [evils] to a confident prediction of the future is largely due to the force of the intervening speech of Oedipus. The Chorus seeks to secure Oedipus' continued high standing by constructing his identity in strictly favorable terms. Unlike Oedipus, who directly confronts the uncertainty of his lineage and does not shy away from expressing this through an exclusively matrilineal designation (also at 1062–63), the Chorus affirms his legitimacy by suggesting indigenous origins (the Theban mountain Cithaeron will be shown to be his mother), by underscoring his continued status within the community (Cithaeron will gain honor for being the fellow-native of Oedipus and be celebrated with dances for the kindnesses she rendered to their ruler), and by ascribing to him the divine patrilineal ancestry typical of royal families (1098–1109; cf. 267–68). Their predictions, while hopelessly optimistic, serve to draw attention to the paradox of Oedipus' true identity: he will indeed prove to be of illustrious stock and to have local origins, but it is these very traits, usually felicitous, that contribute to his downfall.

In one important aspect, Oedipus' conception of [fate] and his characterization of himself as a child of [fate] is vindicated over the course of the play: [fate] is presented not as a random force of chaos, as Jocasta characterizes it (977–83), but as a principle of order that underpins the coincidences of the plot and the vicissitudes of human existence. However, Oedipus must learn through terrible experience that even a "child of fortune" cannot control his fate (1523), and that [fate] can be as cruel as she can be kind. By the end of the play, Oedipus characterizes his miraculous deliverance from death on the mountainside as preserving him for some dreadful evil (1456–57) and no longer seeks to control his fate: * * * "But let my fate go wherever it will go" (1458). In stark contrast to his earlier confident statement of good fortune as his birthright, he now expresses his wish for Creon's good fortune as a prayer: * * * "May you have good fortune, and may a god guide you on this path better than I was guided" (1478–79).

Earlier in the play (813–27), Oedipus expressed what he considered the most terrible possibility imaginable: that the old man he killed at the crossroads may prove to be King Laius, whom he does not yet envisage as his biological father. This possibility would deal him a double-blow. He, the man who enjoys preeminence in two city-states, could no longer set foot in either of them. His exile from Thebes would result from the edict that he himself passed against the murderer. His exile from Corinth, however, he describes not as the penalty for homicide, but as self-imposed exile in the hope of averting the fulfillment of the oracle by avoiding contact with

Polybus and Merope. The reality, however, is far worse than what Oedipus imagines. Oedipus will prove to have killed his father and defiled his mother; this discovery will bring about his mother's suicide and his own immeasurable suffering and exile. He will be an exile not only from Thebes and Corinth, but from all human society (1410–12, 1436–37).

To conclude, the issue of Oedipus' identity is a central concern of the play and the driving force behind its plot. Oedipus' identity, as seen through the eyes of the characters, is constantly in flux. Consideration of practices such as exposure and adoption of neonates, of ceremonies of legitimation and naming * * *, and of factors determining legitimacy in Oedipus' succession to the throne at Corinth and rule at Thebes, helps us understand the actions, questions, and pronouncements of Oedipus from the contextual perspective of the original Athenian audience. In his famous but widely misunderstood "child of *Tychē*" speech, Oedipus attempts to control his public image and respond to a crisis with the proactive poise characteristic of statesmen and of Oedipus in particular; his response reassures his Theban subjects. Although Oedipus eventually comes to the terrible realization of the true identities of his biological parents, Laius and Jocasta, and of his interactions with them, his ties to his foster parents Polybus and Merope are also examined. The play certainly explores the issue of Oedipus' identity as an existential question; but it is also interesting to tease out the social dimensions of the construction of identity in the play.

KIRK ORMAND

From Nature and Its Discontents in the *Oedipus Tyrannus*†

> "It's disquieting to reflect that one's dreams never symbolize one's real wishes, but always something Much Worse." She turned the light on and sat up. "If I really wanted to be passionately embraced by Peter, I should dream of something like dentists or gardening. I wonder what are the unthinkable depths of awfulness that can only be expressed by the polite symbol of Peter's embraces. Damn Peter!"
>
> DOROTHY SAYERS, *Gaudy Night*

† From *Exchange and the Maiden: Marriage in Sophoclean Tragedy* (Austin: U of Texas P, 1999), pp. 124–52. Copyright © 1999 by the University of Texas Press. Reprinted by permission of the University of Texas Press. The author's notes have been omitted.

Few plays have had such a profound influence on the Western literary tradition as the *Oedipus tyrannus*. Whatever we may think of Freud's theories of child development, few would deny that this play, with its central, hidden facts of incest and parricide, has shaped the way that we moderns define the individual. As a result of that long critical history, it is extraordinarily difficult to interpret the play without the specter of Freud's "Oedipus complex" looming over every scene. At the heart of this difficulty is the fact that Freud offers his reading as representing a transcendental, transhistorical truth: Oedipus is posited as Everyman, his forbidden lusts and angers representative of our own developmental stages. As such, some version of Freud's family drama underlies virtually every critical reading of this play, even those that take issue with it.

Feminist critiques of psychoanalysis, however, have pointed out that Freud's (and Lacan's) subject is male, that even when he is discussing "female" sexuality, it turns out to be a reflection of masculine desires. At the same time, duBois has shown that the Freudian model of sexuality (and especially female sexuality) is not supported by numerous ancient texts.[1] My concern throughout this study, similarly, has been to locate questions of marriage in a specific cultural context. Rather than viewing Oedipus's story as a map to the human psyche, I want to see how his birth from one marriage (that of Laius and Jocasta) and participation in another (that of himself and Jocasta) fit into both mythical paradigms and contemporary views of marriage. It is from these two marriages, I argue, that we come to know Oedipus's identity, that he is "hailed" as a subject. In saying this, however, I am referring not to the inner workings of his psyche, but to his place and function in society, and to his recognition of that place and function.

                              *   *   *

*** The center of the *Oedipus tyrannus*, the point upon which all else turns, is Oedipus's incestuous relation with his mother. In this drama, however, the *experience* of marriage is never a question. Indeed, no character ever speaks about what marriage has been like for him or her. Instead, the play assumes a basic structure of marriage, and depends on the fact that Oedipus, in marrying his mother, has violated that structure. Rather than search for traces of Athenian ideology of marriage in this play, therefore, I examine the way that this play constitutes marriage as a structuring institution, and particularly as a producer of biological identity. That is, I analyze the process by which Oedipus becomes recognized as "really" the child of Laius and Jocasta. This recognition is crucial

---

1. See Page Dubois, *Sowing the Body*, Chicago: Chicago UP, 1988—*Editor's note.*

to the play, and, despite its necessity, it takes a surprisingly indirect route. The play suggests that, contrary to general expectations about parentage, biological identity is an unstable category, confirmed by processes of displacement.

I use the term "displacement" in a specialized sense, though derived from its use in psychoanalytic theory. In classic psychoanalysis, a traumatic event is "displaced" onto a parallel, though less traumatic, event. So, for example, a man might demonstrate little grief over the death of a close relative, only to break down in uncontrolled hysteria a few weeks later over the loss of a family pet. In such a case, the grief the man feels over the loss of the pet is real and authentic. But it is simultaneously a marker of another, hidden grief that was not expressed earlier.

Similarly, every work of literature contains rifts in logic, gaps that are not filled in. We shall be looking at a specific type of such an occurrence in this text, one that involves careful misdirection. Such an event stands both as an important event in itself, and as a marker, pointing us to some other "displaced" meaning. The answer to one question, for example, is posited and accepted in place of the answer to the question that was asked. On a more physical level, Oedipus has been displaced from his birth family—cast out to die on Mt. Cithaeron—and this act serves, ironically, both as a marker of his "outcast" status and as confirmation of his identity as the son of Laius and Jocasta. Such processes of misdirection fix Oedipus's place on his family tree and in society throughout this play. I do not mean by this that Sophocles intends us to see Oedipus's identity as Laius and Jocasta's child as invalid, culturally produced, and therefore a sham. Oedipus really is who the play says he is. In this play, however, Oedipus's biological identity asserts itself as natural only insofar as it forcibly displaces other forms of identity. It becomes "natural" through a socially accepted process of recollection and subsequent suppression of other, competing possibilities, and through masking the instability inherent in this process.

In important ways, then, this is an abstract reading of the *Oedipus tyrannus*. I am not so concerned with the action of the play itself as with the way that the play interacts with basic social categories. In such an enterprise, we risk failing to encounter the drama as a moment of dramatic production. We gain, however, a vision of the drama as ideology and in concert with ideology. Such a reading shows us how an apparently natural category of human social behavior— such as biological identity—directs our perception even as it is directed by it. The *Oedipus tyrannus* presents marriage as a mediating institution, one that both creates categories of biological identity and allows for the possibility of violating the rules implicit in those identities. As such, marriage both enables and mirrors those

processes of displacement that confirm Oedipus's identity. I offer
the following, then, in an attempt to break out of the free-floating
psychoanalytic questions about individual development that Freud
postulates. I approach the drama here as representing a social
mechanism, demonstrating the way that we produce both individual identities and interpretive meanings. This, therefore, attempts
both to interpret the play (from my own politically and socially
invested standpoint), and to imply a critique of Freud's ahistorical
reading.

Problems of Interpretation

* * * [R]iddles, especially the sorts of riddle that Oedipus answers,
deny a multiplicity of answers. The answer to the sphinx's riddle,
for example, reduces an apparent plurality of beings to one: What
walks on four legs, and two, and three? Answer: Man, who crawls
as a baby, walks as a man, and walks with a cane as an old man.
Once we know the answer, it seems obvious; and any apparent dis-
parity of meaning is dispelled.

Similarly, the play sets up its crisis—the need to find the killer of
Laius—as two questions rather than one. We spend the play learning not only "Who killed Laius?" but also "Who *is* Oedipus?" And
when it finally comes out (as we knew all along that it would) that
the answer to both questions is "Oedipus, son of Laius and Jocasta,"
interpretation stops. The solutions to the play's problems have all
come to the surface: It was Oedipus who killed his father and married his mother. He is the cause of the plague, and now that he has
revealed himself, civilized structure can be restored. When we
accept the play's own interpretation of events in this manner, however, we also accept a certain logic of displacement. The "obvious"
answer to the play's questions, like the answer to the riddle above,
does not seem to exist in the categories set up by the questions.
When asked the sphinx's riddle, presumably, the unsuspecting victim tries to find an animal that walks on two, three, and four legs
simultaneously. When the answer is revealed, it fits into the question's categories by introducing an answer that we did not think
eligible and, in effect, displaces those categories.

In much the same way, when Oedipus begins his search for the
killer of Laius, he does not consider himself a candidate; still less
does he imagine that in the process he will discover himself to be
Laius's son. Most striking of all, however, the play allows the answer
to one question to stand in for the answer to the other. * * * Is the
crucial question "Who killed Laius?" or "Who is Oedipus?" Before
the herdsman enters the scene, Oedipus focuses on the first, hoping

that he is not the culprit. He pointedly sets up a logical criterion for answering the question:

* * *

You said that he said that *highwaymen*
killed him [Laius]. If therefore he still
will say the same number, I did not kill him;
for it would not happen that one is equal to many. (842–45)

Later, he completely ignores this criterion and, moreover, offers no explanation for doing so: "In the interim between his summoning and his arrival, the Corinthian messenger has appeared and shifted the action to the question of Oedipus's origin. . . . And it is to this issue exclusively that the Herdsman's remarks are addressed." With the benefit of hindsight, it is easy to say that the answer to one question is the answer to the other. Oedipus is both the killer and the dead man's son. But it is far from clear how the second question manages, in the course of the drama, to supplant the first.

Both questions center on Oedipus's identity and provide alternative paradigms for establishing that identity. If asked who Oedipus was, we might say, "The son of Laius and Jocasta," or, equally likely, we might say, "That guy who killed his father and married his mother." The first definition depends on a widespread cultural assumption of biological relationship, the second on identity as a matter of deeds. This play problematizes the question of identity—often a crucial question in Athenian legal cases—by making these two paradigms interchangeable. Oedipus does not simply become distracted by the question of his parentage. Rather, he ignores the single criterion to which, up to this point, he has given considerable weight of credibility. He never once asks the herdsman if one or more than one person killed Laius. He apparently accepts the answer to the question "Who am I?" as sufficient answer to the question that has consumed him, "Who killed Laius?" He actively allows his biological identity to displace the question of what he has done. Like the answer to a riddle, the discovery of Oedipus's identity changes the categories that the original question suggested.

* * *

Sophocles * * * makes Oedipus confirm his self-recognition as *the* answer to both questions that the play poses. Oedipus's marriage to Jocasta creates a social identity for Oedipus, therefore, that goes far beyond the simple implications of incest. He proclaims, in essence, that as the son of Laius, he is by definition both parricide and regicide.

How, then, does Oedipus's apparently natural and unquestioned
self-identification come about?

* * *

Long before he was conceived, he was hailed by an oracle as the man
he turns out to be:

* * *

> For an oracle came to Laius then . . .
> that it was fated for him to be killed by his child,
> who would be born from me and from him. (711–14)

This form of the oracle is specific to Sophocles' version. In Aeschylus's
version of the myth, Laius is warned that he must not have children,
if he wishes to save the city. The oracle is proscriptive rather than
descriptive. Sophocles, then, has made the oracle unavoidable,
creating the appearance that Oedipus-the-subject exists (and must
exist) before Oedipus-the-individual does. His "specific familial
ideological configuration" takes on the form of inevitability.

In referring to the inevitability of Oedipus's identity, I do not
mean to deny his "free will." * * * Oedipus has always-already been
Oedipus; what the play shows us is his active discovery of this obvious fact. At the same time, Oedipus's discovery presents itself as
inevitable, as *the* answer, most significantly through the social process of naming. Many scholars have pointed out important puns on
Oedipus's name. The most crucial, for my purposes, takes place in
the exchange between Oedipus and the messenger:

* * *

> OE.: What pain did I have when you took me in your hands?
> ME.: The joints of your foot would show you.
> OE.: Alas, why do you speak of that old pain?
> ME.: I freed you as you had the tops of your feet pierced
>   through.
> OE.: I picked up that terrible disgrace from my
>   swaddling-clothes.
> ME.: Thus, who you are, you were named from this chance.
>   (1031–36)

This exchange provides the unavoidable proof that Oedipus *is* the
son of Laius, since the messenger, identifying Oedipus by his "swollen feet," can confidently say that this is the baby he saved. At
the same time, these swollen feet are directly responsible for *who
Oedipus is,* that is, his name is a pun on [*oideo*] ("swell") + [*pous*]
("foot"). He does not just discover who he is, then; he discovers
who he *always already* has been. And like the solution to a riddle, this

identity comes as a flash of insight, unarguable, single, and apparently natural.

* * *

To allow Oedipus's biological identity—and subsequent incest—to displace the other questions that the play raises is to accept that "oracular logic" ourselves. If we wish to see beyond the play's self-proclaimed solution, we must step outside of the specific ideology that creates Oedipus's slip in logic. Rather than accept his biological identity as a sort of universal signifier, we must analyze the social structures around marriage that allow that definition of identity to displace all others.

Always-Already Oedipus

Biological identity always presents itself as natural. That is, no culture denies the relationship between a child and his or her parents. In fifth-century Athens, we should remember, this biological identity carried the full force of law: citizens could only be those who were *biologically* identifiable as born of two citizens. In every genetic and social understanding of identity, Oedipus really is the child of Jocasta and Laius. This play forcefully privileges that biological identity. The entire problem of Oedipus's marriage with Jocasta is that he really is her son; contrary to his own fears, it would be of no outstanding consequence if he were to have sex with Merope. At the same time, however, this play presents Oedipus's birth in competition with other forms of identification, a process that emphasizes the cultural baggage that surrounds "natural" identity. And when Oedipus does finally recognize who he really is (thus displacing the question of who killed Laius), he does so through a convoluted series of displacements. Biological identity, this play seems to say, is a cultural fact and potentially unstable.

Oedipus's search for his birth is necessarily convoluted, since that process creates the dramatic tension that sustains the drama. But *our* understanding of Oedipus's identity also takes a serpentine path. Everything in this play depends on our implicit acceptance of Oedipus's parentage, yet Sophocles suggests a surprising number of possible parents for his hero. In addition to the obvious surrogate parents, Polybus and Merope (e.g., 774), we see *Tuchē* ("Luck," 1080), the mountain Cithaeron (1089–91, 1451–54), and Bacchus with some nymphs (1105–09) suggested as possibilities. Tiresias adds yet another, if only metaphorically: * * * "This day will give birth to you and will destroy you" (438). * * *

Going through this list, we are forced to see that the concept of parentage is not the same in each case, though all contain a certain kind of truth. Polybus and Merope have been Oedipus's parents in

social terms. They have raised him and, until he is disabused of his
error, Oedipus derives his social identity from them. Even though
Polybus and Merope know that Oedipus is not "really" their son, for
example, Oedipus inherits their property: the herald arrives to
inform Oedipus that Corinth has pronounced him king (939–40).
Tuchē and Mt. Cithaeron are his parents under a strained metaphor: he survived his exposure thanks to them, so that Oedipus
understands them to have given him life. Bacchus and the nymphs
seem a mythological extension of this metaphor, a divine origin
assigned to a mortal of importance whose "real" origin is not known.
"This day" is perhaps the most complex parent of all. Tiresias means
that on this day, Oedipus will discover his true identity for the first
time. But we spectators may be tempted to suggest another meaning, namely, that this day has given Oedipus life because it is one of
the days of the tragic festival, and his play is on the program.

Most importantly, a metaphor of biological parentage defines each
of these various surrogate births: of *Tuchē*, for example, Oedipus
says, "For I was born (*pephuka*) from her" (1082). All of the "parents" listed above, then, are attempts to replace the horrible truth
that we know lurks just offstage, that Laius and Jocasta are Oedipus's
"real" parents. This misdirection works, to a point: the very surfeit
of alternatives suggests that the identity provided by Laius and
Jocasta can be called into question. We have been playing within
a broad spectrum of meanings for the idea of giving birth. Once
Oedipus's real biological identity is known, however, it must supplant these other playful possibilities. Again, we see the force of
biology as a cultural signifier. It becomes *the* answer to the question
of Oedipus specifically by displacing all other options.

Although biological identity asserts its own authority in this play,
we must bear in mind that in the world of everyday Athens, such
identity could be far from secure, at least as it was socially recognized. The possibility of illegitimacy was a constant threat * * *. This
play picks up on the instability of biological identity, and reverses it,
by discussing Oedipus's birth in terms entirely typical of the law
courts. Oedipus, ironically, is concerned that he will be found of low
birth. * * * It is remarkable that with all the talk of Laius's death, the
oracles, and Oedipus's parentage, it never occurs to him that Jocasta
might be afraid that he is *legitimate* rather than illegitimate. But,
unless we read Oedipus as dissembling in this scene, the possibility
never enters his mind. * * * An essential element of the way the play
works, therefore, is to take this extraordinary situation—Oedipus's
incestuous relations with his mother—and pose it (reversed) in
mundane terms. Issues of paternity, citizenship, and family member-
ship are common in the legal arena, so that Sophocles simply borrows
the expression of class structure that underlies such contests and

puts it in Oedipus's mouth. As a result, we recognize that Oedipus has missed the point completely—it would be far better if Oedipus *were* a slave, and no biological relation to Laius.

In the remarkable inversion of this drama, then, legitimacy is a bigger problem than illegitimacy. * * *

The purpose of legitimacy tests within society, moreover, is to establish difference. *Gnēsioi* children are citizens, eligible to inherit property; *nothoi* are not. When these boundaries are crossed, all social distinctions are threatened. So, in [Demosthenes] 59, Apollodorus argues that if Athens allows a prostitute (Neaira) to be a wife, it will make all Athenian wives into prostitutes. Legitimacy distinguishes one class from another within the city, and one nationality from another outside the city. But Oedipus's legitimacy has the opposite effect—it breaks down difference, and difference on an even more "natural" level than that of class or nationality. Oedipus eliminates distinctions between generations, as any number of lines point out. I cite only one instance here, Tiresias's dire prediction:

* * *

He will turn out, living with his own children,
to be their brother and father, and of the woman from whom
he came, he will be son and husband, of his father,
he will be a sower in the same place, and a murderer. (457–60)

Oedipus's legitimacy, therefore, has an effect structurally opposite to that which legitimacy is supposed to have. Rather than solidifying identity and naturalizing difference, it eliminates it. This particular biological identity creates a multiplicity of identities, and a tangle of relationships that Oedipus would gladly trade for the simplicity of status as a *nothos*. The unfortunate fact of Oedipus's birth creates a fundamental instability in his identity, so that basic terms of familial relationship become interchangeable. The idea of displaced identity, therefore, is essential to Oedipus's experience. Oedipus's crimes depend on the certainty of his biological identity, and we, insofar as we are horrified at his realization of incest, accept that certainty. We do so, however, in the face of the paradox that his unwitting incest has thrown the whole paradigm into question. He fills too many categories at once.

* * *

Supernatural Marriages

* * * Athenian tragedy (like many of the representations of Athenian culture) naturalizes marriage. It describes marriage with a series of metaphors from the wild and agricultural spheres in order to make

the cultural bond between husband and wife appear straightforward, normal, and analogous to other processes of civilization. The
Oedipus tyrannus does the same, but with a twist. It uses these
same naturalizing images to describe the patently "unnatural" marriage of Oedipus and Jocasta. But the play does more than simply
create this juxtaposition. A number of descriptive passages suggest
that, as with Oedipus discovering his identity, this marriage should
have spontaneously discovered and denounced its own perversity.
These conventional images serve here to denaturalize the institution of marriage, to expose the mechanisms by which culture
defines itself.

Early on, the play suggests that something is wrong with Oedipus's marriage through descriptions of the plague, which manifests
itself as an interruption of fertility on all levels. The chorus of suppliants says,

* * *

[The city is] wasting away with the fruit-bearing crops of earth,
wasting away with herds of grazing oxen,
with the unborn children of women. (25–27)

The assumption behind this description is an association with which
we are familiar: often Athenian literature equates the fertility of
the land with the fertility of women. Such images naturalize the
production of children, and woman's role in the *polis*. Here, however, fertility has stopped on both a human and an agricultural
level. For all who know the myth of Oedipus, the perversion of fertility described above has an obvious (we might even say biological)
cause: Oedipus's marriage to his mother, Jocasta. Such an "unnatural" marriage (especially one between the rulers of Thebes) results
in the disruption of everything that marriage represents to the
community.

Surprisingly, then, the *Oedipus tyrannus* presents Oedipus's marriage in the same naturalizing terms that we see elsewhere. The
play contains an unusually high number of images of women as
harbors and plowed fields, both common in descriptions of *parthe-
noi* as they undergo marriage. In some instances, these images
appear to have no sexual connotations at all: Oedipus is several
times characterized as a helmsman, piloting the "ship of state."
Elsewhere, however, this civilizing image is specifically a metaphor
for his marriage. Tiresias, for example, says:

* * *

What harbor will there not be for your cries,
What Mt. Cithaeron will not cry in response quickly,

> when you perceive the wedding, which
> you steered, harborless, into the house, happening on good
>   sailing? (420–23)

Though the syntax here is unusually complex, the notion of a marriage being represented by the image of a ship sailing into safe harbor is a fairly common one. The image also clearly suggests the sexual act of penetration. Oedipus's fateful marriage, then, takes on the same aspect that any normal marriage would, rendering the act of intercourse with the civilized and civilizing images of sailing. Here, however, we should note that it is the wedding that is sailed into the house, and that the same wedding is marked "harborless." This marriage, it seems, is neither safe nor normal.

* * *

The same sort of variation is put on an even more common image of marriage, that of the plowed field. Again, this image occurs in the play with unusual frequency. In an early ironic passage, Oedipus describes his link to Laius in these terms, saying that he is * * * "holding his same-sowed bed and wife" (260). When Oedipus recounts what the oracle told him, the father that he is destined to kill is [described as] "having planted" (793). Later, Oedipus uses the same adjective to describe Polybus and Merope (*phuteusantes*, "having planted," 1007, 1012). After Oedipus knows his identity, the metaphor is used more often and more explicitly, as in lines 1255–57:

* * *

> He rushed in, asking me to provide a sword,
> that he might meet with his wife, no wife,
> and maternal double field where he also begot children.

The idea of sowing a field creates an image of sex and reproduction that is in accord with the world of agriculture. The image is highly ironic here, a suggestion of naturalness just at the point when Oedipus has fully realized how "unnatural" his marriage has been.

* * *

* * * Oedipus's act of incest disrupts the cultural production of marriage just as it disrupts the paradigm of biological identity. In the face of Oedipus's unnatural marriage, neither paradigm sufficiently explains the facts at hand. The incest taboo ceases to operate if a man can marry his mother, and biological identity cannot describe the man who is both father and brother to his offspring. The agricultural metaphors for marriage imply an ordered process of civilized and civilizing fertility. Oedipus's fertility denies that process and the categories that it establishes.

Jocasta : Oedipus :: Excess : Identity

Few critics have much to say about Jocasta, and it is easy to relegate her to the status of a plot device. * * * We know nothing of how she felt when she allowed her child to be exposed, or when she learned that her first husband had died, or when she married Oedipus shortly thereafter. Her experience is masked in the text, overshadowed by Oedipus and protected from public view. Nonetheless, she is important: she is, after all, the relationship center that creates Oedipus as the person he is. And if we cannot recover "her" experience (because Sophocles does not represent it), we can look at the way she serves as a link between key characters, and thereby creates a social identity for others.

I have focused above on the nature of biological identity as a displacing and displaced construct. Jocasta embodies that process of displacement. She fulfills the traditional role of woman-as-other, in that she does not establish an identity for herself so much as she serves as a creator of identities for the men around her. That is, Oedipus obtains his biological identity through her and, as we shall see, also realizes that identity because of Jocasta's pronouncements. Moreover, the male characters in the play try to establish relationships with one another through Jocasta, often invoking the links that have been created by her marriage. In this respect, her marriage in and of itself mirrors the process of displacement: Oedipus is confirmed as king, for example, because he has married the queen, a state that replaces and masks his status as the heir apparent. Such attempted social identities, as we might expect, become superfluous when Jocasta's "real" relationships to Oedipus and Laius become clear. Once again, biological identity displaces other, competing social forms of identity. Most important of all, then, Jocasta's marriage mirrors the process of displacement in that it creates relationships—and categories of relationships—beyond and outside of those that the characters seek.

Before Jocasta arrives on the scene, Creon and Oedipus recognize and validate a relationship to one another through her. At line 551, Oedipus warns Creon that he will receive no special treatment although he is *suggenēs*. The word suggests that the two are tied by blood (as they are, though they do not realize this yet) and indicates the strength of Oedipus's marriage bond with Jocasta. Similarly, Creon emphasizes his relation to Oedipus as he begins his defense: * * * "What? Are you not married to my sister?" (577). He then goes on to argue that as the brother-in-law of the king, he enjoys all the benefits with none of the responsibility of royalty (583ff.). His relationship to Oedipus, which he currently believes to be a simple marriage-tie through Jocasta, creates an unofficial political identity as well.

Even more important, however, is the purely social link that Jocasta creates between Laius and Oedipus. This link exists in both political and personal terms. * * * Marriage to the queen, as we have seen several times before, is one of the signs of "being the king," of ruling over the *polis,* and it is this legacy that Jocasta transfers to the stranger who comes to town. Jocasta and Oedipus fail to realize, however, that she has also transferred her husband's property according to the more usual method, by providing a male heir. The problem, then, is not that Jocasta (like Clytemnestra) has transferred the *oikos* to an enemy or outsider, but that she has transferred it in too many ways to a too-near relative. Oedipus's political legitimacy, then, has been overconfirmed: he cannot both inherit and marry into the kingdom.

* * * The bond of common children carries a hidden threat of being too close, of destroying difference altogether (as we saw earlier). Jocasta becomes a sort of hyper-woman, creating too many links, facilitating too many relationships between men.

Jocasta's speeches, moreover, are analogous to her position. Consistently when she tries to mediate, to smooth things over, she ends up creating an excess of information, just as with Oedipus she creates an excess of relationships. The most obvious example is her attempt to calm Oedipus about the oracle. She offers the oracle she and Laius heard—that he would be killed by his own offspring— as proof that oracles are meaningless. For, she says, Laius was killed by robbers at a crossroads (711–25). This last detail, seemingly inconsequential, catches Oedipus's attention, and he begins at this point to suspect that he is the regicide. In many of Jocasta's speeches we see such elements of excess, and such excess is part of the topos of women as other. For even as they create links between men, women remain in some sense radically outside; they leave a residue—of information, of relationships—that does not dissolve. Significantly, the details that Jocasta first brings to Oedipus's attention—for example, that Laius was killed by *several* people— remain unresolved. Jocasta may be telling Oedipus too much, but even when he follows her clues and accepts the awful truth, what she has said remains outside of his interpretation, unintegrated into the "meaning" of the play.

* * *

* * * Although this play is extraordinary in the emphasis it places on misdirection in the process of signification, it also suggests that

this misdirection is the special province of women. Jocasta is the unspoken center of all the problematic relations in this play: Oedipus and Creon, Oedipus and Laius, Oedipus and his off-spring. As a mediator between households, her role is always over-determined, always potentially doubled (if not duplicitous). Little wonder, then, that so much of Jocasta's speech seems to embody displacement. Possessed of no stable identity of her own, Jocasta creates identities for others through a disturbing process of dis-placement and oversignification.

* * *

* * * On the one hand, we expect that Oedipus will be exiled once he is revealed as the killer of Laius. Because the punishment of exile was pronounced by Oedipus himself, however, Creon must refuse the pronouncement in order to establish his own ascen-dancy. *His* final lines demonstrate this concern: * * * "Do not wish to rule over everything. / For that which you ruled does not follow your [remaining?] life" (1522–23). Creon refuses to honor Oedipus's request to exile him (see especially 1518), therefore, and in so doing establishes himself as the head of the household (and state). His pious control seems to indicate a return to order. But the simultaneous result is that the murderer of Laius, this Oedipus who has become a perversion of fertility on every level, remains within the *oikos* [household]: His blood ties remain symbolically within the house.

It is worth remembering here the difficulty inherent in establish-ing identity in the Athenian legal system. In order to prove oneself a citizen in fifth-century Athens, one had to prove that both father and mother were citizens. The former could be, in some cases, difficult; the latter appears never to have been easy. * * * [T]he process of establishing a woman's identity could only rely on a series of recol-lections of public events during which no citizen stepped forward to deny her citizenship: the marriage ceremony, the introduction of sons into the phratry, the marriage of daughters to citizen men, and the like. The very notion of Athenian citizenship depended on a stable biological identity; that biological identity proved itself, over and over again, impossible to establish with certainty.

Oedipus can transfer his daughters to the son of Menoikeos, but they remain "his" daughters. It seems unlikely that Creon will be able to transfer them to husbands. Their social identity, like Oedipus's, is confirmed by a series of failed displacements, and ultimately rests in their biological link to their father. And that is exactly how ideology—how the production of the subject—works. Against the background of unsuccessful "cultural" productions, it presents itself as "natural," and thus displaces other possible identities. But here, the "natural" relationship is that which is specifically unnatural, a product of excess and a disrupter of difference. The play allows us, if only momentarily and with much effort, to see that even biological identity is potentially unstable, is subject to political and cultural manipulation.

The *Oedipus tyrannus* presents, in this reading, a complex and subtle critique of Athens's insistence on biological citizenship. Oedipus really is the man who killed his father and married his mother. His daughters really are his daughters. But we are unhappy because the play's confirmation of these facts—Oedipus's continued presence in the *oikos*—has now displaced our dramatic and social expectations. The small wrench that we feel as the play fails to achieve closure mirrors the process by which we have seen Oedipus discover who he is. Thus we are afforded a glimpse—perhaps no more—of the workings of ideology. But that perspective does not allow us to escape the world of constructed subjects; like the characters in the play, we have no choice but to leave Oedipus, securely identified, within the house of Laius.

JOSHUA D. SOSIN

From Death on a Road[†]

ABSTRACT: Scholarly consensus holds that a law quoted in Demosthenes (23.53) permitted one to kill a highway robber who had lain in ambush and attacked one on a road. But the relevant phrase * * * says nothing explicit about ambush. * * * It is argued here that they were mistaken and that the [law] referred to those who inadvertently killed a fellow traveler while 'overtaking on a road.' The new interpretation may offer another way to think about the encounter between Oedipus and Laius. *Keywords*: homicide—Athens—law—Harpocration—road—robber

According to a famous passage in Demosthenes, "It was permitted to kill a highwayman who waylaid one on a road." The law is quoted at 23.53:

* * *

> If one kills unwillingly in games, or [on the road], or having failed to recognize (a comrade) in war, or (if one kills a man who is) with a wife, or with a mother, or with a sister, or with daughter, or with a concubine whom he keeps for purpose of

† From *Historia* 65 (2016): 155, 166–68. © Franz Steiner Verlag, Stuttgart 2016. Reprinted by permission of Franz Steiner Verlag and the author. Most of the author's notes have been omitted.

producing free offspring, he shall not, for these (acts) go into exile for having killed.

But the [law] says nothing explicit about highway robbery or ambush, which are generally regarded as the circumstances involved in this claim to lawful homicide. * * *

* * *

Not Oedipus but Laius

* * * Draco's homicide law made it difficult to prosecute the driver of a vehicle who struck and killed a family member. To a modern reader, this might seem an odd exception, not in the same category as boxing accidents or death by friendly fire. But it may have made sense to an Athenian in the seventh century. Mounted and vehicular travel could be treacherous. Horses startle. Ruts could be deep. Roads were often narrow, drop-offs sheer. And chariots at least were notoriously fragile, their crashes a fixture of Greek myth and literature. Moreover, Greeks' agonistic disposition probably did not make road travel any safer.

* * * To force someone off a road was a power to which superiors felt entitled—to be forced from a road an abuse that they felt free to repay with violence.

Draco wrote this clause in a period when violence and the force of social hierarchies loomed large * * *. Elites imposed harsh, even mafia-like, 'protection' regimes on poorer residents of the Attic countryside. * * * Even as civil society began to blossom, the roads of Attica were liminal places where social status dominated, * * * where the big man simply did not yield. This clause in Draco's law, I urge, preserved and protected that old elite entitlement to exercise a particular kind of potentially violent behavior in inherently dangerous circumstances, without fear of reprisal.

Well into the classical period, roads remained places in the Greek literary imagination where a bit of the heroic mindset endured, where elites demanded the right of way, period. Antiquity's most famous highway killing is the backstory to its most famous play. Where three roads meet, father drove at son and son killed father, neither knowing the other's identity, relative social status, or what ills would come. Some have thought that an Athenian audience might regard Oedipus as innocent of murder, for he was waylaid in the road and acted in self-defense. But Harris has argued that Athenian theatergoers would have understood that Laius and driver had not lain in "ambush," so that Athenian law cannot have recognized their killing as justified and lawful; that the driver shoved and Laius goaded, but Oedipus slew, out of rage. No ambush, no self-defense, and a disproportionate response: for the audience member who was inclined to think in terms of Athenian law, Oedipus had no viable claim to lawful killing; he was guilty of homicide.[1]

But if the phrase ["waylaid on the road"] addressed vehicular homicide committed while overtaking someone on a road, then the question of Oedipus' guilt had nothing to do with the absence of ambush. And if we examine the episode through the lens of Athens' archaic homicide law, then we should ask also about the innocence of Laius. For in Oedipus' version of events the old man and driver issued no warning but simply "started driving me off the road," as if exercising the superior man's right and privilege to pass without yielding, and to use force if opposed. What, then, if the man had simply *killed* Oedipus, and lawfully, in his attempt to pass? Father might have incurred neither guilt nor pollution, and so spared the son the very same. An awful thing to ponder. But all the more tragic.

MARTHA C. NUSSBAUM

From The *Oedipus Rex* and the Ancient Unconscious[†]

I shall be discussing the practical nature of the ancient unconscious—its preoccupation with questions of good and bad fortune, control and lack of control, security and insecurity. I shall be arguing that these questions are more central to its workings than questions of sexuality narrowly construed, indeed, that sexual anxieties function as just one species of practical anxiety about control and security. It therefore seems appropriate to begin with a dream, to all appearances sexual, which really has, according to the ancient interpretation, a nonsexual practical significance for the fortunes of most of the contributors to this volume—people, that is, who make a living giving lectures and exchanging arguments. In the first book of Artemidoros of Daldis' work on dream interpretation (*Artemidori Daldiani onicocriticon libri V*), in a section— to which I shall return—on dreams whose content is that which violates convention in sexual matters, Artemidoros, a professional

---

1. [Harris, E.M. 2010. "Is Oedipus Guilty? Sophocles and Athenian Homicide Law." In E.M. Harris et al. (eds.) *Law and Drama in Ancient Greece*. London. 122–146]: 136–137: guilty, at least insofar as the narrative at OT 800–813 suggests. His account in the OC differs in crucial and interesting ways: Harris 2010: 138–139. * * *

† From *Freud and Forbidden Knowledge*, ed. Peter L. Rudnytsky and Ellen Handler Spitz (New York and London: New York UP, 1994), pp. 42–71. Copyright © 1994 by New York University. Reprinted by permission of the publisher. The author's notes have been omitted.

dream analyst of the second century C.E. interprets the dream that one is performing oral sex on a stranger.

In general, Artemidoros says, this dream is a bad one, indicative of some bad fortune to come—this in keeping with the pervasive Greek view that such intercourse is unclean and base * * *. But there is an exception. With his characteristic pragmatism and flexibility, Artemidoros notes that the dream is a happy one, indicative of future good fortune and security, "for those who earn their living by their mouths, I mean flutists, trumpet-players, rhetors, sophists, and whoever else is like them." The sexual act is cheerfully read as a metaphor for the successful practice of one's profession. Beyond the information it imparts, so interesting to the professional academic, this example begins, I hope, to give a sense of some profound differences between ancient Greek and Freudian attitudes toward what the unconscious mind contains and how to decipher its contents. These differences—and also their significance for the reading of Sophocles' *Oedipus Rex*—will be the subject of this essay.

I have often felt discomfort when hearing discussion of the Freudian Oedipus complex in connection with Sophocles' play. For while it seems plain that both Freud's theory and Sophocles' play explore important aspects of human experience and evoke in their readers a valuable sort of reflection about experience, I have (along, I suspect, with many readers of the play) much difficulty finding the closer link that Freudian interpretations of the play wish us to discover. For it seems difficult to avoid the conclusion that the play itself is not very much concerned with sexual desire as such, or with deep-hidden sexual urges toward one's parent, combined with aggressive wishes toward one's parental rival. Its subject matter does very much appear to be that of reversal in fortune. So it has been understood since Aristotle's *Poetics*, where it provides the central illustration of the concept of *peripeteia* [reversal] and, it appears, with good reason. Incest seems to figure in the plot as that which, when discovered, causes Oedipus to plummet from the summit of good fortune to the very bottom. It is, of course, crucial to the plot that Oedipus is not experiencing desire toward the person whom he takes to be his mother, toward the woman who raised him as a mother, nor, indeed, toward any woman who nursed, held, or cared for him at any time. So far as the intentional content of his desire is concerned, Jocasta is simply a well-placed eligible stranger. It is also perfectly clear that his aggressive action against Laios is in and of itself culturally acceptable, a counterattack in self-defense. Nor is there any sign that Oedipus has at any level hidden knowledge about the identity of the stranger he kills. How could he, when he would never have looked upon his face, even in infancy? Finally, the whole question of erotic desire does not appear to be salient in the play's treatment of the marriage to Jocasta. The marriage is a political one, and is never described as motivated by *erôs*. *Erôs* is mentioned frequently in Sophocles—but not in this play. In short: the play *seems*, as Aristotle says, to be concerned with the vulnerability of even the best fortune to abrupt disaster. And it is crucial to its construction that the collocation of circumstances that strikes Oedipus down is not regarded, by him or by anyone else in the play, as the product of his sexual intentions, whether conscious or unconscious.

* * *

* * * I shall examine a portion of the dream book of Artemidoros, which, though written in the second century C.E., gives us the most extensive evidence we have about popular beliefs concerning these matters and testifies, it is clear, to deep and persistent cultural beliefs about the crucial importance of "external goods" in the structure of the mental life. Artemidoros confines his account to the reading of dreams, which is, of course, his trade; he has no theory comparable to Freud's concerning the motivational role of repressed unconscious desires in one's waking life. * * *

* * *

First, some general observations. Artemidoros is important to anyone who wants a better understanding of ancient attitudes to dreaming and sex (and many other things besides) because, although he is himself an expert practitioner with a theory, the theory operates through a detailed understanding of popular cultural symbolism and deeply rooted cultural attitudes * * *. To find out what a dream signifies, Artemidoros needs to know the various symbolic associations of the parts of the dream-content. Usually he does this in general cultural terms, since he is writing a general handbook. But he makes it clear that the good interpreter must really always take into account the peculiarities of the dreamer's own history, his or her own personal variations on the cultural symbolism. In a non-judgmental way he must seek to uncover the facts about the dreamer's own practices and associations, so that no relevant symbolic connection will have been overlooked. In my opening example, the interpreter needs to know the dreamer's profession—for this will inform him that the dream of giving sexual pleasure with one's mouth, which has dire associations for most people, has associations with profit and success for the dreamer, as member of one of the occupational groups named. Elsewhere he makes it clear that he also needs full information about the dreamer's sexual practices, if dreams with a sexual content are to be correctly understood. In two cases where males dreamed, one of performing cunnilingus on

his wife, the other of being fellated by his, Artemidoros at first
expected something bad to happen. He was amazed when it did
not, and this seemed to him most "unreasonable." But later the puzzle
was solved. He discovered (he does not tell us how) that the two
men in question actually had all along had a personal taste for oral-
genital activity, a taste that they had not reported to Artemidoros,
presumably because of the cultural stigma attached to it. "Both
were in the habit of doing that, and not keeping their mouths clean.
So it was plausible that nothing happened to them, since they simply
saw what excited them" (4.59). Thus, though many dreams refer to
future events, their significance must be read—as in the case of
Freudian interpretation—in terms of the dreamer's own personal
history, wishes, and associations * * *.

* * *

* * * [T]he most striking aspect of Artemidoros' view about sexual dreaming, for the post-Freudian reader, is the type of significance he attaches to the sexual in the interpretation of the soul's
deliverances. The post-Freudian interpreter is inclined to seek for a
sexual meaning beneath apparently nonsexual dream-contents.
The deepest point at which one can arrive, in unraveling the mind's
symbolic language, is a point at which one arrives at some sexual
wish. Artemidoros moves, on the whole, in just the opposite direction. For him, even dreams that have an overtly sexual content are,
like all other dreams, read off as having a significance for the rise
and fall of the dreamer's fortunes, his or her command or lack of
command over important items such as money, status, friendships,
and the other important things in life. * * * Dreams, for Artemidoros, and sexual dreams among them, signify the dreamer's (future)
command or lack of command over these significant external goods.

* * *

The account of mother-son incest occurs as part of the analysis
of dreams of sexual intercourse, which itself falls into three sections: dreams about intercourse "according to convention," about
intercourse "contrary to convention," and about intercourse "contrary to nature" * * *. In the first category are dreams of all kinds
of nonincestuous and nonoral intercourse, both active and passive,
with partners of either gender (the one exception being "a woman
penetrating a woman," which, as we shall see, falls in the third category). Although the goodness or badness of the events predicted
by the dream is often connected with the generally approved or
nonapproved nature of its content—thus the dream of penetrating
someone is usually, though not always, more auspicious than the
dream of being penetrated—the whole group is called "according to

convention," regardless of the genders and positions of the actors. "Against convention" are two sorts of dream contents: dreams of incest, and dreams of oral sex. "Against nature" are contents that simply seem to Artemidoros too weird to have any ordinary social signification at all, things that are just off the ordinary map— having sex with a god, having sex with an animal, having sex with oneself (this not in the sense of masturbation, but in the sense of self-penetration and self-fellatio); and, finally, "a woman penetrating a woman." It is important to note that the dream of something "against nature" need not be ill-omened; everything depends on the further analysis of the content, the postures of the actors, etc. (Thus, as we have seen, it can be very good to dream of mounting an animal.)

Artemidoros' account of mother-son incest is longer than any other discussion in the incest section—on account of the fact, he says, that "the analysis of the mother is intricate and elaborate, and susceptible of many discriminations. It has eluded many dream analysts" (1.79). Here is the main part of Artemidoros' account—the ancient analogue, or disanalogue, of Freud's oedipal wishing:

> And if a poor man who lacks the essentials has a rich mother he will receive what he wants from her, or else he will inherit it from her when she dies not long after, and thus he will take pleasure in his mother. Many too have undertaken to care and provide for their mothers, who in turn take pleasure in their sons.
>
> The dream sets right the sick man, signifying that he will return to the natural state, for the common mother of all is nature, and we say that healthy people are in a natural state and sick people are not. Apollodoros of Telmessos, a learned man, also remarks on this. The significance is not the same for sick people if the mother (in the dream) is dead, for the dreamer will die very shortly. For the constitution of the dream woman dissolves into the matter of which it is composed and constituted and most of it being earth-like reverts to its proper material. And "mother" is no less a name for the earth. What else could having sex with a dead mother signify for the sick man but having sex with the earth?
>
> For one who is involved in a suit over land or who wants to buy some land or who desires to farm, it is good to have sex with a dead mother. Some say that it is bad for the farmer alone, saying that he will scatter his seeds on dead land, that is, he will have no yield. But in my opinion this is not at all correct, unless however one repents of the intercourse or feels upset.

Further, he who is in a dispute over his mother's property will win his case after this dream, rejoicing not in his mother's body but in her property.

If one sees this dream in one's native country he will leave the country, for it is not possible after so great an error (*hamartêma*) to remain at the maternal hearths. If he is upset or repents the intercourse he will be exiled from the fatherland, otherwise he will leave voluntarily.

To penetrate one's mother from the rear is not good. For either the mother herself will turn her back on the dreamer or his fatherland or his craft or whatever might be his immediate business. It is also bad if both are standing upright during intercourse, for people adopt such a posture through lack of a bed or blankets. Therefore it signifies pressures and desperate straits. To have sex with one's mother on her knees is bad: it signifies a great lack because of the mother's immobility.

If the mother is on top and "riding cavalry," some say this means death for the dreamer, since the mother is like earth, earth being the nurturer and progenetrix of all, and it lies on top of corpses and not on top of the living. But I have observed that sick men who have this dream always die, but the healthy men live out the remainder of their lives in great ease and just as they choose—a correct and logical outcome, for in the other positions the hard work and heavy breathing are for the most part the male's share and the female role is relatively effortless; but in this posture it is just the opposite—the man takes pleasure without laboring. But it also allows him who is not in the light to be hidden from his neighbors, because most of the telltale heavy breathing is absent. (1.79)

There follows a brief digression on the naturalness of the frontal position; and then, in a transition to the following section on oral sex, Artemidoros analyzes the dream of oral sex with one's mother. To that dream we shall turn later; first, however, some comments on the material just cited.

The strikingly non-Freudian nature of the analysis is evident; but a few concrete observations will help to pin it down. First, there is nothing special about mother-son incest in Artemidoros' account of the soul's inner language. It is just one more signifier, and it is not singled out as playing an especially fundamental role. It is ranked along with other cases of incest, and all incest along with oral sex; and, as we have already said, the entire account of sexual dreaming is a very brief portion of the longer analysis.

Second, the dream of mother-son incest, like other sexual dreams, is significant, not in terms of underlying sexual wishes, but in terms of things like getting control over an estate, having authority in the city, getting on well with one's family and friends, getting or losing one's health, and so forth. The mother's body frequently signifies country or property. Even when, in the opening paragraph, a dispute with one's father is mentioned as one possible significance of such a dream, it is made just one possibility among many, and is not basic to what follows in any sense. Furthermore, the father's jealousy is just ordinary sexual jealousy, "the element of jealousy which would occur no matter who was involved." The dream signifies a rupture in one's fortunes, since good relations with one's family are conventionally taken to be a central part of one's fortunes. But neither its specifically sexual significance nor the identity of the parties is dwelt upon. And we must take note of the fact that very many of the dreams in this section are auspicious—again impossible if they were read as in every case denoting a hostile wish.

Third, the significance of these dreams is to be understood not by focusing exclusively on the fact of incest—to which, of course, the Freudian account single-mindedly directs us—but rather in terms of the specific sexual positions and activities employed. Artemidoros is very insistent about this. Thus, to penetrate one's mother from the front is usually good, to penetrate her from behind usually bad. Standing intercourse, in characteristic fashion, is immediately taken to have an economic significance, in terms of the lack of bedclothes and furniture. The position with the mother on top—in Artemidoros' novel interpretation, of whose cleverness he is evidently proud—is auspicious (for a healthy man) because it is associated with ease and an absence of heavy breathing.

Fourth and finally, there is not the slightest hint here that the dream should be connected to any deep and extended narrative pattern of sexual wishing going far back into one's childhood and repressed in adulthood. Such dreams are read matter-of-factly, like others, in terms of the dreamer's current profession, fortune, and so forth; the mother's significance in the dream frequently comes from his current professional activities. And far from expressing disturbing repressed sexual material, the dream's sexual content is not taken to be especially disturbing. Consider the case of the farmer, whose dream of incest with the *corpse* of his mother is auspicious, "unless one repents of the intercourse or feels upset"—apparently not the usual case! We might add that the range and variety of dreams of this type that were reported to Artemidoros may itself give evidence of an absence of repression of such ideas in Greek culture. For many contemporary people who read this section, what seems oddest is that all these dreams should have occurred at all, in this undisguised form. To the Greeks it seems, apparently, perfectly normal and natural, just as natural as the fact that one's especially deep anxieties about money, health, and citizenship should assume, in a dream, a disguised form. In short, if anything is, here, so disturbing that it invites repression, it is the soul's anxiety about external goods.

Now we must turn to one further dream in the sequence, "the most awful (*deinotaton*) dream of all," says our author. For this dream might seem initially to cast doubt on some of our claims—although more closely inspected, I believe, it supports them. This dream, as I have said, forms the transition between the section on incest dreams and the section on dreams of oral sex. Its analysis goes as follows:

> The most awful dream of all, I have observed, is to be fellated by one's mother. For it signifies the death of children and loss of property and serious illness for the dreamer. I know someone who had this dream and lost his penis; it makes sense that he should be punished in the part of his body which erred. (1.79)

A Freudian interpreter might suppose that Artemidoros here at last betrays the Freudian nature of his, and his patients' concerns. For the "most awful dream," after all, is a dream of intercourse with the mother. And having the dream is linked to the idea of a merited sexual punishment for a transgression that is, apparently, specifically sexual. Sexual error signifies a sexual loss. Don't we have here, after all, the proof that the deepest and most fearful things in the ancient unconscious are, after all, sexual things, and that a repressed thought of incest is, after all, connected in this culture with a fear of the loss of virility?

Things are not so simple. First of all, there is an obvious and striking departure from Freudian concerns in the fact that the dream is terrible not on account of its incestuous content—many incest-dreams, we recall, are auspicious—but on account of the mode of copulation. Here, as elsewhere in the discussion, Artemidoros expresses his culture's view that to perform oral sex is unclean and base; to be made to perform it on someone else is a humiliation. The discussion that ensues makes it plain that the uncleanness of the performer's mouth is thought to make it impossible to share kisses or food with this person any more. (In general, any dream of oral sex with a known person signifies a separation from that person.) Thus the dream of the fellating mother is understood as a dream of the humiliation of the mother by the son, a humiliation that is bound to destroy the household. It is for this reason, and not on account of its specifically incestuous content, that it is so inauspicious. And the son's error, for which he is punished, is not to engage in intercourse with his mother; it is to cause his mother to perform an unclean act after which the household can never be the same. Well might such a dream signify "the death of children and loss of property and serious illness."

Second, what the dream does in fact signify is, as we just said, "the death of children and loss of property and serious illness." The man who loses his penis is just one case of "serious illness," a case picked out by Artemidoros because of its ironically apposite nature. But, as elsewhere, the "real" significance of the dream is in the dreamer's relation to "external goods." And the punishment of the dreamer is the loss, not only of a bodily part, but of the chance to have, in the future, a family of his own. Because he did something destructive and antifamily, he loses the chance to have a family, and to enjoy the position of status and control signified by the penis.

In short: the dream of incest is, at bottom, a code, through which the soul speaks to itself about what it most deeply hopes and fears. Not sex, but control over external goods, are the content of those most basic hopes and fears.

* * *

Oedipus and His Fortune

[Now], all too briefly, I want to make some suggestions about ways in which this set of concerns might illuminate our approach to the *Oedipus Rex*. * * * I would * * * like to suggest that we might fruitfully approach the *Oedipus* as, so to speak, a dream issuing from the unconscious of its citizen watchers, but an unconscious of the ancient, rather than the Freudian, kind. What I mean is that if we ask ourselves how an ancient audience might actually see in the play a kind of possibility for themselves, connecting themselves to the characters through the emotions of pity and fear, which (as Aristotle persuasively says) require, both of them, the belief that one's own possibilities are the same as those of the protagonists—if one asks this question, one is bound to focus, not on the literal events of the play, but on what one might call their Artemidoran symbolism. In the world whose preoccupations I have tried to depict, an average member of the audience is very unlikely to believe it a salient possibility for himself that he would actually do what Oedipus does here, killing his father and marrying his mother. For one thing, the net of circumstances that brought this about in Oedipus' life is too strange and complex to be very likely to be replicated. But if, on the other hand, we see the literal events as representing, as in an Artemidoran dream, possibilities for the rise and fall of human fortunes, we can far more easily see what a citizen would find terrifying here. If someone who enjoys the extreme of control, prosperity, and in general good fortune can be so brought low by events and circumstances beyond his control, then no human life seems safe from this possibility. For most lives start out more vulnerable and less prosperous than his was. * * *

If one turns to the play with these ideas in mind, one is struck by the fact that while, on the one hand, *erôs* seems to be absent from it, *tuchê* is omnipresent. Oedipus is introduced as [fortune], most powerful (40); and yet the city itself has been afflicted by forces beyond its control, so that the citizens can already be addressed as "pitiable children" * * *. At line 145, beginning on his fateful search for the causes of the pollution, Oedipus announces, "We shall either emerge fortunate * * *, with the god's help, or as fallen * * *." Immediately the Chorus, entering, begins to speak of its anxious fear and tension (151ff.). And of course, from the first, Oedipus is present to the audience (through his name alone) as a cripple, someone cast out naked into the world and maimed by its dangers * * *.

* * *

* * * I believe that the ancient views I have discussed are profound and highly plausible in a way that goes beyond strict cultural boundaries; and yet, equally clearly, that they are culture-bound in certain ways, and lack, in some areas, a richness of development that would be required if they were ever to become powerful and plausible for a contemporary understanding. It might emerge, however, that the confrontation between these views and the modern views of thinkers such as Klein, Fairbairn, and Winnicott, and of both with the best of recent cognitively oriented work in experimental psychology, for example the work of Lazarus (1991) and Seligman (1975), might generate a philosophical theory of the human longing for control and self-sufficiency that would preserve the best features of both sources, and link them in a new account of fear, aggression, pity, and love.

MICHAEL ANDREW KICEY

From Road to Nowhere: The Mobility of Oedipus and the Task of Interpretation[†]

I

In many respects, Oedipus' failure to recognize himself simply magnifies our own mundane, everyday failure to recognize properly those things that we see every day—the things that escape our notice precisely because they stand in the plainest sight, in the most intimate relationship to what we think we are and what we think we understand. This inertia of the mundane mind, its failure to make sense again of what seems to make eminently good sense already, plays a key structural role not just in the language of Sophocles' *Oedipus Tyrannus* but also in the language of literary criticism—particularly for a work that has generated as much criticism as this text has, and along such well-worn avenues of proliferation at that. In the process of interpretation, we often speak a language we think we understand, or even one we think we ourselves have invented and therefore one we fully control, but, like Oedipus himself, we sometimes fail to perceive the patterns we obediently reproduce, fail to listen to the words we are actually using.

Let me begin with an example from the play, from which I will work my way back to this point about the language of criticism. In the exchange with Creon upon his return from Delphi, Oedipus describes the murder of Laius figuratively as the bold transgression of a limit set on physical movement: "Unless some intrigue had been worked with bribes from here in Thebes, how would the robber have proceeded * * * to such a point of daring * * *?" (* * * 124–25). Compare this with Oedipus' long speech to the assembled Theban elders (216–75) in which he assures the citizens that he will apply all his resources in pursuing the killer. Here the ambiguity of his language, and its gentle but unmistakable allusion to the idiom of 124–25, characteristically rebound on its speaker: translated literally, he says that he himself "will arrive at all points" or "show up everywhere" (* * * 265). Oedipus' words unintentionally evoke his own, still-unrecognized arrival at the criminal "point of daring" beyond all acceptable limits that he unknowingly described earlier

---

† From *American Journal of Philology* 135 (2014): 29–55. © 2014 Johns Hopkins University Press. Reprinted by permission of Johns Hopkins University Press. The author's notes have been omitted.

at 125. Over and over again, the more Oedipus tries to draw a
boundary in words between the daring of the assassin and the zeal
of the prosecutor, the more they continuously and conspicuously
collapse into one another. And just as Oedipus in his duplicity violates all boundaries imposed on action as well as thought, destroying the "common places" that map out the shared moral and
political life of Thebes, so does the troubling polysemy of Oedipus'
voice willfully violate the "commonplaces" that maintain the integrity of words, meanings, and concepts in moral and political language. This kind of ambiguity or multi-vocality inflects the poetic
language of the *Oedipus Tyrannus* through the conspicuous multi-
plication and dislocation of meaning in not only Oedipus' language
but also the language of his interlocutors. From our viewpoint, the
dramatis personae constantly mean both more and less than they
say: their language is rife with double and triple meanings of which
they are hopelessly unaware, even going so far as to undermine or
contradict the meaning of which they are aware. They all talk a great
deal, but they consistently fail to hear what anyone is saying.

* * *

What if the critic interprets the *Oedipus Tyrannus'* tragic irony
not as a contrived dissonance that the play ultimately resolves into
a default consonance but rather as a means to reflect on the irre-
solvable and ubiquitous dissonance that suffuses interpretive language as such—even our own? What if we read not to congratulate
ourselves for having the resources to steer clear of Oedipus' interpretive morass but instead to see ourselves, who are his interpreters,
as perhaps even more deeply and ignorantly implicated in that
language than he is? To pursue such a course, which seeks not to
avert Oedipus' challenge but to meet it head-on in our own language and practice of interpretation, we must—like Oedipus—
proceed beyond the point where we simply explain how the play's
language lends itself to multiple meanings. We have to ask how the
mutual interferences between these different meanings, the displacing of commonplaces, might put our own practices of interpretation in question or reveal our own critical language as fraught
with overlooked ambiguities. * * * If the fate of Oedipus, the archetypal interpreter of signs, still has meaning for us as we are engaged
in the practical business of interpretation, this possibility cannot
be ignored without incurring serious risk. As the example with
which I began already indicated in part, this article will argue that
the best place to look for this point of contact between the language
of the *Oedipus Tyrannus* and the language of its interpreters lies
in its polysemous and disorienting vocabulary of place, space, and

movement as applied to the interpretive activity of Oedipus. Viewed from this perspective, I will argue that the language of the play invites us to face up to the inescapable and dangerous indeterminacy inherent in the position of the interpreter, who tries to occupy every possible place on the map but thereby risks being cast out of all of them, who tries to outmaneuver and outrun the riddle she seeks to solve, only to discover that she has thereby only outmaneuvered and outrun herself.

To develop this viewpoint on the play, however, only represents half the battle, since what good is an invitation to which nobody responds? I want to argue, furthermore, that we, too, as critics who dwell in the afterlife of Oedipus in more than one sense, are entrenched in the uneasy mixture of location and dislocation, hard certainty and wild indeterminacy, that marks the language of the play. We fail to take up its invitation, I believe, only because we have become too habituated to the words in which that invitation is addressed to us—words drawn from a very specific figurative vocabulary of place, space, and movement. * * *

* * *

If we ask what place Oedipus, that archetypal interpreter, occupies, we are also bound to ask what place we must occupy in order to understand him, in order to become his interpreters. * * * If the tragedy of Oedipus ultimately expresses a profound doubt about the interpreter's secure place in the order of meaning, then we must also finally ask: where does the play itself place the interpretive conversation about its meaning, or, really, any of our conversations about meaning? Where does this text make us stand, what place and perspective does it make us occupy, and what object does it make us take up, if not ourselves and our own processes of interpretation? * * * [T]he play is constructed so as to allow the audience the rare and troubling privilege of simultaneously assuming a human and a super-human perspective on the meaning of language, of perceiving—as we otherwise seldom can—that what appears true and just to the former appears as equivocal and erroneous to the latter. From this equivocation, no interpretive language is immune. This is why both location and dislocation, both vision and blindness, both articulate meaning and arbitary noise confront and interfere with one another constantly in the language of the *Oedipus Tyrannus* * * *. [W]e are destined to reproduce these interferences in our own interpretive conversation about the tragedy—or, indeed, in any interpretive conversation.

* * *

II

In its uneasiness surrounding the question of "where?," in its overlay and interplay of rival interpretive mappings, the *Oedipus Tyrannus* consistently links the indeterminacy of location to the extraordinary power of Oedipus as interpreter to *move*: to cross boundaries, take up new positions, and redefine perspectives. This condition of simultaneous escape and pursuit, arriving and departing, coming and going constitutes the native habitat of Oedipus' conspicuously rootless character, just as it does for the practicing interpreter. More than anything else, what is truly awesome and terrifying about Oedipus is just how much he can and does move across the literal and symbolic landscapes of the drama, how his points of arrival only coincide with new points of departure, how he comes to occupy every possible position on the board and none of them at the same time. Just as his ultimate arrival at truth unmasks his single-minded pursuit as wandering in oblivion, it condemns him outright to undertake the same wandering in full awareness for the rest of his days; the capture that should have triumphantly crowned the interpreter's pursuit of truth has only marked the distance from the truth he has reached in flight. The forms of literal and figurative mobility characteristic of Oedipus and, by analogy, decisive for the activity of interpretation itself I call the power of *kinesis* (* * * "motion"). As an aspect of the poetic language of the *Oedipus Tyrannus*, tracing the effects of kinesis helps us understand how indeterminacies of location and dislocation, place and displacement, come to govern the activity of interpretation. Our pursuit of meaning may in fact put us in flight from it; our arrival at the truth may in fact be a departure from it; we may be all too distantly abroad when we think we are at home; in seeking to assign everything to its proper place, we may be setting it in perpetual motion—these name just a few of the risks that the narrative of Oedipus marks out as conditions of the activity of interpretation. In this section of the [essay], I will investigate how the play defines Oedipus' hermeneutic perspective through the vocabulary of kinesis, and how kinesis introduces a stubborn indeterminacy into not only Oedipus' interpretation of his own career but also our interpretations of his tragedy.

If what is astonishing and frightening about Oedipus is his exceptional ability to move, this begs the simple question: what is he moving towards? At the beginning of the drama, a simple answer presents itself: he moves towards noise. In the initial encounter between interpreter and *interpretandum* captured in his opening speech, Oedipus describes in calm but searching tones the confusing disarray of sensations that confronts him upon entering (1–13):

"the city is as filled with the smoke of burnt offerings / as it is with both songs of prayer and groans of lamentation" (* * * 4–5). Swirling smoke, hopeful singing, desperate cries: the clear and the unclear, the articulate and the inarticulate mingle and interact in the mass of noise that confronts the interpreter and demands his response. The Chorus describes how the women of Thebes "cry out in response to each other for their miserable sufferings" (* * * 184) and how "the song of prayer rings out in concert with the groaning voice" (* * * 186), two figures that render the interaction of sounds within the noise in musical terms, as a kind of polyphonic singing. In its dense interweaving of sounds, the city itself now repeats in changed form that other interpretive enigma confronted by Oedipus not so long ago, the riddling music of the Sphinx, who is characterized throughout the play as a "cruel singer" (* * * 36), a "bitch rhapsode" (* * * 391) who recites "intricate, convoluted song" (* * * 130). Oedipus' first response to the confusion makes conspicuous both the autonomy of his understanding and the boldness of his approach—in interpretive as well as physical terms—by placing upon these the seal of his own name: "not judging it right to hear of these matters from others, I have come here myself—I who am called Oedipus, renowned among all men" (* * * 6–8). * * * Oedipus thus strongly binds his own name, which is heard here in the play for the first time, to his identity and characteristic outlook as a man who moves towards noise in order to hear and interpret it for himself. Just as he did with the riddle of the Sphinx, so now with the riddle of the plague he has voluntarily come forth in order to understand and overcome the disordered music that holds Thebes in its grip. The emphasis laid upon Oedipus' arrival by his self-nomination sounds out for the first time the restless, roving ubiquity, the eagerness to confront and inquire, and the courage to overcome every obstacle that distinguish his interpretive personality. But even in this brief dossier of character traits, the unmistakable mark of kinesis begins to reveal itself.

This exceptional power of movement stands in stark contrast to the group of suppliants he encounters, who seem almost rooted in their positions of desperation in front of the royal palace and at different points around Thebes * * *. The group of youths and old men who have been dispatched to seek Oedipus' help is even described by the priest as if they were flightless birds, the former being "not yet strong enough to take wing" (* * * 16–17) and the latter "weighed down with old age" (* * * 17). The same sense of the dead weight and immobility imposed by the sufferings of the plague takes on a particularly ominous color in the priest's comparison of the city to a ship beleaguered by a storm or a man drowning in the sea: "the city . . . already rocks back and forth violently, and can no longer lift up its head from the depths of the bloody surf" (* * * 22–24; cf. 101). Unlike Oedipus, the city does not freely and adroitly move itself; instead, it either remains motionless or is moved passively by destructive and still obscure forces outside its control. The series of figures that describe the helpless condition of Thebes in terms of being unable to rise, stand upright, or move freely culminates in the priest's emphatically repeated request to Oedipus to "set this city upright so that it cannot fall" (* * * 51; cf. 39, 46, 104). He adds force to this plea and, from our point of view, gives it a presciently ironic turn by reminding Oedipus of his previous triumph over the Sphinx (47–48) and declaring, "let us by no means remember your reign as men who stood upright at first only to fall flat later" (* * * 49–50).

Against the plague's overpowering noise and the dull paralysis of the Theban suppliants, Oedipus asserts his acute awareness of the situation: "you have not roused me awake, as if I were someone fast asleep" (* * * 65). He emphasizes his agile efforts, quite literally, to pursue every possible avenue toward discovering the plague's cause—"you should know that . . . I have walked on many pathways in the wanderings of thought" (* * * 66–67). Far from the drowning man or flightless bird of the priest's language, the efficient and insuperable Oedipus has already set his sense-making mind in motion to confront the crisis. Moreover, he has set others in motion toward this end, namely, his brother-in-law Creon, who opportunely returns from the consultation with the oracle at Delphi that Oedipus had commanded. Creon reports that the plague is a result of the pollution incurred by the city (96–98) in its failure to avenge the murder of Laius, the former king of Thebes, who was killed under mysterious circumstances while traveling back from Delphi (114–15). Immediately upon learning of the murder (105), Oedipus figures his own interpretive role in terms of a hunter reading the tracks of his quarry and following it to its hiding-place—that is, in a figure of active pursuit: "In what part of the country are they now? Where will this indiscernible track of ancient guilt be found?" (* * * 108–9; cf. 220–21). Creon's reply develops the same metaphor and expresses the heuristic principle upon which rest both the hunting-figure itself and the interpretive pursuit for which this figure stands: "[The oracle] was saying that they were in this country [i.e., the province of Thebes]. What is sought after can be captured, but what is neglected escapes" (* * * 110–11). Oedipus' active and agile intellect, already on the trail, is quick to extract from Creon all the information the latter recalls about the circumstances and aftermath of the crime (112–23). Borne along this path of evidence by his own interpretive momentum, Oedipus wonders aloud why the Thebans were not equally nimble in their own pursuit when the

murder came to light: "What kind of unfortunate obstacle * * *
hindered you [ειργε] from finding this out?" (* * * 128–29). Just as
he had done with the hunting-figure at 110–11, Creon again picks
up Oedipus' figure of an obstructed pathway in his understated and
ironic response: "The Sphinx had persuaded * * * us to defer these
obscure matters and attend to what was right under our noses
[* * * lit., "at our feet"]" (* * * 130–31). The obstruction posed by the
Sphinx, of course, was precisely what Oedipus was able to overcome through his own interpretive kinesis before he ascended the
throne of Thebes: his mobile power of sense-making is such that it
recognizes no obstacles and no limits.

Yet herein lies the problem Oedipus poses where his remarkable
freedom of movement is concerned. For it is precisely in the ambiguities surrounding Oedipus' vigorous and, indeed, admirable defiance of all limits that even this comparatively naïve reading of the
drama's opening must acknowledge the points of indeterminacy
that entangle him in the interpretive problem he seeks to overcome.
Ambiguities begin to surface once the language in which Oedipus
describes his own relentless interpretive pursuit, on the one hand,
and the language he applies to the murderer's transgressive flight,
on the other, begin ever so subtly to converge. Here I return to the
pair of passages with which I began this article and place them in a
new light. Oedipus' remarkably quick first conjecture in interpreting the information Creon gives him is to suspect a conspiracy in
Thebes to assassinate Laius. Nonetheless, and as I have already
pointed out, the poetic language Oedipus uses to describe the
crime as the bold transgression of a limit set on physical movement
necessarily implicates his own disregard for limits and defiance of
obstacles as a comparable transgression: "Unless some intrigue had
been worked with bribes from here in Thebes, how would the robber have proceeded [* * * lit., "walked"] to such a point of daring?
[* * * 124–25]. In his long speech to the assembled Theban elders
(216–75), this ambiguity emerges with even greater force when
Oedipus assures the citizens that he will apply all his resources in
pursuit of the killer: translated literally, he says that he "will arrive
at all points" or "show up everywhere" (* * * 265). Just as he unintentionally evokes his own crimes here, his language evinces a
similar ambiguity when he assures the suppliants that he "will leave
nothing untried" (* * * 145). To an audience already well aware of
the enormity of Oedipus' unconscious crimes, his diction would
recall an expression for criminal unscrupulousness used to great
effect elsewhere in Sophoclean tragedy: * * * "to stop at nothing,"
literally "to do everything," i.e., even things that are strictly forbidden (see Soph. *Ant.*, 74). Even at this early point in the drama,
these and other crucial ambiguities provide a clear index of the

indeterminacies that Oedipus' tireless kinesis introduces into the language of interpretation. The agile mobility so central to his method, and so incomparably valuable to both the king himself and his city, may make him indistinguishable from the criminal he is hunting down and even render him complicit in the latter's crimes. After all, both hunter and hunted in Oedipus' language are equally *transgressors* in the etymological sense of the term (*transgredior*): each of them boldly "walks across" boundaries that are set up to contain and control movement, or to distinguish one meaning of a word from another. Just as Oedipus does not know and cannot control the multiplying meanings of his own language, he likewise does not know and cannot fully control the kinesis of his interpreting mind either. Oedipus' risk lies in the fact that he can never be sure where interpretation will take him—nor what it will make him leave behind. In the last analysis, the interpreter can determine neither his point of departure nor his destination: his undertaking has as much to do with the truth he is attempting to escape as it does with the truth he pursues.

As we discover much later in the drama, Oedipus' career of constant, restless kinesis, which began even before his defeat of the Sphinx, provides a paradigmatic instance of how interpretation allows the interpreter both to pursue and to flee from truth by the same means. In the long monologue he delivers to Jocasta relating the story of how he came to Thebes and what happened during the journey (771–833), his language dramatizes his efforts to interpret the riddle of his own origins in terms of aggress and regress, pushing through and falling back—the very same terms he then applies to his murderous encounter with Laius in the Theban countryside. Oedipus relates how he grew up in Corinth and enjoyed a place of preeminence among the citizens there "before a chance event fell upon me" (* * * 776–77). * * * Oedipus * * * describes in terms of a physical attack the unnerving experience in which a drunken companion happened to accuse him of being a "fabricated" (* * * 780) son to Polybus, Oedipus' putative father. In language we already recognize from the plague-induced torpor of Thebes described by the priest, Oedipus tells how he was "heavily burdened" (* * * 781) by this accusation. He reacts to this potentially paralyzing blow, however, with aggression and a pursuit of his own: he can "scarcely hold himself back" (* * * 782) before "approaching" (* * * lit., "coming near to," 782) his parents to demand enlightenment. Polybus and Merope are subsequently enraged at "the one who shot forth this word" (* * * 784) * * *. Although Oedipus is temporarily satisfied with his parents' reaction, the thought continues to "irritate" him (* * * 786), not least of all because the rumor, like an enemy preparing a future ambush, "crept around a great deal in secret"

(* * * 786). His interpretive pursuit compels him to go to Delphi without his parents' knowledge ("I journeyed in secret," * * * 787) and ask Apollo's oracle about his parentage, whereupon the god abruptly repels his approach, "[sending] me away deprived of the answers for which I came" (* * * 788–89). Like the groans and prayers of Thebes Oedipus hears at the opening of the play, the drunkard's accusation is a source of interpretive "noise" that sets Oedipus in motion. Rather than finally solving the riddle of this accusation and, as it were, silencing its noise, Apollo redoubles its impact by forcing Oedipus to "listen" (* * * 794) to even more noise: the terrifying and confusing prophecies about the abominable crimes that still lie in his future (789–93). Although he continues on the same path away from Corinth and toward Thebes, Oedipus' former strategy of attack and pursuit now quite suddenly turns to one of retreat and flight. In order to avoid fulfilling the dreadful oracles he has heard, he resolves never to return home, orienting himself solely by his power to interpret his environment and move within it accordingly: "I fled * * * from the land of Corinth, judging its position from then on by the stars" (* * * 794–96). What began as pursuit continues as flight: his continuing effort to reach the truth about his parentage through interpretation now cannot be separated from his effort to evade the fulfillment of Apollo's oracles, which directly concern his relationship to his parents. Even before he begins the inquiry that drives the dramatic plot, Oedipus is both pursuer of, and fugitive from, himself.

We have seen how what I called Oedipus' virtuoso mobility, driven by his indefatigable will to interpret, does not exist in a vacuum but rather results from his no less extraordinary talent for offering and overcoming resistance, by either physical or intellectual means. Once he enters the vicinity of Thebes, however, he narrates how this talent was put to a very literal and, indeed, violent test. The circumstances of this test demonstrate how the same deliberate drive of interpretive pursuit that took Oedipus to Delphi has all too easily combined itself with the arbitrary drive of flight from Corinth (800–813):

* * *

When in my journeying * * * I was close to that intersection of three roads [which Jocasta has already mentioned as the scene of Laius' murder], there I encountered * * * a herald and a man mounted upon a horse-drawn carriage, just as you described; the leader and the old man himself tried to drive * * * me off the road by force. The one who was trying to turn me aside * * *, the charioteer, I struck out of anger; when the old man saw this, he kept a lookout as I was passing alongside * * * the

> carriage, and then came down hard * * * the crown of my head
> with his double goad. Yet he was paid back with interest: with
> a summary blow from the staff held in this very hand, he rolled
> * * * straight out of the carriage and flat on his back * * *. And
> then I killed them all.

The aggressive tonality of Oedipus' language in describing the
events that led to his departure from Corinth had remained merely
implicit and metaphorical. Now, however, this tonality reasserts
itself in the context of explicit and literal combat—the murder of
the man he later discovers to be his father, Laius. In the verb meaning "I met with, encountered" (* * * 804), the confrontation is represented as hostile even before it becomes hostile in fact. Once this
happens, the passage's verbs vividly capture the highly animated
and physical clash between the opponents: "drive hard" (* * * 805),
"turn aside" or "push out of the way" (* * * 806), "come down hard"
(* * * 809), "roll out flat on one's back" (* * * 811–12). Despite the
fact that it shares with the preceding narrative (771–97) a common
language derived from hostile encounter, the shift from figurative
to literal uses of the same language in this passage throws into
sharp relief the moral stakes of conflating pursuit with flight in the
way that Oedipus does and, indeed, in the way that interpretation
must. Since Oedipus never expresses any specific motivation on his
part to travel to Thebes that would justify particular haste or per-
sistence such as, for instance, he had for his journey to Delphi,
his aggression here seems arbitrary unless we view it both in the
context of the broader pattern of his character and in terms of
the activity of interpretation which, as I argue, the play explores
through its language. By his own admission, Thebes is simply a
place other than Corinth where, in the absence of his parents, he
believes he can safely evade the fulfillment of the Delphic oracle
(796–97)—a place where he can exist indefinitely in perpetual
flight. The term here translated as "journeying" (* * * walking, way-
faring, lit., "making one's way on the road"), in fact, conveys just
this tone of arbitrary perambulation and acquires an even more sin-
ister cast by recalling the Chorus' testimony that the regicide was
carried out by "highwaymen" (* * * 292) * * *. Indeed, Oedipus
never offers any reason external to the moment of confrontation
that would justify such a violent assertion of his own right-of-way
other than his implicit eagerness to flee Corinth—his desire, as
always, to stay in motion. While his assault of Laius and his retinue
escapes legal—and presumably moral—condemnation by virtue of
the fact that it would have been acquitted under contemporary
Athenian law as self-defense—the driver does, after all, provoke
him first (804–5)—the language of Oedipus' narrative indicates

that his primary motivation for going to such extremes was the fact that his victims simply refused to get out of his way. * * * When we compare the figurative aggression that appears in Oedipus' will to interpret after his departure from Corinth with the literal aggression that appears in the confrontation with Laius, we are brought up short by the fact that the cool reportage of Oedipus' narrative tone indicates that he quite literally never gave his actions a second thought: he never paused, never stopped moving long enough to make sense of them. Unlike the figurative aggression he suffers at the hands of the Corinthian drunkard, which becomes the occasion for a fairly ambitious hermeneutic expedition, Oedipus has remained completely unconcerned about the possible larger significance of his own literal aggression—he has never taken it as a point of departure for his interpretive perambulations. Just as Oedipus' interpretive pursuit was motivated by a will to approach and to know, this will becomes inseparably combined with a will to ignore and to evade: his mobility serves flight and pursuit in equal measure. * * * Much as we may be tempted to condemn Oedipus' act by applying our own somewhat more stringent moral standards, doing so would only represent yet another wishful effort to reassert our independence from the condition we share with his character: we would thereby seek to regain in moral superiority what he and we can never possess in interpretive clarity and foresight. The language of Oedipus' narrative brusquely demonstrates that our impassioned pursuit of meaning is at the same time and by the same token a headlong flight. Both the drive to interpret and the drive not to interpret are equally served by the ability to overcome resistance, to ignore whatever does not expedite one's progress, and, above all, to remain in continuous motion. * * *

III

Once we take a step back, however, and see how the turn of events in the investigation of Laius' murder has prompted Oedipus to deliver his narrative of pursuit and flight, it becomes clear that the primary significance of his anecdote lies in the interpretive "second thoughts" that he is finally forced to apply to that narrative and in the risks for his interpretive enterprise that those second thoughts now uncover. As we shall soon see, in order to proceed beyond the point he has reached, Oedipus' kinesis must now turn around, reflect upon itself, and reverse its route, making the object of his pursuit converge with that of his flight. Indeed, when we consider Oedipus' career as an interpreter in the broadest terms, we readily perceive that the meaning or structure of place in the *Oedipus Tyrannus* depends on a sequence of returns and recursions of this

kind, and that such changes lead us to reflect upon our own endlessly recursive efforts as readers to establish, as it were, the place
of place. At the very beginning of the play, as we have seen, the interpretive problem that Oedipus sets for himself lies in the enigma of
the plague. Following just such a recursive pattern, this figurative
riddle returns to and reiterates the literal riddle of the Sphinx under
an altered guise and demands a "solution" (* * * 306 * * *) perhaps
even more urgently. But in the course of Oedipus' headlong, kinetic
rush to reach such a solution, the riddle of the plague eventually
turns back its interpreter to reflect upon his own unforeseen place at
the very center of the first riddle as well as the utterly changed land-
scape of meaning he now confronts. The riddle of the plague, then,
retrospectively uncovers the intractable, or indeed, "incurable" (* * *
98) character of the Sphinx's riddle about man—because the second
riddle turns back not just upon the first riddle, but upon the solver
of riddles himself. In the language and action of the tragedy as a
whole, this same movement of *epistrophy* * * *—a turning-around to
reverse one's direction or to regard again, under an altered guise,
something that has passed from view—precipitates the crisis of place
as it appears in the *Oedipus Tyrannus*. Not just in spatial, but also
in temporal, political, and familial terms, this symptomatic turnaround offers perhaps the neatest summary metaphor for the hermeneutic procedure that occupies the center of the drama, which
hinges on reversal and inversion of every conceivable kind. As the
language of this essay itself constantly demonstrates, the reversing
move of epistrophy has become just as pervasive in the interpretive
language we apply to the play as it is in Oedipus' own dilemma: we
quickly discover that once we turn around to reconsider, we can never
stop turning.

In an effort to refute Teiresias' troubling prophecies about Oedipus' crimes, Jocasta has been relating how comparable prophecies
given to Laius—to the effect that he would be murdered by his own
son—were never fulfilled, since he was killed by highwaymen "at a
place where three roads meet" (* * * 716). She therefore advises
Oedipus to disregard Teiresias' statements, saying "These are the
sorts of things that prophetic statements set forth * * *—but you
should take no heed * * * whatsoever of these things" (* * * 723–24).
If we read Jocasta's idiom as figurative language, she is telling
Oedipus not only to disregard boundaries—something he has
already made a career of, in moral, geographical, and hermeneutic
terms—but also not to turn towards the interpretive statements
that have hampered the momentum of his inquiry the most. Nonetheless, her offhand mention of the place where Laius was killed
has, ironically and quite unforeseeably, delivered a shock to her
husband's momentum—it has compelled him to "epistrophize," to

turn around so as to confront in a new light the literal and figurative terrain he has passed over. The force of this shock has shifted a marginal and near-forgotten past experience to the very center of Oedipus' attention and anxiety, where its bare outlines have suddenly been filled with the horrendous possibilities of meaning and consequence that he dwells on after completing his narrative (813–33). The identification of the place where the crime was committed, furthermore, has made Oedipus' experience alter its place in the context of his interpretation, just as he has constantly altered his own place and his own context all along—by crossing boundaries, overcoming resistances, and solving riddles. The risks of Oedipus' incessant motion have started to come home to him, and they do so by enacting a dramatic reversal in his interpretive direction. We should not be surprised, then, that Oedipus chooses to express the immediate subjective effect of this shift as an intense vertigo that dislodges every object of sense and thought from its place and sets it in headlong motion: "while I was listening to you, my wife, what a wandering of the soul and a stirring-up of the mind just now took hold of me!" (* * * 726–27). The "wandering of the soul" that Oedipus experiences here directly recalls the "wanderings of thought" he undertook on behalf of the plague-ridden city (* * * 67) * * *. Whereas his previous wandering (67) had an active character, however, the same wandering now (726) assumes a passive character (* * * 726), almost as if Oedipus can no longer control his power to move himself or others towards the truth through interpretation—as if his kinesis itself had suddenly turned around to confront him as a powerful and autonomous being, a hostile *daimon* that has done the moving and controlling all along (q.v. 1299–1302). The sudden shift in viewpoint to passivity and trepidation, in fact, may even ironically recall the condition of the city at the play's opening as described by the priest of Zeus: inert, powerless, tossed to and fro like a drowning man (16–17, 22–24, 101). Appropriately, Jocasta's reaction to Oedipus' outburst again describes this abrupt and unsettling turnaround with an epistrophic figure. Her somewhat convoluted question translates literally as "having been turned around by what source of anxiety do you say this?" (* * * 728). The further progress of the inquiry after this point in the play repeats and reinforces, in varied forms, the epistrophic reversal he suffers here—the first crucial "turning point" in Oedipus' perambulations.

Nonetheless, the epistrophy that Oedipus experiences would only be of limited interest if it did not also implicate the experience of the reader and/or spectator in the risks it reveals—that is, if it did not directly pose a challenge to the direction and meaning of our own interpretive moves, our own process of kinesis in making sense of the play. This challenge only becomes clear, in fact, when we interpret epistrophically, re-opening the question of kinesis in the play's opening section from the vantage point of its crisis and discovering how the crisis of the turnaround is inscribed in Oedipus' interpretive mobility—and in our own—from its very beginnings. * * *

* * *

Oedipus quite literally identifies the inquiry into Laius' murder as an epistrophy at its very inception, but not without unwittingly putting his finger on the dangers that accompany his subsequent moves toward the truth. Once Creon admits that the Thebans had neglected the prosecution of Laius' murderer because of their more immediate concern with the Sphinx (130–31), Oedipus says he will open the inquiry afresh: "Then I will bring these same things [sc. the "obscure matters" Creon mentions at 131] to light all over again from the beginning * * *. Most worthily has Phoebus Apollo, and worthily have you insisted upon this regard [ἐπιστοφήν here = attention, respect, regard; lit., "turning-around, twisting"] for the deceased" (* * * 132–34). For Oedipus, on the one hand, this statement means that the kinesis of his inquiry, which proceeds toward the truth and the future deliverance of the city, paradoxically depends upon a recursive epistrophy that recedes ever more deeply into the obscure distances of the past. Hermeneutic progress and regress can no longer be distinguished in this circular path, forged equally of kinesis and epistrophy.

From this viewpoint, Oedipus' travels unfold as if he keeps one foot in continuous motion and the other firmly fixed: the end and the beginning of the interpreter's path coincide, with horrible precision. For the spectator/reader of the play, on the other hand, this same statement proves to be prophetic insofar as we try to approach, understand, and overcome Oedipus himself through our own interpretive moves, and incur the same risks along the way. We only seem to arrive at the ultimate meaning of Oedipus' fate when, like him, we remain in continuous motion: beginning from the beginning over and over again, constantly moving forward in false confidence and turning around again to reconsider in fear and doubt. In the end, though, Oedipus eludes every attempt to make sense of himself because he reveals the degree to which the language of the interpreter—the language we share with him, the language that by definition makes sense—is also unwittingly complicit in the unmaking of sense. When we attempt to apply normative language to Oedipus, when we try to respond adequately to the challenge he poses, we find that such an attempt produces multiple, fragmentary, and divergent evaluations of one and the same phenomenon. Like Oedipus'

voice, the voice of his interpreter—my voice, your voice—ultimately
contains a multitude of voices that arise in many places at once and
may not finally be reconciled with each other. Rather than affirming
the unity and coherence of their origin, they tear themselves apart
in headlong flight and infinite dispersal. Oedipus himself, blinded
and abject, puts it best: "Alas, alas, how miserable I am, where on
earth am I being carried in my misery? Where is my voice being
swept away to, born on the wings of the air? O my spirit, how far
you sprang forth!" (* * * 1308–11).

TERESA M. DANZE

From The Tragedy of Pity in Sophocles'
Oedipus Tyrannus†

The moment at which Oedipus discovers his true identity in Sophocles' *Oedipus Tyrannus* receives Aristotle's admiration as the finest
example of self-recognition in Greek tragedy. The self-recognition
and reversal of fortune coalesce in one simultaneous act, yielding
from the audience either pity or fear, the primary effects of the
mimetic art of tragedy. Pity in this instance is not simply an expected
reaction from the audience, however. It plays a significant role in
both the exposition of the past and the tense moment of dramatic
action in the present. Pity compelled the Theban Herdsman to pass
the infant Oedipus on to the Corinthian Messenger, ensuring
Oedipus' survival and his subsequent downfall (1175–82):

* * *

OED: The wretched woman who bore me [ordered me
        destroyed]?
TH: Yes, it was out of fear of evil prophecies.
OED: What sort?
TH: That he would kill his father was the prophecy.
OED: Why then did you release him to this old man here?
TH: Out of a deep feeling of pity, master, thinking he would
        take it to another country, where he was from; but he
        saved [you] for the greatest evil. For if you are the same
        man whom he says you are, know that you have been
        born ill-fated.
OED: Oh! Oh! Everything has come out clear.

† From *American Journal of Philology* 137 (2017): 565–99. © 2016 by Johns Hopkins University Press. Reprinted by permission of Johns Hopkins University Press. The author's
notes have been omitted.

Surely the innovations in and around the recognition scene should give us pause: Sophocles replaces a critical moment in the traditional tale—the random discovery of the infant by a member of Polybus' household—with an intended transfer motivated by the emotion of a Theban Herdsman. Deep pity is the reason that Oedipus survived and the final link in the mystery of his past, a factor not repeated in other extant accounts of the myth. Ironically, a similar kind of pity is also the primary emotion motivating the play's protagonist from the beginning: Oedipus' deep pity (* * * 13) for plagued Thebes sets him on the quest for a cure that leads to his own demise. Thus the pity that once saved Oedipus' life and ensured his horrific fate is the very emotion we witness onstage that compels him to save his people now. While Aristotle identifies the affective poignancy of this scene, pity plays a larger role here than simply fulfilling the audience's tragic desires: it underscores the very rise and fall of Oedipus himself in Sophocles' tragedy.

* * *

My argument about pity in the *Oedipus Tyrannus* is divided into three parts. In section 1, expressions of * * * pity in the first half of the play—limited to Oedipus alone—establish the centrality of this emotion to his character. Oedipus' pity reflects a largely empathetic understanding of pity displayed through gestures of identification in which he envisions himself to be a father and the people understand him as a savior. In section 2, I argue that Sophocles turns this dynamic on its head by utilizing similar language to identify the pity of the Corinthian Messenger and the Theban Herdsman for the infant Oedipus, reducing the city's tyrant to a suppliant child before self-styled fathers. In doing so, Sophocles brings both the internal and offstage audience to a disturbing and unexpected climax in which Oedipus' moment of recognition and reversal reveals that pity is itself tragic in this Sophoclean world. In section 3, I argue that Oedipus passes on not only his political and paternal authority to Creon in the final speeches of the play but also the power and responsibility of the emotion of pity. Creon, however, receives this symbolic gesture ambiguously, leaving the status of pity uncertain at the final exit.

Before continuing, a brief word should be said about the terminology used to refer to * * * the emotional process of pity discussed in this [essay]. Classicists writing about *oiktos* and *eleos* today use "pity" as a definition of these terms and I do not deviate from this standard. Though pity can connote superiority, pity is understood here to be an all-encompassing translation of *oiktos*, defined as a feeling of pain or sorrow at the knowledge of another person's

suffering. In modern parlance, this definition is commonly understood as "sympathy" or "compassion." In Sophocles, however, *oiktos*
appears to be used in ways that reflect not only a different intensity
of emotion * * * but also two slightly different emotional processes,
i.e., sympathy and empathy. The term "empathy" has only been in
circulation since the nineteenth century and its definition is not at
all static in the fields of philosophy and psychology but the process
of this type of emotional experience is clearly separate from that of
sympathy if understood in the following way: the spectator who
empathizes attempts to feel the same emotion as the object of his
emotion through an imaginative leap into the victim's situation
whereas the one who feels sympathy experiences a removed, unique
sorrow or pain at the misfortune of the other that does not attempt
to resemble the emotions of the object. Because of the nuances in
the definition and use of *oiktos* that the two defined ideas above
identify, i.e. sympathy and empathy, I will use them to distinguish
the way in which the emotional undertone of an exchange or speech
should be understood or the way in which the Greek could be
translated.

Oedipus: A Man Driven by Pity

Many would agree that Oedipus is especially prone to violent fits of
anger. His own account of the murder of Laius states that he retali-
ated "out of anger" (807), and his treatment of Creon and Tiresias
is filled with outbursts understood as wrathful (337–38, 339, 344,
364, 405, 523–24, 673–75). * * * The moments of anger and violence in the play enforce the idea that he must have inherited these
traits from his biological father, Laius, who himself had violent ten-
dencies: e.g., striking unnecessarily at the crossroads, piercing the
ankles of an infant. Anger is not the only emotion that dominates
Sophocles' version of Oedipus, however. In fact, the prologue and
first episode of *Oedipus Tyrannus* depict a leader whose capacity for
pity underlines his political rhetoric and informs his decisions on
behalf of the Theban populace.

Prior to any word spoken onstage, Sophocles conditions the
viewer to anticipate potential appeals to and expressions of pity by
opening with the only scene of its kind in Sophoclean drama: a
silent procession of the Priest of Zeus, select youths, and the elderly
bearing the accoutrements of supplication who then rest at the
altars flanking the *skene* in a suppliant posture. Such ritually
charged activity would lead one to expect suppliants, who articulate both their suffering and their hope for relief, to appear before a
personage with the authority to respond to their needs. Pity is often
the emotional support not only for these appeals but also of the

affirmative responses. Unlike most suppliant displays in tragedy and in Athens where suppliants present themselves before a political body, supplication takes place before the palace of a single individual, intended for his eyes and ears alone. The Priest has arrived with a set of suppliants different from the rest of the group (18–19) who are similarly wreathed at the altars in the marketplace. Indeed, the very innocence and vulnerability of this group has the greatest chance of manipulating the emotions of the viewer as is the case in the Athenian law courts, for example, where children of the convicted are often used to encourage leniency or acquittal. Sophocles thus prepares his audience—internal and offstage—for a familiar scene of *pathos* [suffering] through the silent staging of vulnerable individuals who need say nothing to achieve a pitiful reaction. Oedipus knows why they suffer, of course; he has already sent Creon to Delphi to find answers to the city's troubles. Yet he enters the stage and asks the children alone why they assemble, finally addressing the Priest as a spokesman for the youth. Before anyone has an opportunity to respond, Oedipus assures that he will offer his help out of deep pity (1–13):

* * *

OED: [O] children, young charge of ancient Cadmus,
What in the world compels you to sit before me in
    supplication
with suppliant boughs, wreathed in garlands?
The city is full of incense and at the same time
full of paeans and lamentations:
I have come myself, children, thinking it unjust
to hear these things from other messengers,
I, famous to all, called Oedipus.
But, old man, tell me, since you are fit to
Speak on behalf of these here, for what reason you sit here,
    out of
fear or affection? Know that I would wish to give you every
    sort of aid I can:
for I would be hard of heart if I did not deeply pity
such a show of supplication.

An audience accustomed to suppliant dramas could anticipate the type of dialogue, emotions, and actions the suppliants' entrance affords. Sophocles gives us an opening speech that meets those expectations but before the nature of the suffering is made clear or the reciprocal advantages they bring. Yet the sight of those customarily most vulnerable invigorates Oedipus' initial expression of pity, not an explanation of undeserved misfortunes, immediately marking

Oedipus' susceptibility to pitiful displays and his presumptuous nature. He pities them and promises aid before knowing what he has committed himself to, without formal deliberation or judgment.

Moreover, Oedipus is not simply a detached king, poised to provide formal aid to his citizens given a reasonable request, but an affected father, moved to action by the silent spectacle of his "children." The strikingly familial language Oedipus uses to address the group presupposes his authority and is as much paternal as it is political. By addressing only the most vulnerable members of the group twice in a short number of lines * * * (1, 6) * * * and labeling the group in terms of one element of it rather than the group of suppliants as a whole, Sophocles immediately establishes Oedipus' relationship to the Cadmeans as paternal. A sense of justice and curiosity at the suppliant activity before his doors may compel him to emerge, but his pity for their suppliant efforts moves him to anticipate the suppliants' appeal. His commitment of aid is rooted in * * * a deep feeling of pity without which he would not be a benevolent *tyrannus* but one that is "hard-hearted" or "unfeeling" (12).

The Priest in turn sees Oedipus as a savior: "this land now calls you savior * * * on account of your former zeal" (48). Oedipus' past success at saving the city from a scourge encourages the Theban suppliants to make another explicit appeal for relief. Although the Priest refuses to equate Oedipus with a god (31–32), he refers to him as the best of men (46) and one with privileged access to divine powers (38–39) using language fit for the divine: *sōtēr* ["savior"] is later used to describe Apollo and his prophecies (81, 150). This characterization reverberates in Oedipus' response addressed again to the children. This paternal and salvific positioning, however, now extends beyond their group to the city as a whole in a magnanimous expression of empathy (58–69):

* * *

> O pitiful children, known and not unknown to me
> are the reasons for which you have come, for I know
> well that you are all sick: and though being sick,
> there is no one among you who is equally sick as I.
> For your pain comes on each of you for yourself
> alone and for no one else, but my
> soul laments the city, myself and you altogether.
> Thus, you do not awaken me as if I were lying down in sleep
> but know that I have wept many tears indeed,
> and traveled many roads in wanderings of thought.
> But after proper consideration, the lone cure which I found
> I have applied.

Oedipus reiterates his feeling of pity for the group but now reveals that this is not the first time. He has wept and lamented because of the pain caused by the sickness that engulfs even him. Oedipus is not a victim of the plague, however, but of his emotions. Oedipus likens his feelings of *oiktos* to an illness that he understands to be the pain of every diseased citizen. This imaginative leap conflates the fatal illness that has devastated the city with the pain (* * * 62) which Oedipus feels for everyone who suffers from their own illness or the illness of a [friend or family member]. * * * Moreover, although he himself is not physically ill, Oedipus acknowledges his empathy by using the same term to describe the state of the city—*nosountes* (60)—as he uses to describe himself—*nosei* (61). This imagined illness that Oedipus claims to share with the Thebans through shared language bridges the gap between his wisdom, power, and health and that of the nameless, individual Theban who suffers physically and emotionally (21–30). The medical language not only portrays Oedipus as the ultimate empathizer of the plagued city in his superhuman ability to lament the pain of every citizen but also shows him to be its ideal healer, for he has found the only cure available and applied it, namely, by seeking the advice of the healing god, Apollo (68–69). In doing so, Oedipus elevates himself to the role of divine healer while simultaneously reconnecting with the citizen populace as a shared victim of ravaging Apollo. For the cure itself reveals Oedipus' own weakness—his inability to solve the problem despite his intense emotional experience and rational efforts (66–67). Through his empathy, Oedipus then perfectly embodies the Priest's image of a Theban savior—god-like but human. This type of gesturing continues in the following scene.

Oedipus abides by his promise to give aid to the city and to do as Apollo sees fit by vowing to root out Laius' killer. It is not enough for him to make a decree, however. Instead Oedipus imagines that he is an ally of Laius and Apollo, resolving to act as if the crime were committed against himself (132–41, 244–45):

* * *

OED: Well, starting anew, once again I will shed light.
       For Phoebus is right and you are right
       to put forth such attention on behalf of the dead
       so that justly you will see me also as an ally,
       defending this land and the god at the same time.
       For not on behalf of a distant relative
       but on behalf of myself will I scatter this defilement.
       For whoever was the killer of this man, he may
       wish to take vengeance on me with the selfsame hand
       so that in providing aid for this man [Laius], I am thus

helping myself . . .
In such a way I will then act as an ally to the god
and to the man who died.

Just as he empathized with the city by connecting its disease with
his own emotional distress, so Oedipus takes on the misfortune of
Laius and the responsibility of revenge through another gesture of
identification, vowing to end the pollution and face the vengeful
violence that Laius experienced if necessary. Conceiving of himself
as an allied warrior to Laius and Apollo (* * * 136, 244–45), Oedipus imagines his purpose to be similar to that of men on the battle-
field. The military analogy here recalls instances of alliances built
upon *oiktos* found in epic. * * * In pity for the citizens' loss, Oedipus
becomes indignant, turning his attention to tracking down Laius'
killer and enacting divine justice. Yet Oedipus goes a step further
by acting on his own behalf as well, taking the death of Laius as a
personal attack to be resolved by himself alone (138). When Oedipus enters the stage again with an official decree against Laius'
killer, Oedipus vows to be an ally to the god and to the man who
died (244–45) since he shares those things that Laius once held—
the throne, his wife, even children had Laius sired any. Indeed,
Oedipus promises to act as if Laius were his own father (258–68).
Sophocles provokes the audience with the protagonist's ignorance
of his own truthfulness but also demonstrates how Oedipus connects with the world he inhabits. Oedipus persistently uses pity to
reconcile his foreignness with his position, bearing the suffering of
others by himself alone.

The final expression of pity from Oedipus prior to his self-discovery
appears shortly before the play shifts from a search for the killer to
Oedipus' search for his own identity. Tiresias has revealed that
Oedipus is the source of the city's miasma but Oedipus refuses to
believe it. Instead, he accuses Tiresias and Creon of conspiring
against him for the sake of power and vows to punish Creon with
death or exile (623, 639–41). The Chorus finally intervenes, begging Oedipus to save the city from further strife by dropping the
charges against Creon. Oedipus concedes out of pity (669–72):

* * *

OED: Let him go then, even if it is necessary that I altogether
perish
or that I be driven from this land by force, dishonored.
For I have pity for your pitiful words, not those of
this man [Creon]: he, wherever he is, will be loathed.

Once again, Sophocles' Oedipus expresses pity for suppliants, com-
prised now of a Chorus of Theban elders speaking on behalf of the city.

The effect on the narrative, however, is not to motivate or explain a positive action but to prevent Oedipus from continuing to accuse Creon of conspiracy. This conflict and Oedipus' anger in particular threaten to derail the cohesive and constructive aims of the prologue. The rekindling of Oedipus' pity for the city resolves the potential debilitation of the myth and returns the focus of the drama to the pursuit of Laius' possible killer, i.e. Oedipus himself. Without the plea from the Chorus and the pitiful response from Oedipus, Creon is sent into exile and Oedipus wrongly affirmed. Here the play would end or the narrative would take a highly unusual turn. Instead, Oedipus' pity of the Chorus saves Creon from death or exile and the city from another conflict (660–72). Moreover, it brings the play back in line with its forward trajectory towards the source of the miasma and in doing so shifts the narrative focus away from Oedipus as inquisitor to Oedipus as the subject of inquiry and potential object of pity.

With the above analysis I hope to have illuminated the Sopho-clean vision of pity found at the start of the drama to be paternal and salvific, expressed for suppliants and those innocent of their misfortune. Pursuit of justice driven by a profound understanding of *oiktos* for suffering Thebes motivates Sophocles' eponymous protagonist to the extent that when his pity is lost for anger, the action comes to a standstill and the suspense builds as the narrative threatens to become unhinged as well. Pity preserves the mytho-logical integrity of the drama. More importantly, the specific brand of pity portrayed is deeply empathetic and imaginative, reserved for those who suffer innocently or speak on their behalf, explicitly expressed only by Oedipus in the first half of the play. Although Oedipus proves to be hasty and short-tempered, Sophocles juxta-poses Oedipus' pity in the first 100 lines with his role as a self-proclaimed, affectionate father revered by the city for his god-like ability to save them at the height of their suffering. The conjunc-tion of pity, paternity, and deliverance does not continue to be asso-ciated with the singular figure of Oedipus, however. Instead, these elements unexpectedly and ironically come to define the marginal characters of the drama as the play reaches its climactic revelation and reversal.

The Power of Pity Beyond Status

As established in the first half of the play, the plagued city is an object of pity, an emotion articulated through filial terminology and intense empathetic identification by the city's rightful heir, Oedipus. His intention to save the city and end its suffering, sus-tained by his expressions of deep pity, maintains the course of the narrative even though it means subjecting himself to intense scrutiny. Bringing the past to trial, however, shifts the dramatic focus from the city to Oedipus and with him the focus of suffering and pity. Sophocles manages this turn in part through expressions of pity, past and present, that utilize the paternal and salvific language found in the first part of the drama. These expressions no longer issue from the father and savior of Thebes but rather from the mouths of slaves who attempt to familiarize relationships otherwise greatly divided and to explain their motivations for decisive actions through *oiktos*. Consequently, Sophocles highlights the power that pity can have to eclipse the status of those who pity and the fortune of those who are pitied as well as the illusory nature of such authority.

With the exit of Creon, the attention of the drama turns to the test of prophecies based on experience. Iocasta is convinced that the circumstances of Laius' death proved oracles untrue; Oedipus remains unsure considering his own (presumed) parents still breathe. The Corinthian Messenger, however, proves them both wrong, beginning with a gesture of pity. The Messenger enters excitedly with the news that Oedipus' father, Polybus, is dead and Oedipus is now to be established as the sovereign of Corinth (934, 936–37, 939–40). When Oedipus counters with a vow to never travel where his parents are because of the prophecy that he will kill his father and marry his mother, the Messenger replies, "O child * * *, it's thoroughly clear that you do not know what you are doing" (1008). The Messenger obliquely claims that Oedipus lacks essential facts about his life, and Oedipus' response—that the Messenger educate him in the truth (* * * 1009)—marks the beginning of his openness to learn who he is. In these two lines we witness a shift in authority based on knowledge at the same time as we witness an alteration in the Messenger's emotional tenor. * * *

* * * [B]ecause pity has been reserved for children, the Messenger's reference to Oedipus as a child recalls the paternal connection to suppliants established in Oedipus' own expressions of pity in the prologue. Indeed, this phrasing relocates the position of authority to the one who speaks the line, the Messenger, when he reveals that he harbors an important piece of information. Recall that in his pity Oedipus considers himself the father of Thebes, now present to save the city from its maladies. This dynamic continues now in reverse by the manner in which the Messenger addresses Oedipus—*pai* ["child"]. * * * [I]n the *Oedipus*, children serve the special function of representing the suffering of the innocent city, the entire offspring of Cadmus, for which Oedipus has shown an intensity of feeling. To label Oedipus as a child prepares the audience to see him in the same light—as a suffering offspring in

Thebes, someone he truly though unwittingly is. This exposes the characters to a new configuration of roles that reflects authoritative actions in the past. Through this simple expression the Messenger transforms himself figuratively from a common messenger to a wise father. Tutors and nurses often act in place of and on behalf of a father and the household's interests, but the Messenger's connection with Polybus, not Laius, instantiates the significance of adoptive paternal authority in the life of Oedipus. Moreover, within the context of the narrative itself, the conjunction of pity and paternal authority had, to this point, been located in the figure of Oedipus. Now they point to the role of Polybus' Messenger.

As the exchange between the Messenger and Oedipus progresses, this dynamic of the wise father pitying the ignorant son becomes ever stronger. Oedipus refers to him as an old man in quick succession (* * * 1009; * * * 1013), labels that in themselves show respect (recall that Oedipus refers to the priest of Zeus as *geraie* ["old man" or "sir"] in line 9). It is the Messenger, however, who most clearly begins to identify his role as father and savior when he compares himself to Polybus and explains his part in Oedipus' infancy (1017–20):

* * *

OED: What are you saying? For did not Polybus sire me?
CM: No more than this man here [i.e., himself, the
       Messenger] but equal.
OED: And how can my father be equal to one who means
       nothing?
CM: Well neither that man or I gave you birth.

The Messenger considers himself equal to Polybus insofar as neither of them are related to Oedipus by blood. In effect, he wipes the slate of parentage clean and goes so far as to equate himself with Polybus in terms of their relationship to Oedipus. Neither man can claim a blood relationship and thus both have a potential claim to paternal authority. This alteration in relationship persists in the expository dialogue that follows in which the Messenger slowly reveals that Oedipus was adopted by Polybus and Merope (1029–32):

* * *

OED: Were you then a shepherd wandering in hired service?
CM: Yes but to *you*, child, was I a savior at that time.
OED: What pain was I suffering when you took me in
       your hands?
CM: Your ankles would bear witness to your pains.

The Messenger, bypassing Oedipus' attention to his low status (1029), instead proudly articulates his part in the adoption through more pointed paternal language (* * * 1030), seen before in Oedipus' expressions of pity for the Theban children (1, 6). The Messenger's designation of himself as a savior (* * * 1030), also recalls the earlier references to saviors in the play, namely, Oedipus, Apollo, and Teiresias (304). This compels the viewer to compare the Messenger in a previous time with the current vision of a savior in the play as the one upon whom the hopes for a cure to the plague lie (the Messenger and Herdsman together will in fact provide a "cure" with their knowledge of the past). Up to this point, Oedipus has used this language to refer to Apollo and Teiresias after being labeled a savior himself. Unlike the other "saviors" in the first portion of the play, however, Oedipus was the only one to explicitly verbalize the emotion of pity as well. Now the Corinthian Messenger, who has demonstrated his capacity for pity as shown above, speaks the figurative language that had been reserved for Oedipus. The motivations of the original moment of saving are not made explicitly clear in the language of the Messenger—obsequiousness seems to color his every word—but in the context of the saving father figure in Oedipus and the previous uses of affectionate address, the ambiguity presents the Messenger as a possible agent of pity. This association becomes more likely, at least in the eyes of Sophocles' Oedipus, with his responding question in which Oedipus assumes that he was suffering in some way if he was the object of rescue (1031). The presumption is that one can only be construed as a savior if he acts on behalf of another who suffers (1031–32). It is important to note that the pierced ankles are another Sophoclean innovation to the myth. Given that the known tradition of Oedipus' infancy only involved abandonment and a chance discovery, the need for a compelling reason to incite pity beyond abandonment—and to evoke pity from the audience as well—may have encouraged this addition to the myth apart from the etiological explanation of his name.

Sophocles marks his drama with another innovation that does not continue on in extant literature yet has great effect on the dramatic movement of the tragedy and pity's role within it. Conveying an intense, even sorrowful, feeling of pity * * * acts as both the final example of reversal and the catalyst for Oedipus' horrific self-recognition. In the prevailing myth of Oedipus' survival, the Corinthian Messenger finds the infant Oedipus by chance. This is compatible with the initial story presented by the Messenger (1025–26):

* * *

OED: Did you buy me or did you happen upon me and hand me over to [him]?
CM: I found you in the wooded hills of Cithaeron.

The audience expects to hear the account that Sophocles first presents here. Further inquiry about the name of Oedipus pushes the Messenger to reveal a new element to the story, however, that rejects the accepted tradition. Oedipus notes the inconsistency in the Messenger's account (1037–41):

* * *

OED: By the gods, did my mother or father [name me]? Tell me.
CM: I don't know; the one who handed you over knows this better than me.
OED: So you mean you took me from someone else and didn't *happen upon* [me] yourself?
CM: I did not; rather, another shepherd handed you over to me.
OED: Who is this man? Do you know how to tell this in truth?

This slight alteration in the myth should catch our attention as much as it does Oedipus. Having acknowledged the given tradition of the myth, Sophocles heightens suspense by introducing a new character who participates in a hand-off of the infant. Sophocles marks his change through Oedipus' need for clarification, repeating the prior words of the Messenger and negating them * * *. This mysterious man, responsible for knowing his name and origins, we discover, is none other than the Theban Herdsman whom Oedipus has already called upon for his witness to Laius' murder.

When Aristotle speaks of the Messenger in his *Poetics*, he observes that the Messenger brings a change of situation by identifying who Oedipus is (Arist. *Poet.* 1452a22–26). Yet it is the Herdsman who gives the final and critical points of information. Introducing the Herdsman secures Oedipus' identity beyond a doubt as well as solidifies the role of pity in Oedipus' survival and the Sophoclean vision of the myth. The reluctance of the Herdsman to reveal the reasons and episodes leading to the transfer shapes the movement of the dialogue that ensues, with the revelation of Oedipus' identity taking more than 100 lines to achieve. But Oedipus' discovery of his mother's identity and consequently his own (1175) is not what brings him to his moment of *peripeteia* and *anagnorisis*. Rather, his discovery of why it happened brings the dialogue to its critical point (1175–82):

* * *

OED: The wretched woman who bore me [ordered me destroyed]?
TH: Yes, it was out of fear of evil prophecies.

OED: What sort?

TH: That he would kill his father was the prophecy.

OED: How then did you release him to this old man here?

TH: Out of pity for it, master, thinking he would take it to
another country, where he was from; but he saved
[you] for the greatest evil. For if you are the same
man whom he says you are, know that you have been
born ill-fated.

OED: [O! O!] Everything has come out clear.

The original purpose of the Herdsman's testimony—to identify
who killed Laius at the crossroads—has been completely forgotten.
It is more important to the Sophoclean agenda to know how Oedipus survived, or rather, what force of nature or circumstance
allowed him to live. It is not by fortune or for profit—both possibilities had been rejected already—but rather through pity. For Sophocles, a random moment of discovery did not play the critical role
in Oedipus' survival. A nameless household slave-turned-shepherd
facilitates the survival and downfall of the protagonist because he
once felt pity for him. The cooperation between the shepherds
shows a series of actions performed out of pity, conceived of as saving and paternal. Not only has Oedipus suffered a complete reversal of fortune and self-recognition but the figurative power of father
and savior now tumbles as well in the revelation of the Herdsman's
pity. The Messenger and, by extension, the Herdsman assumed the
magnanimous roles of father and savior for the innocent child.
While the Herdsman attempts to foist the blame for saving Oedipus
onto the Messenger (* * * 1180), the ambiguity of Oedipus' curse
* * * implicates them both: "Curse whoever it was that released me
from the savage fetters . . . and rescued and saved * * * me from
death doing me no favor" (1349–51).

The verbalized emotion that drove Oedipus to the stage, support-
ing his visions of paternity and saving healer, now sends him away
from it, as helpless as he was in his infancy. Oedipus' statement
that all has become clear identifies the error contained within his
sarcastic remark that he could not possibly be ignorant of something that someone else knows (396), but it also acknowledges that
he is not the only one who can feel pity. He once envisioned that
everyone feels pain only for themselves while he alone feels the
pain of everyone who suffers. The Herdsman's confession, however,
reveals to Oedipus that he is not the only one capable of empathy,
to his detriment. For the audience, this final piece of information
would have been equally new. It is not hard to believe that the surprise of such an irony would have been felt in the audience at the
same time that it was presented to Oedipus' surprise onstage, producing the [surprise or wonder] at an unexpected but consequential

occurrence that Aristotle so highly values in tragic plots (Arist. *Poet.* 1452a1–10). While Oedipus' recognition of himself and final reversal of fortune was a revelation reserved for his character alone, the motivation for the action—a factor that preoccupies Oedipus in lines 1025 and 1040—is a moment of revelation for all, audience and Oedipus combined.

Sophocles does offer his audience at least two potential ways to interpret such a moment through references to pity and pitilessness in the drama. These also suggest that the tragedy of Oedipus as Sophocles conceives of it rests partly on the broader implications of pity as an imagined disease and as Sophocles' contemporary Herodotus presents the particular version of the emotion expressed by Oedipus from the start. Oedipus' desire to achieve success alone by insisting that he carried the weight of the city's suffering himself might have been noble but, as the Chorus suggests * * *, his *oiktos* was also perilous in its implications. In this ode, the Chorus of Theban elders provides a concrete, physical connection between pity and disease that contrasts with the more figurative, empathetic expressions of Oedipus' remarks in the prologue. They repeat the Priest's impression of the blight affecting Thebes, focusing on the death of offspring that has been the result of the plague. Pity, or rather pitilessness, defines the relationship between the citizens and their dead (179–81):

* * *

CH: Countless are destroyed and with them the city:
      Pitiless, the offspring lie on the ground
      Bringing death, unpitied.

According to the words of the Chorus, the offspring bring death through contagion as they lie on the ground, pitiless and unpitied. They are "pitiless" (* * * 180) in their participation in the plague, spreading illness as they lie unburied. They are left "unpitied" (* * * 181) by their families who presumably fear they will acquire the disease by performing traditional funeral rites. Contagion by the handling of the diseased was a phenomenon acknowledged by Thucydides and undoubtedly within the realm of experience for a large portion of the Athenian audience who had recently witnessed possibly two plagues by the spring of this performance. The antistrophe continues with the image of suppliant wives and mothers groaning at their losses and singing hymns to Apollo; the Chorus cries out for protection from Apollo as if echoing their words (183– 89). This sad image of the city's offspring lamented by their families yet left alone in their death, surrounded by terms of pitilessness exposes the tragedy of pity itself in Thebes: the one who buries the dead risks acquiring the disease, making pitiful gestures a death sentence. This conceptualization of pitilessness and its resulting comment on pity places a grim shadow on the profuse expressions of *oiktos* demonstrated in the play. On the one hand, Oedipus has answered the pleas of a diseased city in which *oiktos* is necessary for survival. Yet, pity for the victims of the plague comes at a price securing Oedipus' own misfortune. By fashioning Oedipus as the father of Thebes who sympathizes with the Theban suppliants through terms of illness and who vows to be Laius' ally as if the crime were committed against himself, Sophocles' protagonist extends his pity to the living and the dead, the nameless and the famed, but he himself risks becoming a victim of the disease by involving himself in the cure. Pity then seems to be both the salve and the sword for Thebes. The perpetuation of life and death in the city depends upon actions rooted in *oiktos* that subsequently turn in on themselves for the one who pities becomes, in time, an object of pity. Oedipus' pity for the diseased city was doomed from the start given the vision of the Chorus, but without this emotion, Oedipus does not save Thebes.

* * *

For the *Oedipus Tyrannus*, [a] pessimistic vision of pity is not one element among many in the narrative of a life but a part of a thematic thread that defines the protagonist and structures the tragedy onstage. The Herdsman's pity recalls the former confidence, authority, and generosity of the king with which the play began and compels the viewer and Oedipus himself to see not only the great irony in his downfall but also the irony and ultimate failure of pity itself to legitimate the authority of the one who acts upon such a powerful emotion. Instead of abandoning Oedipus for death, following his slavish duties, the Herdsman assumed control over the life of his king's son, imagining himself into a role with such authority, the role of a parent. For both a household slave who pities a cursed and royal infant and an incestuous murderer pitying a dying city, the emotion of pity has allowed them to imagine themselves into positions of power over suffering individuals whom they could not ultimately save without destroying themselves. The pity expressed by the Herdsman and Oedipus suggests that what has been imagined throughout the drama up to this point as an emotion with hopeful and salvific results has actually ensured suffering and a complete reversal of fortune for the play's greatest advocate of pity.

Passing on a Legacy

In the final scenes of many Athenian tragedies, the doors of the
skene will be thrust open and the body of a deceased character will
roll upon the stage to the horror, pity, or satisfaction of the onstage
audience. In the *Oedipus Tyrannus*, however, the Second Messenger prepares the Chorus not for the body of Iocasta, the victim of
suicide, but the spectacle of the self-blinded and bloody Oedipus.
"He needs the strength of some guide, for his sickness is greater
than he can bear" (1292–93), the Second Messenger warns the
Chorus. As the doors open, he continues, "[we] will see such a sight
as to make one who hates [Oedipus] feel pity for him" (1295–96).
Oedipus becomes the object of our pity and that of the Chorus, no
longer able to provide the aid that his pity had promised at the outset of the drama but again, as in his infancy, helpless and physically
suffering. After condemning the Herdsman for saving him from his
injuries (1349–55) and requesting exile or death for himself on
Mount Cithaeron (1409–15), Oedipus turns his thoughts to the
future of his daughters, "poor pitiable ones" (1462), and he seeks
pity for them, passing on his role as father and savior in the process
to Creon. Begging Creon to allow him to touch them since he
cannot see (1466–67, 1469–70), Oedipus becomes the pleading
suppliant and expects from Creon what was once expected of him
as Theban ruler—pity. Promptly hearing the two girls enter the
stage, Oedipus assumes that Creon has indeed taken pity on him
(1472–77):

* * *

    OED: By the gods, do I not hear my two beloved
          ones in tears, and has Creon taken pity on me
          and sent me my two most beloved children?
          Am I right?
    CR: You are. For I am the one who arranged this
          knowing the present pleasure which held you in the past.

The presence of children onstage who are the objects of Oedipus'
pity revives the same dynamic from the opening but under vastly
different circumstances. These children, too, are objects of pity but
the pitier no longer has the ability to act as father and savior without destroying the city. That responsibility is passed on to Creon.
At first glance, Creon appears to accept this responsibility and
respond out of pity. * * * Oedipus assigns pity to his deed and Creon
affirms it. But for Creon, pity could be mere rhetoric coloring a
strictly political or self-interested gesture. While Creon gains only
the accomplishment of his will, this is not an insignificant point
when considering that this is a man whose rule portends disaster

for Oedipus' offspring. The shift in political authority is clear—the Chorus has already assumed as much (1418), but the particular understanding of leadership that Oedipus possessed as *tyrannus* (i.e., as a paternal and salvific figure deeply moved to the point of empathetically suffering along with the city) is not clearly shared by Creon in his first opportunity to profess such emotion. Oedipus attributes pity to Creon who interprets this to mean that he is responsible for bringing the girls onstage as a way to move Oedipus to feel a level of happiness * * * rather than the grief that currently grips him. Although Creon affirms the pattern of pity that the play supports, namely, its association with actions intended to be rehabilitative, bringing the daughters onstage simply appears to be strategic manipulation so that Oedipus will cease from sorrow in the public sphere and quietly retreat within. Creon has already demanded that Oedipus return inside for fear of offending the gods with his cries (1426–29).

Furthermore, given Sophocles' depiction of Creon throughout the play, it is unlikely that Creon harbors the paternal and salvific compassion connected with leadership. When Creon is faced with the accusation of conspiracy, he coolly responds that this is impossible, for political rule is a source of fear for him (584–86) and undesirable for anyone who claims to know how to think prudently (589). He would rather avoid a position in which he would have to act against his will, instead maintaining a royal status that possesses power and influence without pain (* * * 591–93). Is Creon capable of feeling the pangs of pity once expressed by Oedipus for those who do not in some way contribute to what he deems to be "honorable and profitable" for himself (594–95)? Oedipus at least hopes that Creon has such ability for he expends his final efforts onstage securing Creon's promise of pity for his daughters. Oedipus articulates this desire by imagining a life of ridicule and loneliness for his daughters that Creon has the power to alleviate if not eliminate (1500–1510):

* * *

OED: Who then will marry you?
There is no one, children, but most clearly
it is necessary that you die barren and unmarried.
Child of Menoikeus, since you remain the only
father for these girls, since we two, who
nurtured them, are destroyed, do not allow them,
your kinsmen, to wander as beggars, husbandless,
and do not regard these girls as deserving my evils.
Rather pity them, seeing them at such an age
utterly bereft of all things, except as much as you offer.

> Nod your assent, noble one, and touch [them] with your
> hand.

Creon must imagine these girls to be not only Kinsmen in need but
his own children, providing what aid he can for two women subject
to an inherited guilt. The barrenness that has consumed the city
will now inevitably be thrust upon the daughters of Oedipus
because of the fate of their father. Consequently, Oedipus begs
Creon to be the protector, father, and, ultimately, source of pity for
the two girls who might never achieve marriageable status, legally
or socially. His appeal to Creon as the child of Menoikeus, the only
father for his daughters (1503), places Creon within a generational
context in which the daughters become a part of the Menoikean
line, detached from the polluted inheritance of Oedipus. He
reminds Creon that these girls are indeed his kinsmen, not to be
poor outsiders or participants in Oedipus' misfortunes but worthy
of his pity because of their youth and poverty and his ability to provide it (1506–9). Creon, then, bound by blood, must pity them and
adopt them as his own to prevent their potential beggary and what
Oedipus believes to be their present misfortune as poor orphaned
children. His pity for them entails Creon becoming their father and
saving them from isolation. The success of his attempt is entirely
unclear, however. The gesture of acceptance must be performed
with a nod and the touch of his hand (1510), but there is no indication from Oedipus or Creon that the sign has been given—Oedipus
would not have been able to see the nod or feel the touch—nor is it
clear that Creon would respect his promise considering the tone of
the final dialogue and the fate of Oedipus' children, portrayed not
twenty years before in Sophocles' *Antigone*.

Although the ending of the *Oedipus Tyrannus* presents several
challenges, the depiction of Creon remains consistent with the
character Sophocles has already portrayed and emphasizes the contrast in tone to the now-deposed tyrant. Despite the conclusion of
Oedipus' long speeches filled with sorrow and pity, Creon resumes
the impatient and angry speech with which he entered. He is eager
to see Oedipus inside where his weeping can remain private: "You
have cried long enough; go within the house! (1515)" This echoes
his earlier request that Oedipus spare the Sun and Earth his pollution and go inside since only among kin must evils be seen and
heard (1422–31). Creon is not the *tyrannus* that we knew in Oedipus who responded to the lengthy supplication of his subjects with
an empathetic pity bordering on hyperbole. Creon's responses to
Oedipus are laconic and pointed, devoted to orders from the gods
and spoken without frivolity (1516–20). They even run harsh. It
is not with pity that Creon finally sends the deposed *tyrannus*

Oedipus within the house but with the pitiless reminder of Oedipus' inability to rule his own life and now the life of his daughters (1521–23):

* * *

OED: Lead me away from here now already.
CR: March on, then, but leave your children.
OED: No, by no means take them away from me.
CR: Do not desire to rule everything.
   For indeed, being in control did not accompany you in life.

Within the context of pity, this final statement stands true: as an infant, Oedipus had no control over the emotions of his saviors, the Herdsman and Messenger. * * * Scholars agree that the Creon here is intentionally unheroic, a pale comparison to the eloquent and steadfast Oedipus. He is a cool, unaffected, perfunctory ruler, the reflection of moderation that Oedipus could never achieve. At the opening of the play, Oedipus pitied and provided aid to the suppliants at his palace doors without knowledge of their request nor regard for formalities. One could hardly expect such a response from the religiously systematic character of Creon. The possibility that Creon might feel an empathetic form of *oiktos* for the daughters of Oedipus, branded like the contaminated and deceased offspring of Thebes, is thus left ambiguous. Yet Creon appears to take on his role as adoptive father of Oedipus' children with these lines, removing them figuratively and physically from the father who has cursed them.

Conclusion

The word *oiktos* and its cognates operate on multiple planes in the *Oedipus Tyrannus* as I hope to have shown above. The mimetic emotion as displayed and discussed onstage possesses such imaginative power as to transform the least authoritative, least effecting person to the father of a king. Moreover, the rehabilitative assumptions contained within actions rooted in the deepest versions of pity have the ability to blind the one who pities from seeing himself as the very source or perpetuator of the object's suffering. The empathetic form of the emotion expressed by Oedipus connects the paternal and salvific figure of the protagonist in the prologue with the presumptive and saving actions of the two shepherds, compelling both the viewer and Oedipus to reconsider who Oedipus is beyond his biological nature. For his capacity for pity cannot be found in the nature of his biological father but in that exhibited by his figurative fathers—the Corinthian Messenger and the Theban Herdsman.

Narratively speaking, pity advances the movement of the drama in a unique way while preserving the mythological framework of the Oedipus story that sets it apart from other Oedipus accounts, even issuing in reversals, or "changes in situation" as Aristotle understands them. The two mentioned above appear in his discussion of *peripeteia* in the *Poetics* [1452a22]. The first is found in the narrative shift brought on by the Messenger who brings prosperous news about the death of Polybus but then opens up the discussion of Oedipus' identity when he declares that Oedipus does not know what he is doing, a line that appears to reflect pity on the Messenger's part (1008). The reversal ends with the Herdsman's admission of pity for the infant Oedipus. The second is of course the climactic moment that Aristotle praises as superior for the presence of both *anagnorisis* and *peripeteia*. The *peripeteia* is commonly interpreted to mean the downfall of Oedipus at the recognition of who he is biologically, but the reversal can also be located in the downfall of pity, an emotion that assumes a high level of positive agency in the play. It is tempting to think that Aristotle prefers these two scenes in the *Oedipus* for the role that pity plays in their execution, particularly in the denouement that depicts critical moments in the past motivated by pity and fear—the Herdsman's pity for Oedipus and his mother's fear of the prophecy, respectively. Furthermore, the reversal and recognition strike at the core of Aristotle's interest in the tragic effects of mimesis as pity and fear if the characters onstage are seen as emotional exemplars with whom to empathize. Sophocles compels the audience to pity Oedipus for the irony and tragedy in his suffering at the very moment that the Herdsman expresses it or—since this is the only occasion when pity and fear are seen as an "either/or" response in Aristotle's discussion (1452a39)—to fear that their own pity may be fatally misplaced (or they themselves "saved for evils" by pity) eliciting the cries of terror Oedipus himself exclaims.

Oedipus and the Messenger both deemed their responses to pity to be beneficial—for the city in each of Oedipus' expressions of pity and for Oedipus in the expressions of pity by the Messenger and Herdsman both. The association with familial and soterial language supported by the privileged position of one who pities simultaneously reveals the limitations of such imaginings. Sophocles seems to suggest that it is not the unpredictability of Fortune that should excite our deeper anxieties but the necessity and yet blindness of pity, an emotion that humbly recognizes mortal limitations but treacherously inspires the imagination to stretch beyond them.

Sophocles: A Chronology

Sophocles produced over 120 plays, of which only seven survive. Hardly any of the dates of his plays are securely known. We have the titles and some fragmentary quotations from a number of the lost plays. Sophocles was never awarded lower than second place in the Great Dionysia competition, and he was given first prize eighteen times at the Dionysia, and six times at the Lenaea.

? 497–496 B.C.E.	Born, probably in Colonus, outside Athens, to a wealthy family; his father may have manufactured armor.
480	Battle of Salamis: Athens warded off attempted invasion by the Persian emperor Xerxes. Sophocles, then a teenager, was chosen to lead a ritual dance (a *paian*) in celebration.
470	Sophocles' first contribution to the dramatic competition at the Great Dionysia.
468	Sophocles' first victory in the dramatic competition; defeated Aeschylus.
443/442	Sophocles served as one of the financial managers (*Hellenotamiae*) of the city, under Pericles. Served in military campaign against the island of Samos.
441	Elected as one of the ten generals—leaders of the city—along with Pericles.
440s	*Antigone*; *Ajax*.
431	Outbreak of Peloponnesian War.
430	Major plague in Athens.
429 (?)	*Oedipus Tyrannos*.
420	Sophocles set up in his house an image and altar to Asclepius, god of healing and medicine—a new addition to the Athenian pantheon. Received title of Dexios, "Receiver" or "Welcomer" (of the god).
415–413	Disastrous naval expedition from Athens to Sicily; vast casualties and enslavement of Athenian citizens.
413	Sophocles was elected as one of the members of the commission charged with determining the response of

	the city to the disaster, and deciding on appropriate repercussions for those in charge.
409	*Philoctetes*.
406–405	Death.
401	*Oedipus at Colonus*, written by Sophocles, produced by Sophocles' grandson.

Suggestions for Further Reading

There are two good recent collections of essays in English on Sophocles: the Brill *Companion to Sophocles*, edited by Andreas Markantonatos (2012), and the Wiley-Blackwell *Companion to Sophocles*, edited by Kirk Ormand (2012). There is also a recent *Brill Companion to the Reception of Sophocles* (2017). Good single-author introductions to Sophocles include:

Garvie, A. F. *The Plays of Sophocles*, 2nd ed. (London and New York: Bloomsbury, 2016).

Jouanna, Jacques. *Sophocles: A Study of His Theater in Its Political and Social Context* (Princeton, NJ: Princeton UP, 2018). Translated from the French.

Morwood, James. *The Tragedies of Sophocles* (Bristol: Bristol Phoenix P, 2008).

Segal, Charles. *Sophocles' Tragic World* (Cambridge, MA: Harvard UP, 1995).

The recent edition of the Greek text by P. J. Finglass (Cambridge, Eng.: Cambridge UP, 2018) has voluminous notes, many of which can be understood without knowledge of Greek. For discussion of the Oedipus plays from a philosophical perspective, see the recent collection *The Oedipus Plays of Sophocles: Philosophical Perspectives*, edited by Paul Woodruff (Oxford, Eng.: Oxford UP, 2018). On the Oedipus myth beyond Sophocles, see:

Bremmer, J. N. "Oedipus and the Greek Oedipus Complex." In *Interpretations of Greek Mythology*, ed. J. N. Bremmer (London: Croom Helm, 1987), pp. 41–59.

Cigano, Ettore. "Oedipodea." In *The Greek Epic Cycle and Its Ancient Reception: A Companion*, ed. Marco Fantuzzi and Christos Tsagalis (Cambridge, Eng.: Cambridge UP, 2015), pp. 213–25.

Edmunds, Lowell. *Oedipus* (London and New York: Routledge, 2006).

A good general introduction to the themes of the play can be found in Charles Segal, *"Oedipus Tyrannus": Tragic Heroism and the Limits of Knowledge* (Oxford, Eng.: Oxford UP, 2001). The following books and articles are recommended for discussion of more specific issues and particular scenes:

Allan, William. "'Archaic' Guilt in Sophocles' *Oedipus Tyrannus* and *Oedipus at Colonus*." In *Tragedy and Archaic Greek Thought*, ed. Douglas L. Cairns. Swansea: Classical P of Wales, 2013, pp. 173–91.

Bain, David. "A Misunderstood Scene in Sophokles' *Oidipous* (*O.T.* 300–462)." *Greece & Rome* 26.2 (October 1979): 132–45.

Budelmann, Felix. "The Mediated Ending of Sophocles' *Oedipus Tyrannus*." *Materiali e discussioni per l'analisi dei testi classici* 57 (2006): 43–61.

Burkert, Walter. *Oedipus, Oracles, and Meaning: From Sophocles to Umberto Eco.* Toronto: University College, University of Toronto, 1991.

Burton, R. W. B. *The Chorus in Sophocles' Tragedies*. Oxford, Eng.: Clarendon P, 1980.

Cairns, Douglas L. "Divine and Human Action in the *Oedipus Tyrannus*." In *Tragedy and Archaic Greek Thought*, ed. Douglas L. Cairns. Swansea: Classical P of Wales, 2013, pp. 119–71.

Calame, Claude. "Vision, Blindness, and Mask: The Radicalization of the Emotions in Sophocles' *Oedipus Rex*." In *Tragedy and the Tragic: Greek Theatre and Beyond*, ed. M. S. Silk. Oxford, Eng.: Clarendon P, 1996, pp. 17–37.

Dodds, E. R. "On Misunderstanding the *Oedipus Rex*." *Greece & Rome* 13.1 (April 1966): 37–49.

Foley, Helene Peet. "Oedipus as *Pharmakos*." In *Nomodeiktes: Greek Studies in Honor of Martin Ostwald*, ed. Ralph M. Rosen and Joseph Farrell. Ann Arbor: U of Michigan P, 1993, pp. 525–38.

Gould, John. "The Language of Oedipus." In *Sophocles: Modern Critical Views*, ed. Harold Bloom. New York and Philadelphia: Chelsea House, 1990, pp. 207–22.

Halliwell, Stephen. "Where Three Roads Meet: A Neglected Detail in the *Oedipus Tyrannus*." *Journal of Hellenic Studies* 106 (1986): 187–90.

Harris, Edward M. "Is Oedipus Guilty? Sophocles and Athenian Homicide Law." In *Law and Drama in Ancient Greece*, ed. Edward M. Harris, Delfim F. Leão, and P. J. Rhodes. London and New York: Duckworth, 2010, pp. 122–46.

Knox, Bernard M. W. "Why Is Oedipus Called *Tyrannos*?" *Classical Journal* 50.3 (December 1954): 97–102.

Kovacs, David. "The Role of Apollo in *Oedipus Tyrannus*." In *The Play of Texts and Fragments: Essays in Honour of Martin Cropp*, ed. J. R. C. Cousland and James R. Hume. *Mnemosyne* Supplement 314. Leiden, The Netherlands, and Boston: Brill, 2009, pp. 357–68.

Macintosh, Fiona, ed. *Sophocles: "Oedipus Tyrannus."* Cambridge, Eng.: Cambridge UP, 2009.

Sommerstein, Alan H. "Sophocles and the Guilt of Oedipus." *Cuadernos de filología clásica. Estudios griegos e indoeuropeos* 21 (2011): 103–17.